Fresh Water from Old Wells

MERCER
UNIVERSITY PRESS

Endowed by
TOM WATSON BROWN
and
THE WATSON-BROWN FOUNDATION, INC.

Fresh Water from Old Wells

Cindy Henry McMahon

MERCER UNIVERSITY PRESS | *Macon, Georgia*

MUP/ P505

Published by Mercer University Press
1501 Mercer University Drive
Macon, Georgia 31207

9 8 7 6 5 4 3 2 1

Books published by Mercer University Press are printed on acid-free paper
that meets the requirements of the American National Standard for
Information Sciences—Permanence of Paper for Printed Library Materials.

ISBN   978-0-88146-526-6
Cataloging-in-Publication Data is available from the Library of Congress

for my mama

Contents

Prologue

This book is my journey.

It began before daylight: a wide-awake feeling that led me to a quiet room, journal in my lap. My pen told me that I could leave my full-time job and be at home for a while. Find wholeness. Live in hope instead of fear.

I did resign. The rest proved somewhat more elusive.

After watching my dad die and quitting my job, both in the spring of 2004, I spent a year and a half careening from "I'm amazing! If I believe in myself, there's nothing I can't do!" to "What in the world was I thinking?" and back again. In between, I remembered how to play with my children, drove on the Blue Ridge Parkway, and spent a lot of time wondering about *this thing*, this important thing that I could feel waiting out there for me to do. I barely recognized myself: I've always known exactly where I was heading, what was coming next, and what I was going to get done once I got there. Living in indecision, in the unknown, was the hardest thing I've ever done.

Somehow the idea finally bloomed in my head. I could write a book—about my liberal white southern family. About my crazy, idealistic, violent, tree-hugging father who started out as a Baptist preacher, tried to save the world, and ended up living in a tent and criss-crossing the country with his thumb out. About my distinguished maternal grandfather, also a Southern Baptist preacher, who quietly brought factions together without ever making a fuss. And about the women who somehow managed to hold it all together without anybody knowing what it cost them. And I could write about me—maybe I would finally begin to understand where I came from and how in God's name I survived it all in one piece. Perhaps others would one day read my story and find inspiration to shine a light on the dark places from their own pasts.

The thing is, when you have the idea of writing a book, at least in my case, you have to spend many months exploring all the reasons why it's a completely cock-eyed idea. Even if there's a voice deep inside you, first thing in the morning and last thing at night that says, "This is why you're here now. You have a story to tell. Tell it." Even if the first tentative steps are ridiculously easy and you feel like you're being pulled down a path by the hand, you still tell yourself, "Nope. Not me. Can't do it. Don't deserve it. Not good enough." Until the Moment comes.

For me, the Moment was at a February church retreat, in a two-person chair by a roaring fire, snow pouring down outside, in a house on a hill full of burbling women filling their bowls with oatmeal. There were several of us in the conversation at first, talking about trusting the flow—getting into it, being open and prepared, letting it take us where we're meant to go. As I sat quietly with the conversation swirling around me, I found myself getting angry. Flow, schmo. I had been holding my arms out to the flow for the past year and a half, to no avail. I was losing faith in the whole idea.

As others drifted off towards the oatmeal pot, I turned to my friend Jeanine, sitting in the chair with me. "You know—that whole getting in the river thing...I've been letting myself float out there for nearly two years...it's always been clear to me before...I'm caught in some sort of eddy in the shallows. I'm going NOWHERE, and I'm getting frustrated." Jeanine let loose a flow of perceptive questions. What was I resisting? Why was I resisting it? Every reason that I could give her that I shouldn't write a book, all the barriers that I had so carefully constructed over the last many months, got knocked down like glued-together toothpicks. So you're an extrovert? Find non-work ways to meet your social needs. You see yourself as a leader of people? What better way to lead than by telling your story? Worried about money? Trust the process.

She left me with nothing but belief in myself and a clear path ahead. By the time I filled my own bowl with oatmeal, I knew I was going to do it. The sensation was one I had felt before when jumping off a high rock into an icy-cold stream: that moment in mid-air, knowing the splash is coming, followed by the tingling of every pore. I was exhilarated and full of wonder.

And so I devoted myself, heart and soul, to this project. I went through my mother's address book and got in touch with anybody and everybody who might be able to tell me more about my story. I drove up one Georgia road and down the other, knocking on doors of people I'd heard about my whole life but had no memory of, people who welcomed me with open arms, loved me simply because of who I'm related to, and generously shared their stories with my tiny tape recorder and me. I even ventured to the faraway land of Alabama. I dug through church archives and read their histories, visited cemeteries, and found old homes—mine, my grandparents', and my great-grandparents'. And all along the way I shed springs, creeks, and rivers of tears as I watched my mama following her own path away from me into debilitating dementia.

This is my story—fresh water from many old wells. It is the story of an amazing time in my adult life, as well as my childhood and the family who got me here. And it is a goodbye to my beloved mother, who spent my whole childhood making sure our story would never be told. It is out of love that I finally tell my story.

1

Porch Light

It's not easy to be brave in the darkness. If you grow up at the edge of the dark woods, you know better than to look for a streetlight. And you know that the tall mountains and gnarly rhododendrons will obscure the moon. Eyes are useless; only feet and heart will keep you on the path toward home. But if you're wearing my shoes you know that eventually you'll come out of the woods and the light will be on, overcoming the darkness. My mama always remembered to leave the porch light on for me.

Mom doesn't remember much anymore. But remarkably, her earliest memory—from when she wasn't yet three years old—has remained mostly intact. It's an important story in my family, one I grew up hearing though I never really gave it much thought beyond marveling at its real-life heroism.

It was 1933. Miriam, who would be my grandmama many years later, was thirty. She was a petite bundle of energy. I imagine her always smiling and in a hurry in her tiny high-heeled shoes, dusting the fried chicken flour off her hands, her golden hair just a little disheveled. After all, she had three little girls under five years old. Then there was Walter, my future granddaddy. At age twenty-eight, he was an avid hunter and fisherman, scholarly but warm, with a quick, dry sense of humor. As he would be at the churches he served later, he was already beloved at First Baptist Church of Waynesboro, Georgia, where he had been the minister for just over a year.

Of the three girls, Martha was the youngest, just past a year old, toddling around with her red hair blazing. Then Carol (who grew up to be my mama), not quite three, quiet but friendly and inquisitive. I'll bet something about her already seemed like her daddy—it could have been the brown hair or the twinkle in her eye, or maybe it was the dirt under her fingernails. Like her daddy, she loved being outside. And then there was Sunny, the oldest. She wasn't quite five, but probably already protective of her little sisters. She was the only one of the three who was beginning to emerge into girlhood, her legs starting to lengthen and lose their soft baby roundness. And she was the one blonde of the bunch—a tidy cap of shining hair, with bangs straight across her forehead.

Sunny was conceived in Cuba. My grandparents had met at Southwestern Baptist Theological Seminary in Fort Worth, Texas. Walter was there because he had heard the call of the ministry and it was the Southern Baptist seminary closest to his family's cattle farm in Ruston, Louisiana. Miriam traveled to Forth Worth all the way from her family's farm in Ogeechee, Georgia, because it was the only Southern Baptist seminary that offered a degree in sacred music. After a two-year courtship (the second year long-distance), the two were married on Grandmama's birthday in her parents' front room.

Grandmama didn't meet Granddaddy's family until the two of them traveled out to Louisiana after the wedding. It was a long train ride from Georgia and, as she remembered it, "when we got to the house, it was evening. And there was the family under the porch light, waiting to see their new daughter." She laughed delightedly as she recalled, "I was as thrilled as they were."

From Louisiana, my grandparents set off together to be missionaries in Havana, Cuba, where Grandmama's Uncle Moses was director of Southern Baptist mission work.

These two young newlyweds were the opposite sides of each other's coin. He was over six feet, she just barely five. He preached; she played the music and sang like a bird. They played tennis together, learned to speak fluent Spanish, shared a deeply held faith, and within a year had started their family. They stayed in Havana throughout the pregnancy, but when her time drew close, Grandmama felt the call of home and they headed back to Ogeechee. The baby was born in the same room where Grandmama had drawn her own first breath, and Granddaddy chose the name: Miriam. His two best girls, both Miriam. To keep them straight, he nicknamed the little one Sunshine—she was the light of their lives. But Sunshine was a big name for such a little girl, and soon she was known to everybody as Sunny.

Shortly after the birth they went back to Cuba, where Sunny lived up to her nickname from the beginning. After her typical first word ("Da-da") she went on to become very expressive, needing only a couple of "hee-haws" to get her mama to sing her favorite song, "Old Thompson's Mule."

> Old Thompson had an ole gray mule,
> He led him round to the cart.
> He loved that mule and the mule loved him,
> With all his muleish heart.
> Old Thompson knowed when the rooster crowed,
> Day was a 'gwine to break.
> He rubbed that mule with the leg of a stool,
> And he scretched him down with a rake.
> And the mule he said,
> Haw, hee haw, hee haw,
> And he scretched him down with a rake.

I don't know as much about Sunny after toddlerhood. I do know that times weren't always easy. Granddaddy's health suffered, and his doctor in Cuba accompanied the family back to Grandmama's family homeplace in Georgia just a few months before the stock market crashed in 1929. But Granddaddy recovered, and in those hard times folks needed church more than ever. Though the jobs might not pay much, pastorates weren't hard to come by. Granddaddy was called to a little church in Newington, not far from Ogeechee, and the family just managed to make ends meet.

My mama was born in December 1930 (she was their "Christmas Carol"), and less than two years later Granddaddy moved up to a bigger church, First Baptist of Waynesboro. Waynesboro was the county seat of Burke County, the second largest county (square mileage-wise) in the state. I'm sure my granddaddy was happy to be moving there, especially since he was an avid bird hunter and Waynesboro was already known as "The Bird Dog Capital of the World." When the family moved into the pastorium on Academy Avenue in 1932, Grandmama was pregnant again, this time with Martha.

Sunny was still beloved, of course, but no longer the one and only center of her parents' attention. From the pictures Granddaddy took and developed himself, I can tell she didn't mind much—she looks happy to have a sister to play with as she pushes Carol on the swing, plays barefooted with her in the sandbox, wades beside her in the creek, squats on the down side of the seesaw, and smiles into the camera as a younger Carol gazes at her with adoration. They were clearly a contented pair.

And then in an instant, it all changed.

It was November 6, 1933—a Monday—probably Granddaddy's day off after a long Sunday the day before. They were up early, though, with all three girls not yet old enough to be going off to school. They probably had a good southern breakfast: bacon, grits, eggs, and biscuits. And then, when it was all cleared away and cleaned up, I'm guessing that was the time they headed to the washerwoman's house to take the laundry.

It wouldn't have been a long trip, but they all piled into the car to head into what they thought of as the Negro section of town, just a block or two out from where they lived. Leaving Academy Avenue for that other part of town would have felt like going to another country. The street was narrower and dustier, the houses smaller and in poor repair, with outhouses behind. Though my grandparents had trouble reconciling the obvious racial divide with the Christianity they held so close—didn't Jesus say all men were brothers?—it was what they grew up with. They were used to the paradox they'd always known. Going to the washerwoman's was a familiar family ritual, just an errand to be checked off the day's list in Grandmama's loopy handwriting.

And so they drove the short distance, Sunny and Carol probably bouncing in the back, Walter tall in the driver's seat, Miriam holding Martha on her lap in the front. They dropped off the baskets of clothes and then headed home again, parking in front of the house. The doors opened, and this cheerful bunch piled out of the car.

Grandmama headed up the walk first, with Martha on her hip and her list humming in her head—all the other things she wanted to get done that day. Granddaddy came more slowly behind, rounding up the bigger girls, enjoying the morning sun and his day off, slowly following his wife with the children dancing behind him.

And then, as Granddaddy topped the few steps to the front porch with Carol close behind, it happened. A boy's call from across the street. A returning "hi!" and quick little footsteps heading the other way, down the walk, behind the parked car, out into the street. A screech of brakes, the sound of impact, a brief pause, and then the sound of the car, careening off down the street and around the corner, towards that other part of town. Out of sight. Gone.

There was nothing Granddaddy could do. It all happened too fast. In ten of his long, loping strides, he was in the middle of the street himself. His tall frame crumpled beside Sunny's small one, and then he slowly rose, carrying her limp body up the walk and up the stairs to the broad porch, already knowing that she was gone. Blood gushed from her shining blonde head, staining his white shirt. He brought her into the house, laying her gently on the bed.

"No!" shouted Carol, who had seen the whole thing. "She'll stain the guest bed!" Immediately embarrassed, she ran to hide, praying fervently for her childhood Jesus to make it all better.

And what came after? Nobody remembers, and my imagination stops here. I cannot come up with any ideas of what Grandmama would have said or done, how she would have reacted, where she would have stood. Baby Martha must have been crying, responding to the level of panic, tangible in the air she was breathing. Did they call the doctor right away? Did they pray? Were the neighbors there immediately? The scene goes black for me as soon as Sunny is laid on the bed. As it may have gone black for my grandmama.

And then later in the day—I imagine it as dusk—we know that a group of men came to the door. Word would have spread through the little town, especially among those in the church.

5

Footsteps up the wooden stairs. Granddaddy went to answer the knock, probably turned on the porch light. Was Sunny's body still lying on the bed, or had the undertaker already carried her away in preparation for the next morning's funeral? As Granddaddy's frame filled the doorway, one man probably stepped forward, with men behind him that Granddaddy knew well. Men he had hunted and fished with, preached to, visited when they had new babies or their wives were sick.

"Preacher, we found the nigger woman who killed your daughter. We've got a rope and we're ready to string her up." Anger running high, adrenaline, raw masculinity, vengeance. A feeling so different from Grandmama's anguish inside the house, just behind Granddaddy's tall back.

And then his response in the pool of light on the porch—still heartbroken, but kind, praying hard with every word. "Well, fellers, you'll need two ropes. It was just as much my fault as it was hers, and you'll be hanging me, too."

And the scene goes black for me again. Was that all it took? Did those men disperse and go home to their own wives and children, holding them tightly when they got there? Or did they leave shaking their heads, disbelieving that Christianity could make so little sense?

What happened to their murderous rage? And how soon did Granddaddy leave the house to drive across town to the jail? Were the McCalls, Grandmama's parents, already at the house, putting Carol and Martha to bed, warming up milk for Grandmama, stroking her golden head, doing the little they could to help?

I do know that Granddaddy spent the night at the little one-room city jail, just to make sure that two lives weren't lost that day. I feel sure he would have prayed with the woman and assured her that he knew it was just an accident, that he understood why she drove off after it happened. In the dark jail, he would have offered his forgiveness as well as his protection, knowing that God would do the same.

And then morning. The funeral was at eleven o'clock out at Douglas Branch Church in Ogeechee, so the family probably headed out to Grandmama McCall's house early. It's likely that Granddaddy McCall went back to the farm the night before to take care of the animals, leaving his wife to spend the night and make breakfast. Then she or my grandmama would have been in the back seat with Carol, heading out towards the McCalls' house, no Sunny to jump out of the car with them when they got there.

When they all gathered at Douglas Branch Church for the service, the little sanctuary must have been packed. Lots of family, plus dear friends and church members from Newington, Waynesboro, and Ogeechee. T. M. McCall gave the eulogy, and Annie May Kendrick, mother of the little boy who had called to Sunny from across the street, sang a soprano solo. Six deacons from Granddaddy's church served as honorary pallbearers, but only four men actually carried the tiny coffin: Grandmama's oldest brother, Stirling, and three close family friends. Though there was no money for a stone in those lean times, Granddaddy's photo of the grave shows a mountain of flowers, none of them as bright as the life that was lost.

Three weeks later, on the very Sunday that Sunny would have turned five years old, Granddaddy came back to the pulpit. His sermon topic that morning? "Why I Love the Lord."

Grandmama's normally shining eyes were sunken for months, but life went on. There were diapers to change. Meals to make. Lullabies to sing. Clothes to drop off at the washerwoman's house. Walter and Carol, now his oldest daughter and his fellow witness on the porch that fateful day, drew closer. A year later, she was the only one with him as they made the long drive west to Ruston, Louisiana, where his daddy lay dying. Her devotion helped him stay on the road. The next year little Walter Moore, Jr.—Buddy—came along, and the unbelievable grief gradually receded. But it was never gone completely.

Three years after the tragedy, when Carol was just about the age Sunny was when she died, it was time to move on. The family packed up and went back to Cuba for another missionary tour of duty. Their dear friends at First Baptist of Waynesboro were sad to see them go, but there must have been a mixed sense of relief for the Moores as they waved good-bye, stepped onto the train, and put that chapter of life behind them.

~ ~ ~ ~ ~ ~

I had no plan when I went to Waynesboro for the first time. I had directions to get there and had learned from my Uncle Buddy that the Moore family had lived on Academy Avenue. He didn't know the house number. I figured I'd just find my way to the small town, ask for directions to Academy Avenue, and then drive up and down the street, wondering where the accident happened. It had been nearly seventy years since Sunny died, and I knew that the neighborhood had probably changed; I expected a strip of convenience stores and tattoo parlors.

As I drove into the outskirts of Waynesboro, the first logical step popped into my head: *Find the church.* Of course! Granddaddy's old church! They'd surely know the story and be able to tell me where it happened. And First Baptist churches are remarkably easy to find in small Georgia towns. I headed toward what looked like the center of town and then out a few streets, driving up and down a couple of the more affluent-looking boulevards. There it was, between Liberty and Shadrack, a big brick façade with white columns. I parked and walked up to the front of the church. The first thing I noticed was the cornerstone:

FIRST BAPTIST CHURCH
* * *
REBUILT 1935
W. L. MOORE, PASTOR
J. M. BYNE SR.
CHAIRMAN OF DEACONS

I had come to the right place. Next step: *Find people.*

The front door of the sanctuary was obviously not the way in on a weekday, so I headed toward the back, looking for another entrance. I found myself in the middle of a busy child-care center, where a friendly teacher led me through the fellowship hall in a much newer building and on into the church offices.

I introduced myself to the church secretary and told her that my grandfather had been the minister of the church in the early 1930s—in fact, I had seen on the cornerstone that he was the minister when the current sanctuary was built. Walter L. Moore.

I expected recognition. I got nothing. I explained that all I wanted to know was where the pastorium might have been at the time, so I could find where they had lived.

Blank look.

"Uh, I'm new," she said. "Maybe there's a church history file around here somewhere...."

She looked up at the shelves and then glanced helplessly at the file cabinets, but I could tell she had no idea where to start. Fortunately, the minister, Reverend Al Wright, my stereotype of a Southern Baptist preacher, stepped out from the copy room at that moment, having overheard a little of our conversation.

"What are you looking for?"

"Well, my grandfather was Walter L. Moore," I repeated, "the minister of this church back in the early thirties, and I'm trying to figure out where he and his family lived when they were here."

Though he was clearly busy, Reverend Wright was willing to help. He knew of several former pastoriums in the neighborhood, but nothing on Academy Avenue. He found a copy of the church history to give me, and I looked through it while he went back to his office to call the oldest member of the church who might still remember. Yes, there had been a pastorium on Academy Avenue, Reverend Wright told me, and he offered to drive me to it.

On the short ride over, I told him the story of Sunny and the fateful Monday morning on Academy Avenue. I told him about the men on the porch, too, and Granddaddy's response. Al Wright, who had seemed so stereotypical, like he had just stepped out of some over-lit televangelist show with fake plants and big-haired women, began to seem human as I told the story. He said, "I think I'm gonna cry. You know, our church today is the most mixed church I've ever been in. We have black people, white people, and people from many other countries."

Well, I thought, *you may have never heard of Walter L. Moore, but my granddaddy's spirit may somehow live on in your church after all.*

The red pickup truck turned onto Academy Avenue a couple of blocks past the church. My eyes widened. Just as Mom had described, there was the big school on the right. Its windows were now boarded up, with a yard full of weeds and a "for sale" sign out front. But the neighborhood was still residential, and the houses across the street from the school were old and gorgeous. As we drove slowly down Academy Avenue, Reverend Wright pointed out which houses would have been the homes of prominent church members when my grandparents lived there. They had beautiful, generous porches, tall windows, fresh coats of paint, flowering bushes, and well-manicured lawns. I could hardly believe it was so perfectly preserved.

When we got to the last house on the street, Reverend Wright parked the truck.

"This is it."

I couldn't believe my eyes. After the other houses on the street, I expected to see another historic, well-loved home. This one was old, but it was clearly abandoned. Its blue-green paint was faded and peeling, beer cans lay rusting underneath the overgrown bushes, and Virginia Creeper vines climbed across the big, dark windows. The porch, where the group of men had stood surrounded by darkness all those years ago, was beginning to buckle and sag.

It looked like a memory.

The minister had to get back to the church, but I wanted to be there alone, so I stayed. It was only a short walk to my car. I explored around the back of the house, admiring its beautiful dormers and the grace of its now-sagging architecture.

I imagined my mama as a child, playing with Sunny in the yard while Grandmama rested in a rocking chair up on the porch, taking care of some mending while she kept an eye on the girls. I looked across the street, but there was no house as Mom had described. Where had the little boy come from? That crucial piece of the story made no sense to me now.

I climbed onto the porch and looked out, picturing the car coming down the street, Granddaddy's car parked at the curb, how it all would have looked and sounded from his perspective on the front steps. I counted the number of strides from the porch to the middle of the street, noting how close it all was. How immediate.

I stood in the street in front of the house.

This was the spot where my sweet grandmama lost her oldest child, her namesake, her Sunshine. I have a daughter, too, and could easily imagine what Grandmama must have felt in that instant. A sunny morning, a routine errand, the family all together. And then it all cracked open and the darkness poured out. Right in that very spot.

And Granddaddy. So young. Just beginning his career, but already so admired. To lose his golden-haired child, spend the day making arrangements for her funeral, and then, at only twenty-eight years old, to face such darkness in men he loved. And to answer the darkness with so much light.

Finally, sitting on the top step of the porch, I was overcome. I felt like I was drawn back into November 1933. It seemed more real than the present. I wept for Grandmama, losing a daughter whose name she would never speak again. I wept for Granddaddy—as a pastor, he had to be more than a man, sitting all night in the jail with the woman who had accidentally killed his daughter, instead of holding his wife as she slept. I wept for my mama, who had lost her big sister and in that moment became the oldest child herself. Now she was losing her memories as well. How much longer would she remember Sunny? Eventually, I wept for myself.

When I got home from that trip, I wanted to sit down and write the story. But even though I had been to the house on Academy Avenue and had visited the old jail, Sunny's grave, and my great-grandparents' house, something was missing. I could now picture more than the two-dimensional shadow play I had grown up knowing, but I sensed that there was more I needed to know. Who was the woman driving the car?

What happened to her? Who was the little boy across the street? Where was his house? I decided to talk to my mama.

I had taken lots of pictures of the house and the street in Waynesboro, but I waited to show them to Mom. I wanted to review her recollections first.

"So, Mom, your earliest memory is when Sunny died, right?"

"That's right. I remember it like it was yesterday, and I was just tiny."

"Well, when you remember it, when you picture it in your mind, what do you see?"

"Let's see. There was a porch on the front of the house, with steps going down to a straight walk that went toward the street, where Daddy's car was parked. Across the street was the house where that little boy lived, the one who called to Sunny. And there was a big school to the right of that house, with playing fields between it and the little boy's house. I remember I used to watch the kids playing on those fields and I wished I could be big enough to go to school."

I showed her the pictures. With the exception of the missing house across the street, the scene was exactly as she had described: front porch, steps leading to the walk, which led to the street, just a few steps from the house to the spot where Sunny died. Dementia or no, seventy-three years later, Mom remembered it just as it was.

But I needed more. Did anyone else from Waynesboro remember this story or know what happened to the woman driving the car? I had gotten a copy of the front-page article about the incident in Waynesboro's *True Citizen*, but it simply listed the driver as "a colored woman," and said that the Reverend Moore didn't hold her responsible. I contacted the Waynesboro police department, who told me that all the police records from that time had been destroyed. There was nothing left.

I got in touch with the general manager of the *True Citizen*, still published faithfully every week, and she agreed to include Sunny's story in her next local history column, "RFD." Maybe an old-timer I hadn't found would remember and respond. True to her word, the

12

newspaperwoman put Sunny in her column the following week with my questions, but there was no response.

I talked to other people at the newspaper and the Waynesboro police department, and even started up an email correspondence with the mayor, a local history buff. By phone, I chased down every possible lead, waking up elderly Baptists all across the state of Georgia. In this way, I learned about the family across the street, the Kendricks. But the only son anybody remembered had committed suicide as a young man. Was that the little boy who had called out to Sunny? There were no Kendricks left in Waynesboro. I felt stuck at a dead end.

Finally I expressed my frustration to my parents' old college friend, Irvin Cheney, who lived in Washington, Georgia, seventy-five miles from Waynesboro.

"I'm out of ideas. What'll I do?"

"Well, Cindy, my sister lives in Waynesboro. Her husband's family has lived there forever and he surely knows something of the story. If it means this much to you, let me get in touch with them and see what I can find out."

And he certainly followed through. Cheney's brother-in-law had heard the story as a child and still remembered it. He was also pretty sure there was a second Kendrick boy: Neb, Jr. Now I had something to investigate.

With the help of the Internet and after several false starts, I found a listing for Nisbet S. Kendrick, Jr., just outside of Atlanta. Could *he* be the one? I got nervous. What would I say to him? "Are you the person who was responsible for Sunny's death?" What if he *was* the same person, and the incident had scarred him? He had stood there, only five years old, and saw his little friend's head crushed on the road right in front of him. What could I say?

I made myself stop thinking and dialed the phone.

An elderly man answered.

"Hello?"

"Hi. My name is Cindy McMahon, and I'm looking for the Nisbet Kendrick who grew up in Waynesboro."

"That would be me."

Big breath.

"My grandparents lived across the street from your family on Academy Avenue."

He immediately started talking about another family, the Coxes, but I jumped in.

"No, I mean the Moores. My granddaddy was the pastor at First Baptist Church."

"Oh! I remember them! They had a daughter they called Sunshine, who was coming across the street to see me when she got run over."

I could hardly believe it. The "little boy" from the story, now seventy-eight years old, the same age as Sunny would have been had she lived, told me the whole story, corroborating all of Mom's details: his calling out, Sunny running from behind the parked car, the woman driving toward them, Granddaddy getting to Sunny almost immediately, then lifting her and carrying her up the steps and into the house.

"I hate to tell you this," the man said, "but when I think back to that day, the thing I picture is her just lying underneath that car."

The incident, so traumatic, had clearly carved itself just as deeply into his memory as it had into my mama's. But he didn't seem to mind telling me the story.

"Mr. Kendrick, I have one question. If your house was right across the street, why isn't it there now?"

"Oh, the big sycamore tree out front got struck by lightning in the sixties, and the house burned to the ground. That was after our family sold it. There was a picture of the fire in *The True Citizen* that week—you could probably find it."

There it was. The one missing piece from Mom's story. I realized I would probably never be able to find out who was driving the car or what happened to her. Maybe there are some things we aren't supposed to know.

But I had a powerful feeling. This story about my granddaddy's response to the men who were ready to hang the killer of his child had always felt like a family legend. But it was *real*. It forged the extraordinary bond between my mama and her daddy—a bond that would later test the strength of her connection with the only other man she ever loved with all her heart, my daddy. It was also the story that preceded my granddaddy everywhere he went, as he was called from church to church across the Deep South. Though he never would have told the story himself, it moved quietly in Southern Baptist circles, giving him license to speak from the pulpit about "our brothers in black," when others who tried to do the same risked losing their pulpits altogether.

It was a story that needed telling again.

Is the story true? After talking to Neb Kendrick, Jr., I'm convinced that it is. But how much does fact-based "truth" really matter, in the end? Working on a book like this, you spend a lot of time trying to figure out what is "true." Even when you've done your homework, gone to the source, read through the papers, and interviewed the people, have you found the *truth*? Don't people skew what they write in their personal papers and meeting minutes? Aren't church histories subjective? Aren't memories fallible? How valid is anyone's story, anyway? I can shine a light on what happened, but is it the *true* story?

In my case, the questions are magnified due to my mother's illness. As my wise hospice friend describes it, vascular dementia is unique because it's not a progression. It's like trap doors opening and closing all the time. For many events, my mother is the only living witness left, but how can I tell stories based on trap doors? What good does it do to shine my light when the story is no longer there? I can only hope that tomorrow the trap door will open or close again—that the porch light will turn on—and the story will be back. And then will the story be *true*?

As it turns out, I'm finding more truth than I ever imagined. Truth about the present as well as the past. It may or may not be completely factually accurate. But I'm finding that historical accuracy is less meaningful than the deeper truth of the stories themselves. This story-truth is the real truth I'm seeking. Right now, I need as much of that kind of truth as I can get. Last July, my mama finally agreed that she needed more help, and we moved her to a small, family-owned rest home looking out over the mountains, not far from where I live. Her house, though empty, is still in the family. We're trying to find someone to rent it, but it's dark most of the time now. The porch light is rarely on. That's the hardest part. Most of my life, my mama has been the one person I knew I could always count on. But now that has changed. It takes real courage to walk through the dark woods, not knowing whether I'll find the light on or off when I get there.

But maybe I need this darkness, somehow, to find a new source of light.

2

Stained Glass

In 2002, twenty-five years after my grandfather's death, Mercer University in Macon, Georgia, established the Walter L. Moore Humanitarian Award to honor him. The award recognizes Mercer alumni who have shown a lifelong commitment to Christian character, service, and humanitarianism. My mother, Carol Moore Henry, was the first recipient of this distinguished award. She was honored, surprised, and a little embarrassed, having always been a behind-the-scenes humanitarian, never singled out for public recognition. She brought the award home, though, and hung it on the paneled wall of her small, simple living room: a large, limited-edition print of a commissioned painting of the stained-glass windows in Macon's old Tattnall Square Baptist Church (now Mercer's Newton Chapel), triple-matted and surrounded by an ornate gold-colored frame. Needless to stay, it stood out.

Walter Moore always stood out, too, though not in such a pretentious way. By 1959, when my grandparents moved to Macon, Granddaddy had been using the license to speak his truth (grounded in the experience of Sunny's death) from the pulpit for many years. His sermons carried a common theme.

In the 1930s:

> If an African is worthy to carry our crosses, he is worthy to hear what the cross means. Christ does not recognize the barriers of race. If you can't find it in your heart to have a brotherly feeling for the brother in black, I'm afraid you'll have to sit by him in the next world, because some of them are going down there, too.

In the 1940s:

Another evil is war. What are the seeds of war? They are many, but we can mention a few. They are race pride and prejudice, ambition to rule, greed. Whom among us can say that he has no desire for his race to be considered as superior to any other, that he is willing to be the brother on equal terms with every other race?

And in the 1950s:

Interesting how we combine our thoughts of right and wrong with that which will preserve our advantages. The favored always feel that right is on the side of the status quo. Those who have property feel strongly the sacredness of property rights. The whites feel strongly the wickedness of the Negro getting out of his place. . . . It seems to be a part of the fallen estate of man that he must imagine his race superior, so that if he has no other superiority, he is superior in that way. Christian character will be tested by race relations. It will be hard to be Christian in the days ahead. Lip service to Christ will not be enough. Both Negro and white need to be genuinely Christian.

Other men without my grandfather's history—his work as a missionary in Cuba and his experience on that front porch in Waynesboro—were driven from their pulpits for speaking so plainly about race in the Deep South during those years. But Walter Moore, adamant in his quiet way, was rarely challenged.

Soon after he arrived at Vineville Baptist Church in Macon in 1959 (where he was called from First Baptist of Meridian, Mississippi), he participated in a meeting of the ushers. They served as the welcoming face of the church, the people who extended the first hand to any new visitors coming through the doors. The hot item on the agenda that evening was what the ushers would do if a "Negro" showed up on the church's broad front steps some Sunday morning. They were ready to set a policy, make it clear-cut and easy for themselves. And many of the ushers probably leaned toward what other moderate churches were doing: seating such visitors inconspicuously in the back row of the sanctuary.

In most policy-setting situations, my grandfather tended to stand back a little, believing that "the most valuable human asset of any church" is its congregational leaders. On the other hand, Dr. Moore was also convinced that "the pastor has the blessed privilege of encouraging and helping" those leaders, and in this instance, he weighed in. His actual words, chosen carefully and spoken slowly in his educated Louisiana drawl, were long remembered. They were recorded in the church history, many years later: "I will not impose my feelings upon the church, but would rather have the ushers use your Christian discretion in the matter." When he said "Christian discretion," they knew what he meant. He had high expectations for his flock.

Everybody knew where Walter Moore stood, and he was the natural first choice when Rufus Harris, President of Mercer University in Macon, needed a trustee to lead the committee that would examine the issue of integration at Mercer. Due to the 1954 *Brown v. Board of Education* Supreme Court ruling, the question of integration at Mercer was an economic issue as well as a cultural and moral one. Mercer was a private institution, but increasingly, major foundation and federal funding was only available to schools that did not discriminate based on race. Mercer stood to lose considerable monies if the university remained lily white.

It is important to remember the times. This was 1962. Though the gavel had fallen on school segregation eight years earlier, few southern institutions had desegregated, and far fewer had done so without serious external pressure of some kind. That fall, two people had died and scores were injured in the riots at the University of Mississippi before they let in their first black student. Lynching was still woefully common, and the Ku Klux Klan was powerful.

In Macon, geographic center of the state of Georgia, local white leadership was more moderate than in many cities across the Deep South. The mayor, a professor from Mercer's law school, was willing to engage in real talks with black leaders, and gradual changes were being made, though progress was far slower than those who continued to suffer under Jim Crow would prefer. In general, law enforcement responded to protests without violence, and courts, especially when presided over by Judge William Augustus Bootle, tended to be remarkably fair for the times.

Unlike in the more notorious cities across the South (including Albany, Georgia, a hundred miles south, where Martin Luther King, Jr., was jailed in December of 1961 and again the following summer), Macon's civil rights movement was led almost entirely by local people who stayed informed about what was working in other places. No one could dismiss the Macon movement on the grounds that it was caused by "outside agitators" coming in to "stir up trouble," as was the complaint in other southern cities.

Rosa Parks refused to give up her seat on a Montgomery, Alabama, bus in December 1955, sparking Montgomery's year-long boycott followed by bus integration. Five years later, Macon had its own bus boycott, which lasted only three weeks and ended with a favorable ruling by Judge Bootle, followed by the bus company's grudging capitulation.

Macon saw a few relatively quiet lunch counter sit-ins as well, following in the footsteps of the 1960 NC A&T State University students in Greensboro, North Carolina. In the summer of 1961, groups of black teenagers held sit-ins in five Macon department stores. Two people were arrested as a result of a fight—one black and one white. The charges were later dropped for both, and a month later, ten downtown department store lunch counters had integrated.

Unlike in other southern cities, the white leadership in Macon would not respond with violence, and progress continued to inch along. Libraries integrated. Golf courses allowed black golfers. Public parks integrated. Schools were still firmly segregated, though, with the issue mired "in committee" at the school board level. Most of the white folks resisted change, and crosses continued to burn.

On the Mercer campus, surveys showed changing perspectives on "the race issue." In 1961, a student body poll showed that 61 percent of students strongly supported segregation. Later that same year, another poll showed a reversal of the trend: 63 percent said they would be willing to stay in college if blacks were admitted, and 37 percent would not. A year later the liberal arts college faculty voted on the issue, supporting integration with a 95 percent majority.

In 1962 Rufus Harris, Mercer president and a long-time supporter of integration, decided that the time was right to bring the issue before the Board of Trustees. He made an impassioned plea to the trustees at their October 18 meeting, and they responded by unanimously approving his motion to form a "Special Committee" to examine the matter and report back at a later meeting. My grandfather, three-term member of the Board of Trustees, was quickly appointed to chair the committee.

Coincidentally, the next month brought delegates from across the state to attend the annual meeting of the Georgia Baptist Convention, held in Macon that year, not far from Mercer. The trustees' vote to form the Special Committee had hit the grapevine hard—rumor had it that the GBC meeting would include a vote about the integration of Mercer. A plane circled overhead during the proceedings, pulling a banner that read, *"Keep Mercer Segregated."* Granddaddy was at the convention, of course, and he breathed a sigh of relief when controversy was held to a minimum with a simple vote to appoint an "advisory committee" from the Convention to provide counsel to his Special Committee.

Letters poured in from across the state. No doubt my grandfather's keen sense of irony was sparked on a regular basis, such as the day he opened the one from Woodlawn Baptist Church in Savannah. Woodlawn's moderator wrote to the Mercer Board of Trustees to report that on November 7, 1962, "our church met for its monthly conference and at this time a motion was made and seconded that Woodlawn Baptist Church of the Savannah Baptist Association go on record as being opposed to integration at Mercer University, a Baptist financed school." The next paragraph went on to explain their reasoning: "We, the members of this church, are very much interested in seeing the Negroes progress; however, we do feel that they have sufficient schools and colleges available without enrolling in white schools."

The letter was printed on the church letterhead, which proudly bore the church motto across the bottom of the page: "Whosoever Will May Come." As long as "Whosoever" was white, apparently.

One might think that a unanimous affirmative trustee vote to create the Special Committee would mean smooth sailing towards policy change. But all across the South, white people were busily forming committees to "look at the issue" as a way to hang on to Jim Crow as long as they possibly could. Many of the trustees, despite President Harris's heartfelt presentation, probably heard "form a committee" and felt safe. In most circles, this was code for "stall," and so they enthusiastically voted "aye." Not so for Dr. Moore. He intended this committee to take Mercer to the next level, so that it could finally step into line with its stated Christian mission.

Granddaddy was taken aback, therefore, at the outcome of the Special Committee's first meeting. It was just after the holidays: January 4, 1963. This meeting was to be held jointly with the Georgia Baptist Convention's advisory committee, and the agenda, as prepared by the chairman, was to consider four items with implications for the issue at hand: the legal questions, accreditation, Christian ethics, and public relations. But unbeknownst to my grandfather, the GBC advisory committee had met already and came to the joint meeting with a prepared statement, ready to shut down the discussion before it could even begin. It was their consensus, they said, that no action be taken on changing Mercer's admission policies. They then went one step further, advising that in the future, Mercer bring any such proposed plans to the Convention's annual session, where it should be decided by the entire Convention. They wanted the matter out of Mercer's hands altogether.

The meeting went downhill from there: three and a half hours of hesitations, fears, and prejudice. The issue of Christian ethics—the issue that mattered most to Granddaddy—was barely touched, and the meeting ended with a vote "not to consider admission of Negroes at Mercer at this time."

My grandfather, as close as he ever got to furious, was not finished. As far as he was concerned, the members of the GBC committee, who commandeered the process, were using economics—rather than Christian responsibility—as the basis of their argument. They convinced the Special Committee that integration of Mercer was unwise on the basis of integration's potential impact on the Georgia Baptist Convention's overall budget. After the meeting, Granddaddy went home and wrote up his personal notes: "When the time comes that I cannot speak what I believe to be God's word to my day for fear of what the result may be to the offering plate, I'll step out of the pulpit and go to digging ditches or doing whatever it may take to keep body and soul together where I can keep my self-respect." It was time to get busy, and though he didn't know it yet, a fresh wind was sweeping through in his favor.

Just a few days after the hellish meeting of the Special Committee, Granddaddy received two letters from Harris Mobley, a missionary on furlough in Savannah from his Baptist work in Ghana. The first was formal and only one page long:

Dear Brother Moore:

I write you because you are chairman of the group of Mercer trustees asked to study and make recommendations relative to the opening of Mercer to all qualified applicants.

I am a native of Savannah, graduate of Mercer and Southern Baptist missionary to Ghana since 1959. We are home this year on furlough.

No one will be happier than I the day you and the other trustees strike down the racial barriers at Mercer. I only regret your action has not come earlier, but I am thankful that it is being handled now. I think you know that several hundred Southern Baptist missionaries in Africa feel this same way.

Just now our whole missionary structure in Africa is undergoing tension. Knowledge of our pattern of racial segregation is growing. The day may well come when more than a hundred years of missionary labor was stopped in twenty-four hours. I hope that you will open Mercer to all applicants, regardless of race, just for what it will do to boost our churches' mission in Africa.

But, the truth is I want to ask you to open Mercer because it is right, Christian and necessary if we seriously intend staying in the business of "Christian education."

My sincere prayers for all of the trustees as you make this decision, I am

Sincerely yours,

Harris Mobley

There was a second letter from the missionary as well, this one of a more personal nature. It had big news:

> Also, you ought to know that we have a boy waiting in Ghana to come to Mercer this Spring or next Fall. His name is Sam Oni, a Baptist, known by the missionaries, A-1, attended our high school, worked with the missionaries. This past July 1962 he handled lots of the translation at the annual meeting of the Ghana Baptist Convention in Sekondi. Here is a picture of Sam (with tie) with another friend and two of the BSU summer students. I think he would make an excellent student, perhaps very good transitional material.
>
> Sam could go to school in Ghana on a scholarship if he were interested in doing technology or science, but he is interested in doing English language and literature. He can pay his way here, but some church or churches, individuals would have to take care of his stay at Mercer. What is it now, about $1500 a year? I have not talked about this with Mercer, I mean finance, I wanted to take care of first things first. Sam has finished his application papers, paid his fees, and is anxious to hear if he has been admitted, but I have told him to stay quiet, and be patient. I just wanted to share this other part of Sam's coming with somebody who might be able to help. His coming here, getting properly trained, returning home full of Christian influences, could amount to many missionary families going, and a whole lot cheaper financially, too.

Granddaddy wrote back immediately, seizing on this new direction for his own mission:

> Dear Brother Mobley:
> I am deeply grateful to you for both of your letters and also for the copy of the resolution.[1] I plan to have the shorter letter together with part of the longer one and also the resolution sent to the members of my

---

[1] I was not able to find a copy of the resolution that Harris Mobley sent with his letters.

24

committee and also to the advisory group from the Executive Committee of the Georgia Baptist Convention.

If you are to be in this area at any time, I would appreciate the privilege of discussing with you this problem. We might not be able to do anything more than cry on each other's shoulders, but that would be something.

I know you will be praying for our committee and the Board of Trustees.

Sincerely yours,

Walter L. Moore

And in his packet to the two committees, Granddaddy included not only Mobley's description of Sam Oni but also another story from the missionary's second letter. Mobley wrote,

I heard David Jester tell this story a few weeks ago over in Alabama. He was invited to speak at commencement exercises in one of the high schools in Nigeria, one of our own I suppose, since he is principal of one there himself. He said that on the night of commencement he went to speak, but the Russian embassy had sent up eight full scholarships, inviting the top eight graduates, cream of the group, to Russia for a college education. One of these happened to be the son of the president of the Nigerian Baptist Convention. The boy argued with this father about going, "Daddy, if I don't take it I won't get any more education." But his father cautioned him "not to sell his soul for a mess of communist pottage."

David said five of the eight did accept. We had none available here....

Walter Moore was ready to play Christian hardball. If it took invoking the fear of communism to open Mercer's doors, then so be it.

He also decided it was time to gently rally the support of other liberal Georgia Baptist ministers. Responding to one of the positive letters he got amid the pile of letters objecting to integration, Granddaddy wrote to his friend Francis E. Stewart, minister of Monticello Baptist Church.

Dear Francis:

Thank you for your excellent letter. No, I have not complained about pastors not writing me in regard to the admission of Negro students to Mercer. I have been pained at some of the expressions of bigotry, but feel that the pastors have not been greatly involved in these matters.

I do not wish to inspire a letter writing campaign of any kind, but do feel that letters to the members of the committee would be worth far more than letters addressed to me. And I particularly think they need to be made aware of the interest of our pastors concerning the African student. I am attaching a slip of paper with the names and addresses of the members of the committee if you wish to write to any of them.

Thank you for your letter, and I thank God for your being in Georgia now.

Sincerely yours,
Walter L. Moore

There was no way the Special Committee chairman would walk into the next meeting and be blindsided, especially now that Mercer's integration had a name and a face: Sam Oni, product of Georgia Baptist missions. The timing was perfect.

The next meeting of the trustees' Special Committee was planned for the same day as their general meeting, Thursday, April 18, 1963, six months after the trustees approved the formation of the committee. The plan was for the Special Committee to meet early, and then move straight into the larger meeting, with no time for politicking in between.

The timing was tight, and Granddaddy must have felt the pressure as he opened the Special Committee meeting with a prayer. Given the application of Sam Oni as well as another application for a black student who wished to attend Mercer's Southern College of Pharmacy in Atlanta, Dr. Moore presented the committee with what he saw as their five options. They could (1) recommend that only Sam Oni be accepted; (2) recommend that the pharmacy student be accepted; (3) recommend that the Law School be integrated; (4) recommend some combination of the first three options; or (5) recommend accepting students without regard to race throughout all schools under Mercer's umbrella. The last option was clearly the one he preferred. As far as he was concerned, keeping Mercer's status quo was not even on the table.

The committee only had one hour to make a decision, and the debate was hot. Two members were absent but they still had a quorum, and Granddaddy sincerely hoped that this would be the day to push the issue all the way to its conclusion. After forty minutes, with a scant twenty minutes until the trustee meeting, no decision had been made. Mr. G. Van Greene finally jumped forward with a motion: "I move the following: 'The Committee recommends to the board of trustees at their meeting today, April 18, 1963, that Mercer University consider applicants for admission based on qualifications, without regard to race, color of skin, creed, or place of origin.'" Mr. C. C. Giddens quickly seconded the motion, and the chairman called the vote: five affirmative, two negative. It was not the unanimous vote that Granddaddy would have hoped for, but it was enough to get it to the next level. The next meeting was scheduled to start in five minutes.

Rufus Harris, President of Mercer, presided over the much larger meeting of the trustees. He walked the group through the lengthy agenda of routine business before finally coming to the last item: the report of the Special Committee. Dr. Moore took the floor and explained in some detail the process of the committee, emphasizing their consideration of "the Baptist convert from Ghana," Sam Oni. Finally, the Special Committee chairman calmly stated the committee's recommendation: Mercer University should consider applicants for admission based on qualifications, without regard to race, color of skin, creed, or place of origin.

He made a formal motion that this policy change be adopted, and Mr. J. Warren Timmerman, member of the Special Committee, quickly seconded the motion. Granddaddy sat down.

At that point the meeting exploded with objections, delaying motions shouted out and defeated, substitute motions proposed, trustees resigning and storming out, and the president calmly presiding over all. Dr. Moore was silent. The discussion, if it could be called that, lasted for nearly two hours. Finally Dr. Harris, who had strongly recommended already that the trustees "do a brave thing" and vote to drop the color barrier at Mercer, stood to speak.

> I work hard to do the best I can. I pray for guidance. I can be useful to you if I state precisely what I think on all our issues. This is what I propose to do. If ever you reach any point where you don't agree with my views, that will be all right with me, for that is the democratic way. I try to be infinitely fair, and at the same time to state what I think is right. If I must be called bad names, that is all right, too. I want you, my brethren, to be able to work with me in love and in interest. Such is my regard for you.

He sat down, the vote was called, and the motion passed: thirteen ayes, five nays, and three abstentions. Though Macon's federally funded public schools were still completely segregated and would not desegregate until forced to do so by Judge Bootle's court order a year and a half later, Mercer University changed its ways on April 18, 1963. That same day, a letter was sent from the Admissions Office to Sam Oni in Ghana. He was accepted to Mercer University, to begin his freshman year in the fall term.

Mercer's student-run newspaper, *The Mercer Cluster*, trumpeted college pride from the rooftops in the next day's editorial:

> Time will judge the far-reaching effect of yesterday's trustee resolution, but already the decision has demonstrated a new spirit of leadership and decisiveness that has long been absent from Southern Baptist Schools. At a time when many of our sister colleges struggle to avoid the desegregation issue, Mercer's trustees have taken their own initiative and made the decision that rightly belongs only to themselves.
>
> The critics of the trustees will be loud and angry, but derision is to be expected. A clear-cut policy on a controversial issue can never be popular.
>
> It would be naive to think that the application of the Ghana student, Sam Jerry Oni, had no direct effect on the trustee action. Oni's application placed the only real issue before the university, the issue of Christian relevance to our social character.
>
> But while Oni's application presented the issue, it was the trustees who made the issue vital. They could have easily avoided the basic

question and admitted Oni as a foreign student, but they chose instead to draw the lines of policy clearly by ruling on the entire desegregation issue.

The strength and directness of the resolution passing testifies to purposefulness of the action. There was no blinking at the shadow of a state convention. There was no frantic concern over alumni reaction. In the words of trustee member Dr. Walter L. Moore, "each member made his own evaluation of the facts and acted with his own conscience."

This attitude toward an avenue of responsible leadership is a precious thing. Its demonstration marks a high point in Mercer's history.

That day was certainly a high point for my grandfather as well, but there was still much work to be done.

In September, Sam Jerry Oni (who had adopted an American-sounding middle name in honor of the occasion) made his way across the globe, eager to experience the "southern hospitality" he had heard so much about. My grandfather, anticipating the next round of challenges, had been busy. Where would the student from Ghana attend church?

The issue was first raised formally at the meeting of Vineville's deacons on Wednesday, August 14, 1963. But first, the minutes report another important event coming up for the church: Double Day.

> Previously approved by Church Council and Finance Committee the Pastor proposed that September, 22, 1963 be designated as DOUBLE DAY, when we would seek to have every able-bodied member attending at least one of the day's services, when those behind with pledges would be urged to bring them up to date, and when every member would be asked to double their tithe for this day. To avoid any pressure, a blank ballot was provided for each Deacon to secretly vote. When the votes were counted, it was found that every Deacon present approved and pledged 100% support to DOUBLE DAY.

Surely Granddaddy, as Mercer trustee, knew good and well that September 22 would be the first Sunday of Mercer's fall term. He wanted to make sure no one could say that there was not a majority. On that day, he wanted the Lord's house to be *full*.

Then came the next item on the agenda, written in an unusually passive voice. Who made this announcement? Did everybody vote?

.

Deacons were alerted to the fact that Jerry Oni, a new Mercer University student from Ghana, might decide to attend our Church. After lengthy discussion, every Deacon voting approved Frank Groce's motion, seconded by Claude Joiner, that we accept Oni if he comes to worship in our Church.

It was the last item on the agenda. Walter Moore had the unanimity he wanted. The meeting closed with a prayer.

A month later, on September 11, the deacons met again. By this time, Oni's arrival was not even a matter for discussion—simply an announcement:

> Chairman Small discussed the fact that Jerry Oni, the Ghana student who is enrolled at Mercer University would be welcomed to worship at Vineville Baptist. This was reported to the people at the regular business meeting at Prayer Service Wednesday, August 28, 1963. There was no discussion and no vote was taken.
>
> Dr. Moore expressed gratitude for the attitude of the Deacons toward the Ghana student. He stated that he hoped very much for Jerry to receive a good Christian Education and to have a good impression of America to carry back to Africa.

Oni's arrival would not be a surprise: if you didn't know about it, you hadn't been coming to church.

Sam's arrival at Mercer was carefully prepared for and orchestrated as well; the first day, he was shepherded across campus, from train station, to dorm, to snack bar, and back by Joe Hendricks, Mercer's Dean of Men. Don Baxter, Sam's new roommate and Mercer's star basketball player, also extended a welcoming hand.

But this southern hospitality, real though it was, could only provide a thin veneer over the reality of the times. In the first week, the minister of Tattnall Square Baptist Church summoned Don Baxter to his office. Don had attended Tattnall Square, the church on the edge of Mercer's campus, during his first two years at Mercer and had even served as a student preacher. But the minister wanted to make sure Don knew that if he came to Tattnall Square with his roommate Sam Oni, they would not be welcome. That same week, my grandfather sent word that Vineville's doors would be wide open. When Sunday came, Sam and Don boarded the student bus to Vineville.

September 22, 1963, was a big day at Vineville Baptist Church. The word about Double Day had gotten out: the sanctuary was packed to overflowing at the eleven o'clock service. Well into the service, the invitation hymn was sung and all those who wanted to join the church that day came forward. Including Sam Oni and Don Baxter, there were thirty-one in all, a huge number for one Sunday. But Vineville was always popular with the Mercer students, and this was the first Sunday of the school year. Granddaddy called all the names except Sam's, the group of students stepped forward, and there was a motion and a quick second that the new members be received. All were already Baptists, so they could be received into the membership without the ritual of baptism. The voice vote to accept them was unanimous. They all sat down, leaving Sam standing alone in front of my grandfather. Walter Moore gently turned him around to face the congregation. "I am presenting the next person separately because he is special."

Granddaddy proceeded to introduce Sam individually to the standing-room-only crowd, telling the story of Sam's conversion by Baptist missionaries, his acceptance at Mercer, and his arrival in Macon from Ghana. Coming to the end of his story, Dr. Moore presented Sam Oni, with skin as dark and beautiful as a moonless night, for membership at Vineville Baptist Church. The sanctuary exploded.

"Reverend Moore, I am not going to sit here and watch you destroy this church by bringing niggers into the congregation! My grandfather helped found this church, and I'm not going to allow you to bring niggers into the congregation!"

"Outsiders are tryin' to integrate our church! Mercer couldn't be satisfied to go out on the streets and get a Macon nigger. They had to go all the way to Africa!"

Throughout the turmoil, Walter Moore and Sam Oni stood facing the congregation. The pastor did not disagree or counter any of the arguments. He simply waited and then said, in the democratically Baptist way, "Let's put the matter to a vote. Those in favor, please put up your right hand." The hands went up. Only the pastor and the young man from Africa faced the congregation, so they alone could see the total number of hands. It was a slim majority, so Dr. Moore called for the vote a second time. Still, the majority was slim. He called for a standing vote this time, and the fence-sitters, those who were only raising their hands halfway, truly had to declare themselves. Though not unanimous by any means, it was a decisive victory.

Sam Oni, dark skin and all, would join the church. In so doing, he would be the first black person to join a Southern Baptist church in the state of Georgia. He would make history again several years later, when he tried to attend Tattnall Square Baptist Church at the edge of Mercer's campus and was physically rebuffed by the ushers before he could even enter the front door. At Tattnall Square, he ended up sitting in the back seat of a police car. At Vineville, he was a *member*.

Having heard a little of this legendary tale in my childhood (I can still hear Sam Oni's name spoken in my grandmother's awe-filled, hushed southern voice), it always ended there. Ticker tape. Fireworks. A Victory for Good in the World. The Good Guys Win Again.

But no. It did make major news, from the *Atlanta Constitution* to the *New York Times* and all the way out to the *Mankato Free Press* in Mankato, Minnesota. But Granddaddy had to hold fast to keep his church together in those treacherous waters, and the message in his "One Moore Word" column in that week's church newsletter was one of reconciliation:

> Our church has been in that uncomfortable location, the spotlight, this week. For those who are most hurt it has been rubbing salt in the wounds, and all of us have cringed. We do not blame the news media. They have been proved correct in their view that our action was news. We regret some of the inaccuracies, especially the repeated statement that the vote was unanimous. It was decisive enough to make a count unnecessary, but it was not unanimous.
>
> Brother Sam Oni has now been accepted for membership in our church, pending receipt of his church letter from Ghana. He understands

the reason for the divided vote, and hopes to make us a worthy member. We earnestly pray that our church may make a real contribution to his Christian growth and preparation for service.

I have been greatly heartened by telephone calls and letters from many of our people since Sunday. Naturally those who favored the action rejoiced in it. But I have been even more impressed by the number who voted "no," but wanted to assure me of their love and loyalty to me and the church. More than ever I am convinced of the basic soundness and genuine commitment to Christ that exist in Vineville Baptist Church.

The response of our people to the "Double Day" idea was magnificent. The offering of more than $12,000 was impressive. What a joy it was to receive 31 people into our fellowship.

I believe that God is leading us; that he has great things in store for us. As best we can, let us follow him.

In a personal letter that week to his dear friend Chauncey Daley in Kentucky, Granddaddy shared a little of what was in his heart: "I do not know what the future holds, but I could not have acted differently if I had known I would be out of a job the next morning."

Through the storm of phone calls, threats, and letters that followed, it was this unwavering sense of what was right that kept my granddaddy on his feet. Ultimately he weathered the storm, drew the Vineville Church community together, and never lost his position in the church or even among Southern Baptists. In 1968, he was elected to the highest Baptist office in the state of Georgia: President of the Georgia Baptist Convention.

~ ~ ~ ~ ~ ~

My grandmama loved birds. One of my favorite things at her house was a plastic wren that lived on the windowsill above the kitchen sink. It had a hole in its back, and when you filled it with water and blew into its tail, it twittered a bubbly song. Grandmama, too, was musical and bubbly.

She was tiny—I passed her early and I'm pretty small myself. She was a bit round, though not fat by any means, and she moved quickly, always in high heels, whether her "bedroom shoes" or Sunday best. But the best part was when you'd first get to her house and poke your head in the door. You'd call out, "Grandmama?" The response, from whatever part of the house she happened to be, was always her characteristic soprano squeal: *hoohoohoohoohoo*! Welcome to the nest.

When I visited Vineville Baptist Church many years after my granddaddy served there as pastor, I had no idea where to go. The place is big and the front door isn't obvious. But I found my way to the office, and after a few minutes of fluttering around me ("did you hear who her grandfather was?"), a nice member of the staff graciously led me down and around to the depths of the church. Down to the History Room.

You go through many doors to get to the History Room. After passing through the room of mirrors, we went to the back of a larger gathering room and stopped at a set of double doors with a sign that read HISTORY ROOM. Big breath. We stepped through these doors, and I found myself at the bottom of a stairway, with a pointed archway to my left and another door beyond it. That was the last door to open before entering the History Room. And just to the right of this last door, above my eye level (she would be tickled to be so tall), was a large framed portrait of my little grandmama. *Hoohoohoohoohoo*! Welcome to the History Room.

As I stepped through that door, an inexplicable feeling of love washed over me, a warmth that had been closed up in the room with the old files, pictures, and church memorabilia for many years. I could tell before I touched a single folder that the sentiment for my grandparents was still strong in this church. They were a beloved pair, and the feeling lingered in the air, nearly tangible. I breathed it in and felt blessed.

One of Granddaddy's columns in the weekly church newsletter expressed his own appreciation of his calling and the Vineville community:

ONE MOORE WORD

What is it like to be a pastor?

It is trying to lead people in worship, knowing that some are nearer to God than you are, and some entirely uninterested.

It is an earnest search for God's message to His people, very imperfect preaching, and the hope that some seed falls on good ground.

It is listening with compassion and without condemnation as people confess their weaknesses, tragedies, and sins.

It is trying to pray for hundreds of people, some of whom you hardly know.

It is seeing people you love grow more faithful and happier in their religious lives.

It is being disappointed in some from whom you have expected too much.

It is being called, sometimes at midnight, to be with loved ones in their hour of sorrow.

It is being praised for virtues you do not possess and criticized for things for which you are not to blame.

It is being remembered at Christmas with greetings, gifts, and kindnesses which you can never repay.

It is being honored for all that God has done for His church while you have been permitted to serve it.

It is—No; I give up. It is something new and different every day, and if I should keep writing on and on, I could not say all that it means.

But not for the world would I be anything else, and serving as pastor at Vineville is a joy and privilege for which I daily thank God.

I learned about Granddaddy's role at Mercer and Vineville in 2006, when I went to Macon on my first research trip for this book. But there was more to learn. I had heard that Sam Oni had returned to the United States from Africa several years ago, and my trusty friend the Internet led me to his phone number and an Atlanta address. I was planning my next trip to Atlanta to visit old haunts, and marveled at the possibility of meeting the real person I had always thought of as a superhero. But the idea of calling him out of the blue, as with Neb Kendrick, was unnerving.

Fingers on the keypad. *I can do this.* One ring, two, three—*oh good, I'll get the answering machine. Quick, think of what to say.* I hear his beautiful, lilting accent on the answering machine—*yes, this must be the right number!* "Hi, my name is Cindy McMahon, and my grandfather was Walter Moore, the pastor at Vineville Baptist Church in Macon, and—"

Click. *A person!*

"Ohhhhh," he breathed, after a pause, "you are an answer to prayer."

I never thought to ask what his prayer had been—I was too busy feeling thankful myself.

When I found Sam at his apartment complex a few weeks later, he greeted me with a warm hug in the hallway and then welcomed me inside, ready to share his story. As I stepped into the living room, I was dumbfounded to be faced with the same picture that hangs at Mom's house: the stained-glass windows at Tattnall Square Baptist Church, the church on the edge of the Mercer campus where Sam Oni was barred from worship forty years before. But it was too soon to broach that subject. I turned on my tiny tape recorder and listened.

Joining Vineville Baptist Church, Sam told me, was "a faith-shattering experience." He continued going to worship there for a year or more after that September day in 1963, but never felt accepted. After the racial epithets were hurled towards where he stood at the front of the church the day he joined, he always felt self-conscious, looked-at. As he said, "The climate was not exactly conducive for reflection, for meditation, for just being in the presence of God."

If he happened to arrive at church early and sit in an empty pew, no one else would sit there. No one in the church reached out to him, invited him for Sunday dinner, asked him about his family or his studies at school. He never experienced the legendary "southern hospitality" that he felt he so richly deserved. Where was the warm welcome for this young man who had traveled across the world, the fruit of the Baptists' own labor in the missions field?

As soon as he graduated from Mercer, Sam turned his back on Georgia and the South altogether to head for Berkeley, California. Graduate school, flower children, Black Power, accepted at last. As Sam told me, it was the beginning of a love affair with a city as far from Georgia as he could get.

Finally, once Sam had generously answered all my other questions, I couldn't hold out any longer. After everything that had happened with Tattnall Square Baptist Church, I asked him why that picture, of all possible pictures, was hanging on his wall.

He told me the story.

I'm here, just minding my own business. I got a letter, return address Mike Griffin, something like that. And I'm scratching my head. Could this have been one of my classmates that I didn't remember, that just found out I was in Atlanta? Anyway, it turned out to be a member of Tattnall Square Baptist Church. And this guy was effusive, trying to apologize for what had happened. This was just about three years ago.

Anyway, I then responded and it turned out that he was kind of a one-man campaign trying to right the wrong of the past in regard to the church's position towards me. He broached the idea to the minister and the deacons. As far as they were concerned, I was the one who brought the church to rack and ruin, and it nearly led to another fracture. So this guy persisted, and got a few members of the church. He was going to invite me to speak. And then reconciliation.

But some of the die-hards were members when the event happened in '66. So he organized a group of the like-minded people. The minister didn't take any leadership role because the ministers are simply the wage-earners, you know.

We met in a restaurant. We met, and Betty and Joe [Hendricks] came to this restaurant, and a handful of people from the church came, and we had this dinner. That's when this [gesturing to the picture] was presented to me.

Now, for me, Cindy, I don't know about you, but forgiveness is so therapeutic. It heals the forgiver as well as the forgiven: Let me labor the obvious. Whether you realize it or not, the only time that we live is really and truly the here and now. So people can latch onto incidents of the past, and let that affect them whichever way, and in fact maybe even retard their growth and progress. Or be obsessed with the future, and be made insecure by it. But really and truly, the time one lives, is here and now.

With those words, I felt like I had been brought by the hand to Sam's small apartment in Lenox Square specifically for this purpose: to come face to face with yet another story of radical forgiveness. Like my grandfather, whom Sam said "was a man of courage, a man of faith," Sam had been able to forgive those who had hurt him most deeply, and had found healing in the process. He had learned to live in the here and now. Where was *I* living?

Driving away, after bidding my good-byes to Sam, I continued to ponder that question. I thought of the picture of stained-glass windows that hung in Sam's apartment in the city as well as in my mother's house, far back in the mountains. We are all stained; we are all as fragile as those large windows, made up of shards left over from past hurts and injustices. They are left to each one of us. To me. Can I let go of the past, forgive, and live in the here and now? Can I pick up the shards and make them into something beautiful? Can I let the hurt out of the dark places where I've kept it all these years, and allow the light to shine through?

I was beginning to understand, finally, that this forgiveness—letting go of the pain and protective anger left over from my childhood—could be the greatest gift I would ever give myself.

It would be freedom. At last.

3

Steel

In the hot southern autumn of 1962, when Walter Moore was just pulling together his Special Committee for Mercer, my father, Al Henry, was in Mississippi. And he was getting restless.

As Head Chaplain at Mississippi State Hospital, a psychiatric facility in Whitfield, Dad felt cooped up within the walls of the hospital campus, where our family lived in a nice neighborhood of hospital employees. He kept a close eye on the news reports from 175 miles north in Oxford: the federal marshals, days of rioting, the governor decrying integration, two people dead, and many wounded before James Meredith was finally allowed to register as the first black student at the University of Mississippi.

The State Sovereignty Commission, created to "protect the sovereignty of the State of Mississippi and her sister states" from federal interference, had recently reached a bony arm even into the enclave of the State Hospital at Whitfield, investigating claims that another chaplain had organized an integrated church summer camp. Dad could no longer justify his position as a state employee, working for such an unashamedly racist Mississippi state government. And it wasn't just Mississippi he was straining against—Dad also felt restricted by the conservatism of his lifetime church brethren, the Southern Baptists. He was ready for *change*.

The ripple of Dad's restlessness, especially about the Baptist conservatism, reached to the heart of the family. Granddaddy Moore, as a lifelong Southern Baptist himself, was sensitive to Dad's struggle, and wrote about it that fall in a letter to Walter, Jr., my Uncle Buddy.

Yes, I think Al has definitely made up his mind to join the Congregational Church. I don't know how much the Elliott controversy[2] and the race matter weigh with him, but they must have some influence. He says that there are pressures in any Baptist pastorate that he can't live with, and that he can't find a supportive fellowship for intelligent inquirers. I hope he is not disappointed. I have written him two or three letters, primarily to allay any feeling on his part that he is moving away from us.

By the time James Meredith set foot in his first class at Ole Miss and Mercer took the step of forming the Special Committee, Al Henry was ready to step out of the fold. The first of January 1963 would be the hundredth anniversary of Lincoln's Emancipation Proclamation. Dad needed to be in a place where he could exercise his freedom to speak out.

The Congregational Church, founded in the North and known for its liberalism and open-mindedness, was a natural new church home. Dad applied to transfer his ordination from the Southern Baptist Convention to the United Church of Christ, the new denomination formed in 1957 when the Congregationalists joined with the Evangelical and Reformed Church. His formal UCC "Privilege of Call" was signed by James Lightbourne, Jr., of the UCC Southeast Convention, and Ben Herbster, UCC President, on December 1, 1962. It was time to get out of Mississippi.

I don't know how Mom felt about the prospect of the move, and those memories are gone for her, but I imagine it was like all the others—just as she finally felt settled in a place and it began to feel like home, Dad was ready to go. Mom liked their little community at Whitfield. It felt safe on the campus, and their brick ranch house fit nicely with the others on the street, all filled with mothers and children while the fathers worked in the big hospital.

---

[2] Ralph Elliott was a Baptist theologian who had recently authored a book, *The Message of Genesis,* that seemed to question the historical accuracy of the story of Adam and Eve. The book, which was published and then removed from circulation by the publishing arm of the Southern Baptist Convention, caused quite a furor among Baptists. Elliott was invited to speak at Vineville Baptist Church in 1963.

But on the other hand, she had gotten married with the idea of becoming a minister's wife like her mother, and the role felt natural for the short time that Dad was a young minister at University Baptist in Baton Rouge, Louisiana, in the mid-1950s. Even though they would be leaving the Baptist tradition of her childhood and her daddy, she must have looked forward to returning to her role as first lady of a church. It fit her like an Easter glove, a comfortable role for the mother of three young girls: Janet was three years old, Nancy was seven, and Linda was ten (I would come along several years later).

Mom and Dad were both outgoing, though in different ways. They made new friends as Dad looked for a pastorate in the United Church of Christ. Ed Brown, who worked for the UCC Southeast Convention in Atlanta, introduced Dad to an entrepreneurial young UCC layman in Montgomery, Alabama—Millard Fuller. Millard and his wife, Linda, were involved with a group of others who were starting a UCC church in Montgomery. Since their church wasn't yet large enough to have their own minister, they had visiting ministers preach on Sundays. As it turned out, this arrangement provided the opportunity for the Pulpit Committee at Pilgrim Congregational UCC Church in Birmingham to travel down and quietly get a look at potential ministers for their own empty pulpit. The day that Al Henry preached, with his wife and daughters sitting with the Fullers in the congregation, Pilgrim's Pulpit Committee liked what they saw. By springtime 1963, the Henry family was moving to Birmingham. It was nearly Easter, time for new life.

But it wasn't just spring blossoms that were exploding in Birmingham that spring. Birmingham at that time was known far and wide as "Bombingham."

While Macon had always been a textile town, with Old South cotton mills near the river, Birmingham was a steel town. It was a gritty industry. The hills around Birmingham had the perfect geological makeup: black prisoners mined rich veins of iron ore, coal, and limestone, the three primary ingredients for steelmaking. And the culture of the city had grown up around this hot industry, with the white power structure becoming just as rigid as the steel beams their mills forged, providing structure for skyscrapers across the country.

Like the confluence of minerals in the ground, Birmingham's culture in 1963 had all the ingredients for a powerful civil rights movement. The fearless and outspoken Reverend Fred Shuttlesworth, with his direct ties to Martin Luther King, Jr.'s Southern Christian Leadership Conference, was ready for an all-out campaign after the struggles of Albany. Mr. A. J. Gaston, an affluent black businessman, may have been hesitant to stir up the white power brokers, but he had plenty of money to support the movement and a motel to provide shelter to its planners. Crowds of black children were willing to climb over fences to escape their segregated schoolyards and march for freedom, facing snarling German shepherds and powerful fire hoses. And then there was the aptly named Eugene "Bull" Connor, Birmingham's infamous Police Commissioner and a virulent racist always ready for a fight. Together, these provided all the ingredients necessary for a powerful media sweep that would shake the nation.

My family arrived in Birmingham on Good Friday, April 11, 1963, and spent the night at the Birmingham Motel. The moving van arrived on Saturday, and movers carried our belongings into the manse on Gaywood Circle in Mountain Brook, the affluent white suburb where Pilgrim Congregational Church was nestled among the pines.

On Saturday, April 12, the Southern Christian Leadership Conference began leading marches in Birmingham, in spite of a new state court injunction against demonstrations. Martin Luther King, Jr., marched at the head of the line and was arrested, to be thrown into solitary confinement. Over the course of the next several days in that cell, he would write his famous "Letter from a Birmingham Jail," countering the criticisms of moderate white clergy in Birmingham who had published an open letter in the *Birmingham News* that called for the black leadership to postpone the campaign.

The next day, Easter Sunday, April 13, Dad preached his first sermon as pastor at Pilgrim Congregational Church. He was out of Mississippi, he was in a liberal denomination, and he was on the edge of the biggest drama of the day in the civil rights movement. I have no doubt that, for my daddy at least, resurrection was in the air. He must have been exhilarated.

Unlike the large and prosperous Vineville Baptist Church in Macon, Pilgrim Congregational had always struggled to survive. Its church history tells story after story of financial problems, near-fatal congregational conflict, and church buildings that threatened to cave in around the worshipers. The fact that the church community continued to stick with it, in spite of the obstacles, is a testament to their commitment if not their common sense. But on that Easter Sunday, they, too, must have felt that their luck was changing at last.

After nearly a year with an interim minister, they finally had a young, energetic pastor. There had been strife in the church, which was basically split down the middle over race issues: those who had come to Birmingham from northern liberal churches were adamantly in favor of integration, and those who had grown up nearby were just as firmly saying, "wait, wait." Here was a minister who might have some liberal leanings (I don't think they knew the extent of Dad's vision), but he was a son of the South, had come from the Baptists, and could surely bring the two sides together. And his wife was a lovely person, daughter of a prominent Baptist minister. Not only did they have a minister at last, but they also had a shiny new church home. The church was modern, completed just two years earlier. It was an A-frame, with a huge steel roof—bright blue—that was already a landmark in Mountain Brook. The roof was a testament to Birmingham's livelihood, and had won awards in the steel industry. The building's many windows let the light stream in, and it had enough room for the day school they planned to open for Mountain Brook preschoolers. It was a time of promise.

Dad must have felt the promise continuing when a letter soon came across his desk, forwarded by Robbins Strong at the United Church Board for World Ministries. The letterhead was from Carrs Lane Church, Birmingham 4, England.

16th May 1963
The Minister,
The Congregational Church,
Birmingham,
Alabama, U.S.A.
Dear Pastor,

I am a young Congregational minister at a fairly large city church. I am the leader of a group of young people called the Seventy Club (Luke 10:1) whose members come from a variety of backgrounds—junior school teachers, secretaries, etc. Our age range is 20 to 30 years old.

Carrs Lane Church has a link with the Congregational church in Birmingham, Alabama. In 1934 the minister, the late Rev Leyton Richards, presented the church in Birmingham with the pulpit Bible which had been used at Carrs Lane by the Rev Dr. R. W Dale, minister 1859-95.

Each year the Seventy Club has a residential conference lasting a long weekend. This year the conference is to take place from November 15th–17th under the title of Race Relations and Problems, and we wonder if you and your young people could help us? Alabama has figured much in our English newspapers in recent weeks over the question of race relations; we have seen films on our T.V. programmes of the recent disturbances which have taken place in Birmingham. All this would be very relevant to our conference. Would it be possible for you to send us a tape recording, made by a group of your young church members, of their thoughts, reactions and opinions to these racial difficulties and tensions? We should then play the recording at our conference and use it as a basis for discussion. I wonder if you could help us in this way?

If there is any other information you would require perhaps you would kindly let me know. I would just add that the main aim of the Seventy Club is similar to that of the original seventy sent out by Jesus—to serve the community in which we live. We have a variety of groups which read to blind children, decorate old people's homes, visit elderly housebound people, etc. We hope that our coming conference will assist us to understand and help in our own city's race relations and problems. Birmingham, U.K. has a population of one million people of whom 60,000 are from overseas.

With kind regards,
Yours sincerely,
Michael F. Hubbard

I imagine my dad in the small church office, tapping his pencil excitedly on the gray steel desk. Here was the perfect opportunity to get the church talking openly about race issues, and the finger would not be pointed at him as the instigator! He quickly shared the letter with Harold Long, his new friend and the minister at the black First Congregational Church across town, and the two of them got busy, strategizing about the best way to present this opportunity to the two congregations. By late June, they were ready to respond. Dad wrote to Robbins Strong at the United Church Board for World Ministries in New York City, who had forwarded that first letter from England:

> This is to advise you that Harold Long and I have had two conferences with regard to the possibility of our people preparing a tape recording for the church in Birmingham, England.
>
> Harold and I have also conferred with our members about this matter. We have both received a favorable response in regard to the project. Today we are writing a joint letter to the church in Birmingham, England to get more specific information from them regarding the information they need, and to advise them that we are working together on this project.
>
> Though I have only been in the church since Easter, Harold and I are rapidly becoming fast friends. We find that we have many interests in common, and we believe that we can accomplish much through our mutual efforts.

The same day, these differently complected but like-minded ministers sent a joint letter to the sister church in England, asking for more specific guidance to frame their discussions, and assuring Reverend Hubbard that they would have something to send him in time for the Seventy Club's conference in November.

Reverend Hubbard, excited that his idea for the young people was coming to fruition, responded promptly with an outline to guide the discussions:

1) Could you start by each participant giving brief personal details of himself/herself—name, age, occupation, etc. Also, could we be told the size of Birmingham, Alabama, and its approximate racial composition.

2) Could we then hear something about the two Congregational churches in Birmingham; their situation—why there are two—is this due to geographical and historical reasons. What is the racial composition of each congregation? If one church is for one race and the other for another could the team make some comment about it?

3) We should then like to hear something about education in Birmingham, Alabama. Are the schools/universities integrated or segregated? Could any comment on this also include comment on integration/segregation in public places—parks, cinemas, buses, restaurants, etc.?

4) The letter written by Martin Luther King from Birmingham City Jail has been widely publicised in this country in both the religious and secular press.

a) It would seem that the demonstration which he led was criticised as 'untimely'. Could the team comment on this?

b) What comment would the team make on Dr. King's general statements about the treatment of Negroes?

c) Have any changes been made by the new administration to ease racial difficulties?

5) Does the team have any comments to make on inter-marriage?

6) What has been the attitude and what activities have the two churches taken in respect of integration or segregation?

7) Do members of the team wish to make any comments about the racial situation in England as they know it?

8) We find it very difficult to understand and countenance the policy of apartheid as carried out by the government of South Africa. What do you think of this policy and ought the Christian Church to speak and act against it?

Again, I imagine Dad chuckling with glee as he read the letter from England. These were not superficial questions—the British Congregationalists had done their homework and were getting to the heart of the matter. These were not questions that could be sidestepped with the usual niceties. This was going to be *real talk*. It was Dad's favorite kind.

Because of the general tension of the time, it was decided that there would be two panel discussions, one at each church, and they would send two tapes back to England. Though individuals from the two churches had already begun a series of unofficial biracial meetings, with members from both churches coming together at First Congregational to get to know each other, it was dangerous and they started out gently. During the meetings, as Dad and the other members from Pilgrim Church sat in First Church (located on "Dynamite Hill" near downtown), police officers patrolled the parking lot, recording license plate numbers so that they could track the names of the white people attending meetings at this "Negro church." The tapes for England would reflect the segregation of the churches themselves.

By a stroke of amazing luck, I came across a copy of the original reel-to-reel tape of members of Pilgrim Congregational Church, tucked in a box in the storage room off the basement choir room.[3] With permission, I borrowed the tape and had it copied to a CD so I could listen to it, and was transported back to a time before my birth, when my father's personality was being forged in the fires of Birmingham. He spoke very little on the tape, but gave a heartfelt statement at the end of the hour-long discussion. It was powerful to hear his young voice, calmly but adamantly speaking his truth:

> We've mentioned various factors that have fed into the Birmingham racial situation, and different ones have referred to different factors. Some of the factors we've mentioned are the emotional, economic, moral, educational, political, medical and cultural factors. My one concern is

---

[3] When I found the tape, I did not yet know that the two churches had held separate panel discussions. Then, when I was finally able to listen to the recording, I was disappointed to hear only members of Pilgrim Church. I have not been able to find the tape from First Church, though I've contacted their church, as well as Carrs Lane Church in England. The black perspective, which must have been very different from the hesitant perspectives of the white folk in Mountain Brook, will remain a mystery.

that we be sure not to use the other factors, for which we share a responsibility, to avoid our moral duty.

The teaching of the Old Testament scriptures is clear that we are our brother's keeper. We know from the New Testament record that Jesus crossed racial barriers in mixing with the hated Samaritans. The Christian faith always involves a risk and the possibility of a cross. Jesus mixing with the Samaritans may have been one of the reasons he was crucified.

We know that Jesus himself taught and practiced a respect for the dignity and the worth of an individual person as a child of God. I believe that we know also that Paul, in interpreting the mind of Christ, indicated that we were to be neither slave nor free, and we might paraphrase this to say that we are to be considered neither white nor negro in the Christian faith, but we are all children of God, and we are all one in Christ Jesus. We all have one God, and we are all members of the body of Christ. As long as the body of Christ is divided in that the brothers are alienated from one another, we know that this must cause God heartache.

I think that we must take the mind and the heart of Christ as our final guide in these matters.

If the Pulpit Committee or anybody else in Dad's church still had questions about where he stood on the issue of civil rights and integration, there was no doubt now. He could not be considered a "moderate" when it came to what he believed was carrying out the will of God.

The tape was mailed to England on October 26, 1963, Dad's thirty-seventh birthday. By the time it was mailed, his long-overdue installation had taken place at the church, and there was no going back. But the installation service itself, and especially the circumstances surrounding it, touched him profoundly and deepened his commitment to the cause of justice in Birmingham.

Dad's installation service was planned for the evening of Sunday, September 15, less than three weeks after the historic March on Washington. Martin Luther King, Jr.'s "I have a dream" speech was still ringing in everybody's ears. But the service would be, of course, a different kind of occasion. It was not a time to make waves—there would probably be no black faces in the congregation, though it would have meant much to Dad to have his friend Reverend Harold Long as a part of the service.

There were plenty of other "personalities" listed on the bulletin, though, with five UCC ministers from Alabama, one from Georgia, and two from Florida, plus the Moderator of the Southeast Convention of the UCC, as well as James Lightbourne (known as Jimmy), the Superintendent of the Southeast Convention. The one Dad was most excited about, though, was his old college buddy, Irvin Cheney, now a UCC minister in Daytona. Cheney had agreed to give the sermon at the evening installation service.

Cheney arrived the day before and spent the night at the manse with my family. When he got up the next morning, he informed Dad that he wouldn't be worshiping at Pilgrim that morning because he felt led to go over and hear Harold Long preach at First Church. Cheney told me the story of that morning, and I captured his words in my tape recorder:

> I said, "Al, I'm going over to First Congregational Church today. I'm not gon' be in Birmingham and go to your church on Sunday morning and Sunday night at this time in history. And not go to Harold Long's church." I said, "I've got to do this." He was completely supportive. He thought it was the right thing to do.
>
> So Sunday morning I got up early, got myself ready, and was going across the mountain into downtown. I noticed all these police cars in eerie silence, racing around, racing around, all over downtown Birmingham. Not a siren, not a horn, not an anything. It was as if someone had muted the universe. And there was this frenetic activity going on. And you knew something major was underway. And the fact that they were so quiet about it made it even more so.
>
> So I get to the First Congregational Church while they're having Sunday School, and I'm sitting in the parking lot. Some good welcomer of the church saw me out there and told Harold I was out there, and I guess they figured they needed to find out who this was. At the time, you wouldn't blame them for it. So Harold came out and saw who I was, and we had a nice visit for a moment, and he says, "We're in terrible shock."

He said, "the Baptist Church a few blocks away was just bombed, and we don't know how many people were injured or killed. We have many interconnections, families all interwoven, and this congregation is just shaken terribly."

I went in to the worship service, the only pale face in the whole area. And during the service, people kept bringing him little pieces of paper with updates, and he finally announced, about halfway through the service, there had been four teenage girls who were killed, and an undetermined number injured. Well, I'm telling you, I felt like I was a spot of leprosy on the body politic or something like that. That was a lonely feeling. Because there was shock and anger and hostility and fear and apprehension, and "what's this white boy doing here anyway?" probably, though they were too polite to say that. And I existed through that service, and made proper courteous visits, and they were properly courteous, and I left and went back over to Al's and Carol's for Sunday dinner.

I walked in, and Al says, "You look like you've seen a ghost." I said, "I might as well have, after what-all happened." And he said, "What happened?" I said, "Al, you haven't heard?" "No."

I told him the whole story. And he sat there, and he said, "What a lesson. I might as well have been in South Africa instead of just over the mountain." And it was moving to realize—now here's Al, as dedicated as he was to the same thing that they were, and yet there, in Birmingham, two sister churches. By the time I get home, it's about three or four hours after the incident, and he hadn't heard 'til I told him. And we both learned a lot about what the situation really was. It really shook us. Naturally the next Sunday morning, my sermon topic was "The Other Side of the Mountain." Had to be. It was incredible.

The aftershocks of that bomb blast at Sixteenth Street Baptist Church in Birmingham echoed across the country, including the relatively quiet Macon, Georgia, where Sam Oni joined Vineville Baptist Church just one week later. In the Henry family, I'm sure my mama hugged her own three little girls just a little bit closer. They might be over the mountain, but it was all mighty close.

The next spring brought another Sunday evening UCC occasion: a Birmingham visit from Dr. Ben Herbster, President of the National

United Church of Christ. He was welcomed to Birmingham by both UCC churches, and a controversy arose within Pilgrim about whether they would host the biracial service.

On May 11, 1964, the following letter went out from Pilgrim Church to all its members:

> Dear Fellow-member:
> At a regular meeting of the Board of Trustees the following resolution was moved, seconded, and unanimously voted by those present:
> The Board of Trustees, being responsible for the church properties, hereby resolves that in the future there shall be no integrated meetings or gatherings in the church or at the manse unless such affairs are cleared by both the Board of Trustees and the Board of Deacons and approved by the congregation; except as provided in the constitution by direct petition to the congregation.
> Yours very truly,
> David A. Booth, Chairman
> Board of Trustees

The question of where Dr. Herbster would speak had been resolved, though indirectly. From then on, Dad could not even invite his friend Harold Long to dinner at the manse without defying the trustees' resolution. He must have been furious.

Dr. Herbster did speak at First Congregational, the black church, on May 24, though, and Dad participated in the service. Dad's role was to read the scriptures:

> And God said, Let us make man in our image, after our likeness; and let them have dominion over the fish of the sea, and over the fowl of the air, and over the cattle, and over all the earth, and over every creeping thing that creepeth on the earth. So God created man in his own image, in the image of God created he him; male and female created he them. And God blessed them, and God said unto them, Be fruitful, and multiply, and replenish the earth, and subdue it: and have dominion over the fish of the sea, and over the fowl of the air, and over every living thing that moveth upon the earth. ...And God saw every thing that he had made,

and, behold, it was very good. And the evening and the morning were the sixth day. (Genesis 1:26-28, 31)

Wherefore the law was our schoolmaster to bring us unto Christ, that we might be justified by faith. But after that faith is come, we are no longer under a school master. For ye are all the children of God by faith in Christ Jesus. For as many of you as have been baptized into Christ have put on Christ. There is neither Jew nor Greek, there is neither bond nor free, there is neither male nor female: for ye are all one in Jesus Christ. (Galatians 3:24-28)

No matter what might be happening over at Pilgrim, for the folks gathered that evening at First Church, the message was clear: all were equal in the sight of God. Five weeks later, in a direct response to the Birmingham civil rights campaign, the US government agreed. President Lyndon B. Johnson signed the Civil Rights Act of 1964 into law on Thursday, July 2. Independence Day that year had a whole new ring.

But the issue still wasn't settled at Pilgrim. Though the church facilities were officially white-only now, many members were angry enough about the whole thing that they were ready to separate entirely from the UCC denomination. Less than a week after Dr. Herbster's visit, another letter went out to the congregation, this one announcing a special business meeting a week later:

A special business meeting of the congregation of the Pilgrim Congregational Church is hereby called to be held immediately after the morning worship service on Sunday, June 7, as requested by the May 24 petition of thirty-three members of the church: "for the purpose of determining the future relationship of the Pilgrim Congregational Church to the United Church of Christ."

The title of Dad's sermon that Sunday, June 7, was "Teach us to Pray," and I'm sure he had been doing a lot of praying about the issue himself. He had gotten considerable support from the Southeast Convention for his efforts on behalf of civil rights, and a disaffiliation vote would pull the rug right out from under him.

David Booth, Chairman of the Board of Trustees, was fairly moderate, and came to the June 7 meeting with a lengthy motion already prepared, requesting that the congregation not hastily vote to disaffiliate, but instead form a Church Program Committee to look at all aspects of the church, and to formulate "an overall Church Program to which we can all truly unite in furtherance of our mutual Christian obligations." It was a noble attempt to defuse the situation and redirect attention, but it failed. Instead, the following motion passed: "We move that the Board of Deacons and the Board of Trustees and the minister be instructed by this Congregation to make a full study of our relationship to the UCC and that they further be instructed to bring such a plan before the Congregation." Immediate disaster was averted, but the issue was still on the table.

The deacons and trustees held their joint meeting on August 25, at the end of a long, hot summer. At that meeting, which must have been extremely contentious, the following resolution was duly moved, seconded, and passed:

> Resolved that a Congregational Meeting be called for Wednesday night, September 16, 1964 at 7:30 P.M. for the purpose of amending our By-Laws by deleting Article III, Paragraph 3, which reads as follows: "While this church is amenable to no ecclesiastical judicatory, it accepts the obligation of mutual council, comity, and co-operation involved in the free fellowship of the United Church of Christ, and pledges itself to share their common aims and works."
>
> Further, that following the determination of this proposed amendment, if that amendment is carried, motions will be entertained to determine our future relationship with the United Church of Christ.

With eleven people present, including Dad, the resolution passed by a vote of six to five. If the momentum for this effort continued, Pilgrim would surely divorce itself from the United Church of Christ.

In the meantime, Al Henry and David Booth turned to the one strategy that always seemed to work: money. The church had been in financial straits for some time, forced to refinance its mortgage and cut spending in order to keep afloat. As David Booth reported in a letter to the congregation on August 6, collections consistently fell short of expenses, and for the month of August, they did not have enough funds to pay both salaries and the mortgage without borrowing money. It didn't look like September would be any better.

But there was one piece of the puzzle the leadership hadn't yet shared: if the church decided to disaffiliate, the financial situation could become far graver—they had learned that the United Church of Christ had a grant mortgage on the total property of Pilgrim Church in the amount of $19,500. As a grant, it could be deferred indefinitely, but it would become immediately payable under three conditions: (1) if the church sold its property; (2) if the church went out of existence; or (3) if the church withdrew from the denomination.

In the end, as is often the case, money carried the day. The church simply could not afford to divorce itself from the national UCC; if they did, they would have to close the doors. At the September 16 meeting, the congregation voted to stay with the UCC. After yet another contentious and divisive meeting, Dad must have decided he deserved a break. He went fishing the next day—all day long.

Within a month, the church received a flood of resignation letters, including letters from the church treasurer and two of the church leaders who had voted for disaffiliation at the joint meeting on August 25. The rift between the two factions of the church continued to widen, with wills as unbending as the two sides of the church's tall steel roof.

With the matter of UCC affiliation settled, the church leadership turned its attention more completely to solving the financial crisis. By this time, it was apparent that even the steel roof was beginning to deteriorate. David Booth presented a financial report to the Church Council on September 23, 1964, saying that "nothing short of complete replacement of the sloped roof will solve our problem." The roof, it seemed, was becoming a large blue symbol of the general problems plaguing the church. In the tall A-frame building, the roof *was* the church.

Since Pilgrim was still affiliated with the UCC, the leadership decided to turn to the denomination for emergency support, and in November, David Booth wrote a long letter to Jimmy Lightbourne at the

Southeast Convention, explaining Pilgrim's financial woes in detail and requesting assistance. At the end of the three-page business-like missive, Booth changed his tone:

> I have watched our Minister and a large number of hard-working and loyal members of this Congregation work very hard to accomplish the stated policies of our "Denomination." I have heard representatives of our Denomination state that this "Civil Rights Program" (for want of a better title) is one of the most important programs of our national group. Let's face it, "this Civil Rights Program" accounts for the largest part of our problem today in Birmingham, and our problem has arisen because we have worked aggressively to pursue the stated policies of the Denomination. It quite frankly irks me to have to approach the Denomination "hat-in-hand" for assistance to get us out of a financial hole that came about, largely, by an attempt to put their programs into action. Speaking personally, I feel the Denomination owes this Congregation assistance—and in a substantial amount.

For Booth, at least, there was a direct and logical connection between the divisive political issues and the church's ongoing financial difficulties.

The situation continued to decline, and by January, the trustees faced the possibility of complete bankruptcy. The situation was dire. But whether or not Booth's assessment of the root cause was correct, his impassioned plea eventually resonated with the national UCC leadership. At the end of January 1965, the church received word that the Board for Homeland Ministries would send $2,500, barely enough to cover basic expenses for the remainder of the fiscal year. It was a far cry from the $12,000 that Vineville Baptist had raised from the collection plate on one "Double Day" Sunday a year before, but it was a statement from the denomination in support of my father's leadership. A letter from Jimmy Lightbourne, enclosing the first grant installment, reflected the UCC's sensitivity to David Booth's concerns and made a strong statement to the divided church:

> The members of the Board of Trustees, the Board of Deacons and the congregation should be aware that this contribution is made by the Board for Homeland Ministries of the United Church of Christ in recognition

of the fact the church is experiencing difficulties because it is seeking to face up to its Christian responsibility at this particular time and in its particular place. In addition, it is recognition of the leadership the Rev. Albert Henry is giving to the congregation.

The date was March 26, 1965.

Hearing the story of the political and financial problems within Pilgrim Church, one might think that my dad had no time for anything aside from writing sermons, visiting the sick, and dealing with Pilgrim's multiple problems. But he could keep a frenetic pace, and he was still active in the ongoing (though now lower profile) civil rights movement in Birmingham. His calendar from those days shows weekly contact with Harold Long and lists biracial meetings of the Alabama Council for Human Relations, the Concerned White Citizens of Alabama, and regular meals and get-togethers with others involved in the movement, mostly from the ministerial perspective.

After "Bloody Sunday" in Selma, when police officers on horseback, wielding billy clubs and tear gas, advanced on unarmed marchers standing on the Edmund Pettus Bridge, the call went out to movement supporters across the country: "Come and show your support!" Dad could not stand idly by. The following Tuesday, March 9, Dad drove to Selma for the march that was later named "the Tuesday Turnaround," when Martin Luther King, Jr., led supporters up and across the bridge again. This time, though, when the marchers came to the barricade of law enforcement at the end of the bridge, with the road to Montgomery spreading out beyond, Dr. King led the long line in a U-turn, heading back toward Brown Chapel where they had begun.

Dad went again to Brown Chapel the following Monday, to attend the service Dr. King led for slain white Unitarian minister James Reeb, who had traveled to Selma from Boston in support of the movement and been clubbed to death by a white racist on the evening of Tuesday's turnaround march.

The next week, Mom's brother Buddy responded to the call as well, arriving with a friend from Boston, and Dad returned to Selma to march with them. Buddy remembers that as they drove to Selma, his friend said, "Al, you've done this before. What are you thinking as you face the long line of stone-faced police in riot gear?" With a twinkle in his eye, Dad responded, "I just silently chant, 'don't wet your pants, don't wet your pants.'" Their laughter, echoing through the VW bus as it barreled toward Selma, eased the tension of a fearful day.

Finally, Martin Luther King, Jr., and the Southern Christian Leadership Conference got permission to march from Selma all the way to the state capitol in Montgomery, a distance of fifty-four miles. Only three hundred marchers would be allowed to make the entire march, but all supporters were welcome for the final leg into Montgomery, and, on Thursday, March 25, the long march neared its destination. Dad drove the ninety miles from Birmingham to Montgomery to join the march in its final demonstration and cheer for King's culmination speech for voting rights.

> How long?
> Not long, because the arc of the moral universe is long, but it bends toward justice.
> How long?
> Not long, because:
> Mine eyes have seen the glory of the coming of the Lord;
> He is trampling out the vintage where the grapes of wrath are stored;
> He has loosed the fateful lightning of his terrible swift sword;
> His truth is marching on.
> He has sounded forth the trumpet that shall never call retreat;
> He is sifting out the hearts of men before His judgment seat.
> O, be swift, my soul to answer Him! Be jubilant my feet!
> Our God is marching on.
> Glory, hallelujah! Glory, hallelujah!
> Glory, hallelujah! Glory, hallelujah!
> His truth is marching on!

By the following Monday, March 29, it was clear that Al Henry would not be able to stay at Pilgrim. The national UCC had declared its wholehearted support of his leadership and direction (with hard cash to back it up), but his unapologetic participation in the Selma march, even on his own time, could not be countenanced by the conservative members of Pilgrim Congregational Church. Divided against itself, the church was threatening to collapse. The note on Dad's calendar for that next Monday read, "letter to church." And the note for the following Sunday simply read, "mtg. resig." It was over. My father was resigning from Pilgrim.

Over a tearful cup of coffee at her friend Fran's kitchen table, Mom poured out her heart. It hardly seemed believable that two weeks later, Easter Sunday, would be the second anniversary of the Easter they arrived in Birmingham. So much had happened. Resurrection had been turned inside out. And she felt as if she had, too. Once again, just as a new place began to feel like home, it was time to pack up the girls and move on. Sixty days later, in accordance with the terms of Dad's original contract with the church, my family was on the road.

~ ~ ~ ~ ~ ~

Once again, going to the actual place, sitting in a pew under the tall blue roof of that church, gave me a new understanding of my family's history "at that particular time and in that particular place." I walked through the Birmingham Civil Rights Institute, and the movement became real to me. I stood transfixed by the steel sculptures in Kelly Ingram Park, just across the street from the still-beautiful Sixteenth Street Baptist Church. I could imagine the steel German shepherds snarling as they snapped at the shirt of a young man. I could feel the children's fear and pride as they stood behind the bars of the jail. I shared in the moment of the young girl hiding behind the tree, trying desperately to escape the force of the water cannons, frozen forever in that 1963 moment.

As I spoke to old friends of my parents at Pilgrim Church—Pat, Fran, Ethel—I learned that although Dad's strategy faltered at times, his courage never did. They loved and admired him for it, but their deepest fondness was saved for my mama.

She had weathered so much. There were harassing phone calls and more, like the time the exterminator showed up, saying that he had been called with a report of "pests in the parsonage." Next it was a moving company van pulling into the driveway, months before my parents decided to go, ordered by someone who said that the minister was leaving and needed help. And the *piece de resistance*—one day a hearse appeared, driving slowly down Gaywood Circle toward the house. The ominous message was clear.

It must have been doubly hard for Mom because of her natural gifts for diplomacy and reconciliation, learned early as she watched her father gracefully weaving together differing factions in every church he led. She innately understood that sometimes fellowship is more important than justice, especially in the life of a church. But she felt that it was her job to support her husband, not to question or guide him. It was her job to take care of the girls, have dinner on the table when he got home from a meeting, and keep his shirts starched and ironed, always wondering if they would someday be stained with his blood. It was her job to be strong and supportive, ever the classic Southern steel magnolia.

After I visited the History Room at Vineville Baptist Church, Granddaddy's last pastorate, I found my way to the Walter L. Moore Education Building and remembered being there the day it was dedicated to him, when I wore pigtails and kneesocks. The bronzed plaque on the wall there is engraved with Granddaddy's favorite Scripture of all, from the Sermon on the Mount: "Seek ye first the kingdom of God and his righteousness, and all these things shall be given unto you" (Matthew 6:33). Granddaddy truly believed that if you do what is right, everything will work out in the end. And his legacy at Vineville proved it.

Like Granddaddy, my dad felt led by the Scriptures. But his legacy at Pilgrim, his last church, was very different. No buildings were dedicated to his memory. No plaques. But when I went through what was left of his papers in musty old trunks at the back of my sister's storage shed, I found something as close to a plaque as Dad ever got: two pieces of white paper in his most careful printing, with holes in the corners as if they had been hung up on a wall somewhere. Written in red marker were these words:

The Lord
Thy God
A
Consuming Fire
Deut. 4:24   Heb. 12:29

And then came these words in green:

Flee like a
bird to the
mountain—
Psalm 11:1

That was my daddy, all right. Fire. Flight. That was his legacy.

The Pilgrim Church history describes the Reverend Albert L. Henry III as "sincere, earnest, and dedicated," but "he nevertheless proved unequal to guiding the church through the storms, and under his leadership, it only became more polarized." Dad was brave, but his legacy in Birmingham is one of failure.

I have always admired his courage from that time, and have wondered why the experience left him with so much bitterness. It was his first big failure, I think, and because of his insecurities, he was wounded rather than forged by its fires. He carried that bitterness with him from that point forward. He never was able to let it go and feel the freedom of forgiveness.

I often think about failure. Whenever you take a great risk, the possibility of failure looms large. Perhaps the secret is to have true courage not only when facing danger but also—especially—in the face of abject failure. To be willing to face failure head-on, admit that it didn't work, and move on afterward without a life's worth of bitterness. To forgive ourselves as well as others who hurt us or contributed to our failures.

I may be a Southern woman, but I'm not a Southern lady. My hair and nails are a mess, and I don't wear makeup most of the time. I don't *want* to be the quintessential steel magnolia, rigid with strength. I want to be the real, living tree, with strength of flexibility, bending in the wind, losing branches when I need to, and continuing to grow in spite of—*or because of*—my losses.

4

Exodus to Genesis

Sometimes leaving everything behind is the best option, even if you're not clear about where you're heading. But when you leave it all behind and head for the wilderness, you've got to be prepared for that wandering feeling, not knowing where you're headed or whether you'll reach a destination at all. Wandering in the wilderness is a lot like being lost. And that's what my family's next chapter felt like. The Henrys' focus changed completely, along with everything else.

In the last few weeks of his job at Pilgrim, Dad spent a lot of time driving back and forth to a place called Koinonia Farm, near Americus, Georgia. It was a refuge from Birmingham, a place where he could catch his breath among like-minded people. While he was there, he discovered a new way of living.

For twenty years, people had lived communally on this farm in southwest Georgia, picking cotton, shelling pecans, fertilizing the soil, and living according to their Christian beliefs. Unlike most other Christians in Sumter County, for residents of Koinonia that didn't mean shining up their Sunday shoes, giving generously when the plate came down the pew, going to Bible study on Wednesday night, or even sitting through long deacons' meetings. At Koinonia, they lived their Christian faith day in, day out, in a whole different way.

This different way of living didn't always sit well with the neighbors. Clarence Jordan, my Grandmama Henry's first cousin and the man who founded Koinonia with Martin England in 1942, best described the local folks' suspicion of Koinonia in his book, *Sermon on the Mount*. Interpreting Matthew 5:10-12 ("Blessed are they that have been persecuted for righteousness' sake"), he wrote,

It is difficult to be indifferent to a wide-awake Christian, a real live son of God. It is even more difficult to be indifferent to a whole body of Christians. You can hate them, or you can love them, but one thing is certain—you can't ignore them. There's something about them that just won't let you. It isn't so much what they say or what they do. The thing that seems to haunt you is what they are. You can't put them out of your mind any more than you can shake off your shadow.

They confront you with an entirely different way of life, a new way of thinking, a changed set of values, and a higher standard of righteousness. In short, they face you with the kingdom of God on earth, and you have to accept or reject it. There's no washing of hands. These people must be crowned or crucified, for they are either mighty right or mighty wrong.

To men whose loyalty is to the world, these citizens of the kingdom of heaven are subversive agents, dangerous enemies who must not be tolerated.

As far as Clarence was concerned, Koinonia Farm was none other than "the kingdom of God on earth," a beloved community, with all its attendant and resultant difficulties—not the least of which was the fact that black people and white people lived and worked side by side at Koinonia. They even ate at the same table every day.

In the late 1940s and early 1950s when Koinonia was just getting started, the locals thought it was strange, but most people weren't too upset about it. The Englands and Jordans bought the land (with significant help from a benefactor) and started farming. Originally, it was a true commune. (The name, Koinonia, is a Greek word that appears in the New Testament Book of Acts, basically meaning "fellowship." It describes the way the apostles lived communally.) Prospective members of Koinonia Farm were to arrive "flat broke"—they had to give away everything before they arrived or else give it all to the community, and each family got an allowance to live on. Everybody worked on the farm, caring for animals such as chickens, cows, and pigs, and farming pecans and many other crops. The community shared a daily midday meal in the dining hall. Other meals were eaten as individual families.

Koinonia was very much a Christian place. In addition to his bachelor's degree in agriculture, Clarence had a Ph.D. in New Testament

Greek from the Southern Baptist Theological Seminary, and by the time my dad came to visit Koinonia, Clarence was waist-deep in the project of writing his own translation of the New Testament set in mid-twentieth-century Georgia, *The Cotton Patch Gospel*. Though most Koinonians weren't welcome at local churches, they considered Koinonia itself their church, viewing themselves as the apostles in the New Testament book of Acts. Koinonia members had regular Bible study groups and worshipped together on Sundays, taking turns offering a sermon or sitting together in silence, Quaker-style.

After the 1954 *Brown v. Board of Education* decision, which declared school segregation unconstitutional, the larger Sumter County community began to take notice of what was going on at Koinonia. Almost overnight, Koinonia went from being weird but harmless to posing an honest threat to the American way of life that white folks were accustomed to.

That was when the violence started.

Cars would drive slowly by the farm, shooting as they went, blowing out windows, shooting through a hat on a bedside table, firing rounds directly into the midst of children playing ball in the yard. The little roadside stand where the farm sold hams, pecans, and peanuts was dynamited more than once and finally leveled completely. The Ku Klux Klan burned crosses out front and drove menacingly by the farm in long lines of cars with stone-faced men at the wheel. Koinonians stacked wood against their houses to protect the children from bullets as they slept inside, and the men took turns every night keeping unarmed watch in a car at the edge of the property. They were a stubborn bunch, convinced that such persecution was the lot of all true Christians. They didn't give in.

What nearly destroyed Koinonia was not a violent attack but an economic one. The Sumter County business community launched an unofficial but effective boycott of Koinonia, refusing to sell the farm anything it needed to survive: fertilizer, animal feed, tractor parts, and more. It was a complete embargo. Koinonia could neither buy nor sell products locally. It was then that they launched the mail-order pecan business that survives to this day, with an advertising slogan that expressed Clarence's wry sense of humor: "Help us ship the nuts out of Georgia." And they did. The boycott was still going strong in 1965, and Dad worked in the pecan plant when he came to visit.

Though they neither marched nor demonstrated but simply lived their values while farming the sandy soil of Sumter County, Koinonia back then was, as Jimmy Carter has said, "a beacon light for people who believed in racial equality." Though the beacon light was wavering a bit by 1965, it was still shining, and it caught my daddy's eye.

I picture Dad driving fast along the 250 miles of road between Americus and Birmingham, thinking about the possibilities at Koinonia, living among those who agreed about the basic humanity of all people, escaping what he saw as hypocrisy in the insulated Pilgrim Church perched on the hill above Birmingham. I see him imagining the whole family living according to Christ's teachings, leaving materialism behind, working the land side by side with their differently complected brothers and sisters. This was the answer. It was time to stop preaching it and start living it. It was time for the Henrys to "leave all to follow Jesus."

But when Dad got home, the sparks flew. Mom put her foot down. Stomped it, in fact. Every other time Dad had wanted to move just as she was beginning to feel at home, Mom went along without putting up a fuss. But this time was different. She knew they would have to leave Pilgrim, but leave *all*? Not just their home, the church, her friends, and the girls' schools, but the very way of life she had always known? To live on a dirt farm in south Georgia that endured regular drive-by shootings? It was too much. In their three beds, my sisters heard the shouting in the darkness, and felt the ground shifting underneath them. But in the end there was no defying my father. Our mama was still the wife, and she was expected to defer to her husband. Yet again, she gave in, swallowed her anger, and put on a cheerful face for the rest of the world. She was good at that by now.

At first, leaving Birmingham felt like a here-we-go-again experience to my sisters. After all, they'd never lived anyplace longer than a couple of years. In each new place, it didn't seem to take long for Dad to get restless, see all the problems, grumble about the people, and be ready to pack up and go again. My sisters were used to the "new kid" feeling, not having the history the other kids had, feeling on the outside, starting over.

Nancy was nine, and she went through the old familiar ritual of saying good-bye to her best friend, promising to write, knowing deep-down that it wouldn't matter because she'd still be gone. But she made the best of it. Linda, who was twelve, stood in the doorway and recognized that echoing, empty house feeling and the answering emptiness in her own chest. Janet, only five, was wide-eyed in the midst of the rapid changes.

Soon, though, this move began to look different than the others. Our parents had been getting rid of things, like the nice living room furniture and fancy knick-knacks. They kept saying, "We can only take what will fit on the truck."

But hadn't there been a truck last time, and the time before that?

Then came the truck—not a big moving company vehicle operated by men in matching shirts, but a beat-up old farm truck, with a couple of big guys from Koinonia, one black, one white. In previous moves, the family had set out ahead while the movers did the loading. This time, even the kids were expected to pitch in and help. It was beginning to feel like an adventure.

Once everything was packed up, the manse swept clean, and the door locked for the last time, they headed out, the old truck and the VW bus staying close together all the way. It was Saturday, June 5, 1965, and they were on their way to Georgia. They were headed into the wilderness—my sisters were probably picturing Moses from the drawings in their Sunday school books, with his long beard and tall staff. Would the VW bus have to cross the Red Sea between Birmingham and Koinonia? As long as Pharaoh's army didn't catch up, they figured they'd be okay. When they got to Koinonia and everybody piled out, my sisters must have found that, as they were beginning to suspect, life would be very different now.

Even though they'd moved a lot and Dad had been involved in things they didn't completely understand, their lives had always been similar to other kids' lives. They had always lived in a nice house in a nice neighborhood. Daddy had dressed in a suit every morning and gone off to work. Mama had made sure everybody did their homework and got clean behind the ears. Not anymore. Now our family would live in an old farmhouse with bare light bulbs on the ceiling and no central heat or even a bathtub. They would bathe in a big metal washtub!

Daddy was trading his business suits for overalls, and Mama would be working, too. Not only that, but even the girls would have jobs— milking the cows, setting the long tables for community dinners, making breakfast for the family, working in the pecan plant. There weren't many people at Koinonia then, and it was a huge farm. Everybody had to pitch in.

But the farm. Oh, the farm! It was a childhood paradise. A sandy road encircled the commune, perfect for round-and-round bike riding. A light comes into my sisters' eyes when they tell me about the chinaberry tree they could climb, the swimming hole deep enough for diving, the hay barn to tunnel through, and industrial-sized fruitcake bowls to lick. It was summertime, school was out, and when the chores were done, there was nothing but freedom and the big, wide sky. Linda found an old guitar and a Joan Baez songbook, and started teaching herself some chords. Still-tiny Janet loved to talk to the massive cows by the fence behind the house while she stroked their big noses and spoke in a soothing, sing-song voice: "You don't have to be afraid. I won't hurt you." And Nancy loved the kitchens, watching the big black ladies stirring the fruitcake batter with the big paddles in the huge, stainless steel vat.

Though he was technically their first cousin twice removed, Clarence Jordan, Koinonia's founder, was like a big loving uncle to my sisters. He took them on motorcycle rides on the country roads around the farm, or they rode on the back of the motorcycle across the fields, rounding up the cows. Other days he gathered up all the kids to read the best Winnie the Pooh they could ever hope to listen to. Slow, sad

Eeyore. Piglet with the eager, high voice. And friendly, drawling Pooh. Clarence did them all, a Hundred Acre Wood in the Deep South.

And then there was Florence, Clarence's wife and mother of their four children, all but one already grown up and gone. My sisters remember that they could always count on Florence for two cookies, "one for each hand." Compared to our mama, Florence seemed huge and powerful, tossing enormous pots around in the kitchen and plunging her big hands into water that was sterilizer-hot. My sisters were in awe.

Koinonia had dwindled from its heyday, and the Wittkampers were the only other family still living on the farm. Will and Margaret were somewhat elderly by that time, and their three teenaged sons ran a bit wild. There were few other kids, so Linda and Nancy wanted to hang out with those boys. But they had learned a thing or two by watching the bulls with the cows in the field, and they figured you could never be too sure about teenaged boys and hay lofts. The freedom they loved felt dangerous at times. That was the other side of the farm coin.

The only other person who lived on the farm full-time was Collins McGee. Collins was a young man then, in his early twenties. He was the only black person who lived at Koinonia, though others worked there. He was beloved by everybody, especially my sisters. He was their safe place. As long as Collins was around, they knew nothing bad could happen. Collins had a twinkle, too, and used it to his advantage. One time, when visitors were coming to stay, Florence asked Collins to clean the toilet in the guesthouse. "Happy to do it, Florence," he answered. "Where do you keep the starch?" He drove the tractor that afternoon instead. Collins had a special way of letting life roll off his back, even though Koinonia's mission was more real to him than to anybody else who lived there.

Though they thought they were heading into the wilderness, my sisters found that Koinonia was more like the Garden of Eden that summer. They enjoyed a freedom they had never felt before. And the whole community must have celebrated the Voting Rights Act of 1965, signed into law on August 6, the result of the Selma-to-Montgomery March and the final piece of legislation that Dr. King and the Southern

Christian Leadership Conference had been pushing for. It was a big day. Three weeks later, my parents celebrated their fifteenth wedding anniversary. They had come a long way.

Though my sisters managed to avoid the forbidden fruit, their long, golden days in this Garden of Eden came to an abrupt end. Summer was over. Janet and Nancy were sent off to elementary school, and Linda boarded the school bus for junior high. Unlike the grownups, relatively insulated at Koinonia, the kids had to come face to face with the outside world every single day of the week.

The school year began calmly. Janet made friends with a little girl in her first grade class, Kay Chappell. Kay and Janet recognized each other as kindred spirits from the beginning, learning in the same class, eating lunch together, sharing secrets and smiles. They hatched a plan to have a sleepover and were both excited to ask their parents about it.

Kay went home to ask her daddy, the sheriff of Sumter County, if she could spend the night with Janet. When he heard where Janet lived—that detested, communist Koinonia place—he told Kay in no uncertain terms that could she not spend the night with her friend and, furthermore, she was never to speak to Janet again. The next morning, when the two little heads came together at school, Kay shared the answer, and both girls were confused and heartbroken. After that, Janet's best friend in Sumter County was a brick. Literally a brick, wrapped in a baby blanket. And Janet wasn't surprised to learn, when I told her forty years later, that Martin Luther King, Jr., had called Sheriff Chappell "the meanest man I ever met" after his stay in the Sumter County Jail during the Albany Campaign. Though she never had the opportunity to meet the sheriff, Janet always felt the same way about him.

Nancy, who managed every move by finding a best friend as soon as possible, made friends with a girl in her class, too. They planned to go to the carnival together. On the appointed afternoon, Nancy dressed in her best carnival clothes, carefully put her allowance in her pocket to pay for the rides, and walked out to the Koinonia sign where she and her friend had agreed to meet. She waited, sitting on a rock, watching the sign swing back and forth, back and forth. After more than an hour passed,

Mama came out and told her that she might as well come back; clearly her friend wasn't going to come. But Nancy didn't believe it, so she kept on waiting. When it finally began to get dark, she walked slowly home, pushing her glasses up her nose to hold back the tears. How could anybody let down her best friend that way? She never forgot it.

But Linda, who turned thirteen at the beginning of the school year, faced the worst of it. Once the word got out that the new kid lived on "that commie farm," the name-calling began. She always sat in the front seat on the school bus, imagining that if she crouched low enough she could completely disappear and would never again feel the humiliation of a spitball on the back of her neck. After weeks of standing exposed and alone every day on the playing field during recess, one day she realized that she could go inside to the bathroom, where she could stand in a stall until the bell rang and it was time to go back to class. So, from that point forward, that's what she did every day, standing in the bathroom stall and waiting in her brown loafers, grateful for the protection of the close walls around her.

My sisters weren't the only ones having a hard time at Koinonia. For Dad, who was so eager to get out of Birmingham, leaving its tumultuous pace for the slow farming rhythms of Koinonia must have felt like hitting a concrete block wall. Dad was used to being a mover and shaker in Birmingham, leader of the church, and a familiar figure in biracial civil rights activities. He was used to feeling important, having an independent identity, being the breadwinner of the family. And now here he was, sorting pecans, answering to Clarence, stuck in this backwater place with no outlet for his powerful energies. His frustration began to bubble over, burning the ones he loved the most.

One afternoon after school, Linda was in the pecan plant, working with Lenny Jordan and David Wittkamper. David filled the bags from the chute, Lenny folded and heat-sealed them, then handed them to Linda to stack for shipping. But they were teenagers and had fun as they worked. Joking, flirting, tossing the bags in a pile, often being less than careful. Then Dad walked in, a dark cloud across the sun. As soon as he saw what was happening, he became enraged, his face red, eyes blazing, yelling at Linda, barely able to control himself. The boys stopped working, eyes wide, machines still running. Linda looked down and apologized quietly, seeming to shrink as they watched. Dad stormed out. Linda wiped her eyes, lifted her chin, and started straightening the pile. They resumed their work in silence. Lenny, who told me this story on a North Carolina mountaintop many years later, had never experienced anger like that, and he never forgot it. Linda had to forget. It was the only way she could survive it.

The family had only been at Koinonia a few months when their lives began to unravel. Dad was straining within the limitations of the small community, craving the excitement he had left behind, wanting to be more involved in the struggle. Mom was trying to make the best of it while watching Linda's torment, wishing she could wave a magic wand and offer her firstborn the carefree happiness of her own teenage years. Mom and Dad were thirty-four and thirty-eight years old, and three girls was plenty. Having lost two other babies, they felt no need to try again. If there was any certainty in those uncertain times, it was this: there would be no more children in the Henry family. The circle around the supper table was complete. Though my parents were nowhere near the advanced ages of Abraham and Sarah in Genesis, they felt like it some days, and the idea of a new baby for my parents was equally ridiculous.

On a Tuesday morning in September, when all the girls were in school, Mom drove the green Volkswagen bus the eight miles into town to the A&P. She had finished her shopping, loaded all the brown bags into the back, and was waiting for the car in front of her to turn out of the parking lot, when a car came up behind her and didn't stop. BOOM—VW sandwich. The police came, of course, and everybody agreed that it was the fault of the lady behind her. But then, somehow, when they all got out their driver's licenses and gave their addresses, the story changed. The policeman figured out that Mom was a Koinonian, and he charged her with failure to have her car under control. It was Mom's first bald-faced experience of the prejudice that Koinonia had battled since its beginning.

A few weeks later, Mom noticed that she was feeling strange, and her period was late. She figured that she had injured herself somehow in the fender-bender. Not knowing if any doctor in Americus would see her, she called her friend Lib Willoughby.

Lib and her husband Broadus were close friends from my parents' college days, and they lived in Americus, where Broadus owned an auto parts store and served on the school board. With Koinonia's reputation and the tension of the times, the two families could only visit back and forth under cover of deep darkness. But they kept up their close friendship nonetheless, and it felt natural for Mom to call Lib. "Don't you worry," Lib said, "we'll take care of it."

Lib called Dr. Gatewood, the only OB/GYN in town, who had delivered her three children. When she told him about her friend at Koinonia, he responded gravely, "Now Miz Willoughby, you know how dangerous these things can be." "Oh, yes, Dr. Gatewood, we face that every day with Broadus's store, wondering if we're going to get a call some night telling us it's been bombed, just because Broadus has supported integration on the school board. But Carol's not the type to make a big scene, and frankly, I'm worried about her."

That was all it took. Dr. Gatewood agreed to see my mother. At the office, Mama told Dr. Gatewood about the A&P accident, and he conducted a thorough examination with plenty of tests. She waited nervously in the exam room for quite some time, until Dr. Gatewood finally returned and folded his six-foot-five frame into the chair across from her. He opened her chart and looked thoughtful. Until dementia finally erased it, Mama would tell me this story on my birthday every year, her alto voice dropping to a bass at this point, in imitation of Dr. Gatewood's pronouncement.

"Well, Miz Henry," he said, "you have had an accident, it's true. But it's an entirely different kind. You're expecting."

And that was the beginning of me. Oops. Genesis, indeed.

Unlike Sarah, my mama didn't laugh when she heard about this new twist in her life. Driving back to Koinonia, she was in turmoil. Any new life was supposed to be wonderful, and she felt like she ought to be happy. But here? Now? In the midst of all that was going on? Her husband was restless in another new place, clearly fraying around the edges. Her oldest was suffering no less than daily torture at the fragile age of thirteen. Koinonia was struggling under the weight of the boycott. The Civil Rights Movement had accomplished its legislative goals, but Americus and the whole South still felt as racist and violent as ever. Who would bring a new life into this kind of world? Besides, her last two pregnancies had ended abruptly, two months early. The first of these two was a boy who only lived for two days. The second, Janet, weighed a scant three pounds and spent five weeks in an incubator. But tiny Janet used every ounce of stubbornness she had, fighting to stay alive, and she made it. The likelihood of carrying another baby full term seemed slim at best.

All alone in that beat-up VW, driving on the back roads of Sumter County, the tears must have flowed, sobs racking her thin shoulders. But knowing my mama, by the time she drove in past the wooden Koinonia sign, her tears were dry, the cheerful smile back on her face. No one would be the wiser.

Dad, for his part, was thrilled when she told him. As he told his buddy Cheney down in Daytona (also the father of three girls), "This time it's gonna be a boy!"

It was still early in the pregnancy, though, and soon another surprise took their minds off the tiny new life that would be me. Since the time my family had moved from Mississippi to Birmingham, my parents had kept up their friendship with Millard and Linda Fuller, the Montgomery couple involved in starting a new UCC church where Dad had preached when he was interviewing with the Pilgrim Pulpit Committee.

Dad had preached several times at the Montgomery UCC church after my family moved to Birmingham as well, and my parents and sisters usually went to the Fullers' house for Sunday dinner afterward. Though the Fullers were far wealthier than the Henrys, the two families were compatible from the beginning. Linda Fuller remembers Mom wearing a little hat with a veil and Dad looking "like how you would imagine one of the disciples looked—just so genuine, so authentic." Millard saw in them a religious version of his own family: "they looked like a rather typical young couple on the way up in the ecclesiastical world." At the time, Millard and Linda were on the other side of the civil rights fence, but they were beginning to question the ethics of their Old South position and wanted to hear about Dad's involvement with the movement in Birmingham.

As with Dad, the Selma march became a turning point for Millard, though he didn't march and it caught him almost completely off guard. He was at his office one day when the secretary put a caller through whom he'd never heard of. "You don't know me," the man said, "but I'm a UCC pastor from Philadelphia and I'm at the Jeff Davis Hotel downtown. I'm here with another UCC pastor from Colorado, and we both want to go march with Martin Luther King over in Selma, but we can't get there. Nobody will take us. There are no buses running, and no taxi will take us. We haven't been able to find anybody who will take us over there, and I have been told that you are a UCC layman. Will you please take us?"

Millard, who knew as well as anybody the danger of the situation in Selma and the huge impact that this small decision could have on his thriving business, simply answered, "I will." Morris Dees, his business partner and friend (and later the founder of the Southern Poverty Law Center) rode along, and from that point forward, the two were on the other side. According to Millard, it was a defining moment in both of their lives.

Not long after, Millard got a letter from my dad saying that the Henrys were leaving Birmingham to move to some Christian community in South Georgia with an unpronounceable name. Millard thought, "I guess he just couldn't stand the heat in Birmingham any longer. They're headed for the wilderness." The letter ended up at the bottom of a pile, and Millard hardly gave it another thought.

But then came the train wreck for the Fuller family, along with their own version of Exodus.

The Fullers' marriage had suffered for some time, but Millard was too busy riding the wave to notice. He was gone all the time, making money hand over fist to buy bigger houses, fancier cars, expensive toys for his children, and lovely clothes and jewelry for Linda. But, in the middle of all that wealth, the main thing Linda felt was loneliness. She finally boarded a plane, leaving everything and everybody she knew in Montgomery to seclude herself in complete anonymity in New York City. She had to figure out where she was heading.

Millard was never one to accept a loss. Leaving the children in good hands in Montgomery, he went north himself, and the two finally laid it all bare. She confessed her complete disenchantment with their lifestyle. He realized that none of it meant as much to him as she did, and together they agreed to leave it all behind, to give it all away. The problem, though, was that they had no idea what to do next.

When in doubt, go on vacation. So they did, spending two weeks in Florida with their children Chris and Kim, then five and three years old. Though the direction of their lives was completely up in the air, Linda told me, she was elated that at last they could be a real family.

The unknowns started crowding the car when they finally dusted off the sand to head back to Montgomery. It was the beginning of December. What next? Over breakfast in an Albany diner, Millard asked, "You remember that letter I got from Al Henry a few months ago? Didn't it say they were going to some Christian community with a strange name down here in South Georgia somewhere? We ought to stop by and see them." Linda agreed, and Millard got the operator on the diner pay phone. "Is there some Christian farm down here somewhere, something with a foreign-sounding name?" The operator answered, "Nothing I know of, not here in Albany. Let me see…." Millard heard the flipping of phone-book pages, and she got back on the line. "No, nothing in Albany. But I see a Koinonia Farm over in Americus."

"That's it!"

The operator connected Millard to the farm, and he got directions. He and Linda agreed that they'd stay for two hours at most, because by then it would be about eleven, and they knew that in the South if you're visiting someone at lunchtime, your hosts will feel obliged to invite you to stay and eat. They didn't want to impose.

They drove the thirty-five miles from Albany. Millard pulled their long, gray Lincoln Continental onto the sandy drive of the farm, and they never looked back. After a nice visit with my parents, they agreed that, yes, they guessed they would stay for lunch. They stayed for a month.

Millard and Linda found just what they were seeking at Koinonia: a group of people living simply, unafraid to live life based wholly on their understanding of Christian principles. They found kindred spirits who understood their need to give away their wealth, rather than treating them like they had lost their marbles. At Koinonia, after all, letting go of your shiny marbles was the first step to true apostleship.

During the day, Millard worked as close to Clarence as he could get, in the fields or in the pecan plant, soaking up the vision and marveling at the potentials. Linda mostly looked after Chris and Kim, who loved to run wild on the farm, stretching their arms and legs, getting dirty, reveling in the freedom from the stuffy lifestyle they'd left behind. Linda also spent time with my mama, enjoying the female companionship, bending over Mama's slim black Singer sewing machine to make her a calico skirt and blouse, since Mama had long ago discarded the stylish maternity outfits of a minister's wife and was quickly running out of things to wear.

This was a chance for the Fullers and Henrys to reknit their bonds, and they shared many simple suppers at our round wooden table, talking on and on about new understandings of Scripture, the difference between "churchianity" and the real thing, and how they might finally live up to the lessons they'd been absorbing in Sunday school their whole lives. Dad and Millard, both naturally gregarious, could go on for hours—their wives did most of the listening.

Millard idealized our family at that time:

One evening I had some reason to go over there, and there was a soft light on in the living room, and your dad was sitting there reading by this soft light. I can see it in my mind right now.... I didn't go in the house— I saw him through the window. And I thought, "What a wonderful family! What a wonderful picture of a man at peace! He's a man at peace,

76

a man at peace. Look at him sitting in there, just so peaceful, and reading. And the light is soft, and everybody is quiet in the house, and obviously everybody is so happy in this house."

Having the Fullers around must have relieved some of the pressure for Dad. For the moment, he didn't have that feeling of leaving the boiling pot of Birmingham to get stuck in the sludge at Koinonia, isolated from the rest of the world. Here were other young people who wanted to *talk* about all of it.

For Dad, the Fullers provided an oasis in the wilderness. But for the Fuller family, this visit would lead to the genesis that shaped the rest of their lives and the lives of countless others. When they returned to Koinonia to stay a few years later, they worked with Clarence to plant the seeds of Habitat for Humanity, which they eventually nurtured into a worldwide movement. It was the Fullers' exodus, a complete break with everything they had known, which opened their minds to the possibilities lying ahead.

All that, of course, would come later. For the moment, Mom appreciated the respite and sighed her relief. Maybe everything would all be okay after all.

~ ~ ~ ~ ~ ~

When I visited Koinonia, I followed my usual pattern, heading first to their little room of community archives. There's not much there; I learned that all of Clarence's papers and many of the old community documents were donated to Special Collections at the University of Georgia in Athens. But I dove into the boxes and drawers, discovering newsletters and articles about Koinonia from the time my family lived there. I was looking for one particular story that has been told and retold in my family, a story of my father Al Henry, my grandfather Walter Moore, and a few others.

I found it in the Koinonia newsletter from April 1966, one month before my birth.

Just before Christmas the Baptists of this area held a district rally at the First Baptist Church in Americus. The principal speaker, a prominent Southern Baptist clergyman, was the father of one of our members. Since the announcement of the event in the local paper stated that the public was invited, a number of us decided to attend. As the first ones in our group, who were white, entered the door each was handed a card on which to write his name and church. Clarence entered first, then Linda and Millard, then Collins (who is Negro). A card was automatically handed to Collins but when the usher noticed that his hand was black he just froze, and so Greg, Carol and Al, who came in next were not given cards, even though they are white. When it was clear that all had gotten past the door, the group walked down the aisle nearly midway, found a vacant bench and sat down together. The congregation was singing "Gloria in Excelsis, Deo." Hardly had we taken our seats when the people in the pew in front of us started holding a conference with one another, and as soon as the congregation finished singing "Gloria," they moved into the aisle and found seats elsewhere. This made an island of the Koinonia group, with a vacant bench in front and rear, and an aisle on right and left. This, however, did not prevent us from joining in the next hymn, "It came upon the midnight clear, that glorious song of old...of Peace on Earth, Good will to Men." About mid-way the first verse, the frozen usher, now thoroughly thawed, came down the aisle next to Al and said, "He [pointing to Collins] can't stay in here." When Al ignored him and continued to sing "Peace on Earth...," the usher entered the vacant pew and stood in front of Collins and said, "Come on, nigger; get out of here; you can't stay in here." Then Collins, who sings Christmas carols like a buzz saw, discovered that he too could sing "Peace on Earth...." Finally the usher said, "Am I going to have to drag you out of here? You're disturbing divine worship and I'm gonna have you arrested." With this he grabbed Collins and started to drag him over the bench. Clarence then stopped him and asked, "Do you have the authority to do this?" "Yes." "May we see the pastor?" "No, you've got to get out of here; you're disturbing divine worship."

The congregation was still singing "Peace...." We moved into the aisle and out the door. Standing on the steps outside, with about a dozen laymen and the pastor between us and the door, the head usher told us, "This is our church. We own it and we control it. The Federal Government didn't put one dime in it and can't tell us who we can let in." Clarence said he thought the Holy Spirit controlled a church, and the reply was, "That's beside the point. This is our church; we own it." "But doesn't God own the church?" "I told you that was beside the point." The pastor said that he and some others didn't personally agree with this policy of turning Negroes away, but that the church had adopted it and that it would be best for us to leave. Carol asked him to please tell her daddy that she came to hear him but was turned away. He said he would. We left.

I was there, too, that Advent evening. My mama was four months pregnant with little me. I wonder if I could feel her sorrow from within.

The way mama told the story, she had read about her daddy coming in the paper. She hadn't wanted to make a big deal of it—she just wanted to hear her daddy preach. My father had the idea of making it a community event and bringing Collins along. The plan must have thrilled him. Action at last!

Trouble had been brewing between Dad and Granddaddy for a while, at least on Dad's side. Dad had always resented Granddaddy a little, even as he admired him. After all, Granddaddy was prominent among Georgia Baptists, was universally loved, and had an almost magical bond with his oldest daughter, my mama. Dad must have wondered why he never felt the warmth that Granddaddy directed toward others in the family, why his father-in-law always seemed a bit guarded around him. And though Granddaddy had been gracious about my father leaving the Baptists when our family went to Birmingham, Dad was always skeptical about Granddaddy's true feelings.

Then Sam Oni joined my grandfather's Baptist church, while Dad never could get the supposedly liberal Congregationalists to budge an inch towards inviting their black brothers into the fellowship. Finally, when Dad left the organized church altogether, he was ready to end his relationship with anybody associated with the church at all, especially the leaders. That included my granddaddy.

My mother's heart was broken. Her biggest fear was that she would be forced to choose between the two men she loved most in the world. She knew she couldn't do it.

As far as Dad was concerned, here was a chance to expose the hypocrisy of First Baptist of Americus, the whole "Friendship" Association of Sumter County Baptists, and the guest speaker himself. Since the newspaper said "the public is invited," he knew Clarence wouldn't object to it as a demonstration. Supposedly, all were welcome. The paper also publicized that the theme was "Toward Mature Discipleship." The ironies went on and on. Dad must have been practically giddy. He couldn't wait to set foot in the sanctuary.

Years later, on Palm Sunday 2006, I set foot in that sanctuary myself. I arrived alone, appropriately dressed, and was barely noticed. I fit right in. I passed. I sat in approximately the same pew where the visitors from Koinonia had sat during Advent in 1965. I looked around the big, white neoclassical sanctuary and imagined what it was like to sit down and watch people clear the pews around me. When the usher handed me a visitor card with a big smile, I pictured him grabbing the collar of my friend instead, threatening to drag him out of the church. I felt my mother's fear, disappointment, sadness, and humiliation. I understood her turmoil in a whole new way.

I understood it because when I walked into that church, I felt comfort. I have grown to understand the comfort of familiar worship rituals: reading the bulletin, holding the hymnal, sitting in the pew, listening to the choir. Blending my voice with all the others as we sing the old familiar hymns. Going to church can feel like coming home—even more so if you know your daddy's going to preach.

Until my family left Birmingham, my mother had gone to church every Sunday of her life, most of them with her daddy in the pulpit. But when they moved to Koinonia, that familiar comfort was jerked roughly away from her. The evening Advent service at First Baptist Americus was her first chance to go to church since the family's move, and she must have leapt at it. How much more painful, then, to have it all dissolve before her eyes. I finally understood that it wasn't just embarrassment she felt, or worry about making a scene. It was grief. I know about grief.

I also learned about another side of the story. During my research trip to Americus, I visited with my parents' old friends, Broadus and Lib Willoughby. Lib told me the story of sitting on the front pew that evening, right next to my little grandmother as they waited for Granddaddy to come out to the pulpit. Mom had told them that the Koinonia group was coming, so they expected an uproar. From their spot up front, they could barely tell what was happening toward the back. But Lib, who barely knew Grandmama, could sense her anxiety. I can picture Grandmama's small, strong hands wringing her white handkerchief as she silently worried about the dangerous life her daughter was living.

The incident took less than ten minutes of their lives, the length of two Christmas carols, but those seven people from Koinonia never forgot it. As Clarence later said, "Well, everything in Americus is integrated now except the churches and the jails, and I have hope for the jails." But for Mom, there was little hope. The segregation cut to the heart of her family.

South Georgia winters are usually mild, but it was a stormy one in the Henry household after the Fullers left at the beginning of January. Dad's frustration built to the point where he could no longer hold it back. I only know the outlines of this story, but I imagine it was a gray February afternoon. The girls were at school, and Mom came out of the community office to stretch her aching back after long hours of sitting at the typewriter, transcribing Clarence's *Cotton Patch* notes. Now six months pregnant, she found that work was harder than it used to be. Soon, Dad approached her from the pecan plant where he'd been running the shelling machines. He was concerned about the company my sisters were keeping.

"Carol, I've been in there thinking about those Wittkamper boys. They're not good boys. We need to tell the girls that they just can't play with them anymore. I don't trust them."

Clarence was there too—maybe he was walking up from the field, a broken tractor part in his hand.

"Oh, Al," Mom answered, "they're just boys. They're not gonna do the girls any harm. And the girls can't bring home friends from school—who else will they play with?"

That was all it took. My father ignited. "Carol, you can't *trust* these people!" In the middle of his sentence, when he said the word *trust*, his big right hand struck her across the face. Already out of balance with a swelling torso, she stumbled backwards, nearly falling, but caught herself on a picnic table and stood there, silent, stunned, wondering what could possibly come next.

"*Now look what you've made me do!*" Dad shouted, and he ran down the long straight line of pecan trees, away toward the woods beyond.

Mom and Clarence stood in silence for several minutes, watching the towering, bare trees where Dad had gone, neither one quite believing what had happened. Finally, Clarence spoke, softly and slowly. "You know, Carol, you don't have to put up with that. Nobody deserves to be treated that way." Mom didn't answer. She simply turned and walked home. It was a new kind of beginning, a new genesis.

Not all beginnings are good.

Though it seemed like everything was broken, the seasons remembered their cycles. Spring arrived, and the pecan trees began to show buds, then tender green leaves, then the tiny beginnings of nuts. Linda was playing real songs on the guitar now—"On a wagon, bound for market, there's a calf with a mournful eye...." It was warm enough for the girls to go barefoot and splash in the creek, and the days were getting longer again.

The end of the school year was a welcome relief for my sisters. Full, long, golden days on the farm stretched ahead again like a ribbon road. Then, just as the school year was ending and the summer opening up, change came again, this time in the form of a seven-pound, eleven-ounce baby sister. Me.

Mama always told this part of the story in the same way. It, too, is now gone from her memory. It was Sunday, two or three days past her due date, and time for the midday meal that everybody shared in the big community dining hall across the way. Mama felt ill and stayed at home, sending the rest of the family over for dinner. It wasn't long before her water broke with a whoosh. She made her way to the window and called over to the dining hall, "Al! It's time to go to the hospital!" He hurried across the sandy yard, still wiping his mouth, and they climbed into the VW.

Like the pregnancy (but unlike most everything else at that time), the labor and delivery went smoothly. At 8:55 p.m., Dr. Gatewood pronounced the verdict: "It's a girl!" Though the doctor had delivered thousands of babies, Mama had to be certain he wasn't confused. "Are you sure?" "Yep!" "Well, *thank goodness!*" At that late date, she didn't think she could start over and learn how to raise a boy. But she could manage a girl. She knew girls. And if Daddy was disappointed, he never let on.

By Tuesday, Mama was home from the hospital and the family was back together. Grandmama and Granddaddy Moore drove the eighty miles down from Macon to meet the new baby and help take care of everybody else. I can't help but wonder about the tension, with Dad's resentment toward Granddaddy growing ever larger as his own place in the world felt smaller and less significant. I have a feeling my father spent a lot of time in the fields that week.

As he did at every family gathering, Granddaddy had his camera. In the dim blue light of his dark room back home several days later, he must have been thrilled to see the picture he had captured. Two-day-old Cindy in her grandmama's arms, smiling right at the camera. A miraculous shot. At that moment, the title of his sermon from the morning of my birth may have drifted through his head—"Fresh Water from Old Wells." He had preached the Genesis story about Isaac digging new wells. Fresh water indeed.

When Irvin Cheney, down in Daytona, heard about the newly arrived Cynthia Marie, he couldn't resist the opportunity to get the last word on his old friend. A telegram arrived that same week:

"CONGRATULATIONS-STOP-
BUTTHATSAHELLUVANAMEFORABOY!"

In the next issue, the Koinonia newsletter announced my birth to the world: "Al and Carol's new baby arrived on May 29. Her name is Cynthia Marie and she's the fourth girl in a row for the Henrys. All indications now are that she is going to be a redhead—and a good-looking one."

Invited or not, I had arrived.

~ ~ ~ ~ ~ ~

Unlike my parents, who gave up everything they owned to belong to Koinonia, I visited the farm in 2006 as an observer. A sponge.

When I got there, I left my belongings at the sunny yellow house where I would spend the night, and I hung on to my sense of detachment as Button, my spry and cheerful host, explained that she kept a gallon of water sitting on the bathtub drain to keep critters out at night. "Usually just ants," she said, "and a couple of frogs, which is great. I really love the frogs. And then there were the two pit vipers. Don't you worry, though—we disposed of them without killing them." What a relief.

From there, I started my exploration.

I crawled into the archives and mined out all the relevant ore I could find. I stood in the door of Clarence's writing shack. Aside from the coat of garish green paint on the exterior walls, it seemed relatively untouched since his heart had stopped beating there thirty-seven years earlier. I breathed in the air off the crop fields—deep South Georgia springtime breaths—as sunset pink faded from the clouds. I stood in the center of the little Koinonia library, imagining Dad poring over the sections that would draw him in if he were there with me: New Age, Alternative Medicine, Hebrew and Greek. I followed a map of the farm, winding my way through the pecan groves to Picnic Hill, where the Jordans' graves are marked by a big sandy stone uncomfortably bearing a formal-looking plaque. At that point I did step out of my observer shoes momentarily, building a small cairn of rock shards on top of the big one. After all, I'm family, and you don't visit a grave without leaving a little something behind.

Then, after my early morning walk that Sunday, I stepped into Button's kitchen, and everything changed.

Button was there with two friends, Emory and Nashua, having a cheerful breakfast and discussing an article in the paper about the "new" gospel of Judas. It was obvious that I had stepped into an oft-rehearsed scene. They all had their roles—Button spiritual and optimistic, Nashua dark and brooding, Emory challenging. I brought my simple bread, cheese, and tea, and sat down at the table, intending to listen and enjoy.

From what seemed like out of the blue, Nashua said, "Well, the Bible says we're supposed to leave all, family and everything, to follow Jesus."

My head whipped around, and I snapped into engagement: "What is this, a *Koinonia thing*?" Observer no longer.

At that, the words tumbled out of my mouth, and I told my whole story—being born at Koinonia, Dad's activism, his mental illness, my journey. What it feels like to be six years old and on the other side of "leave all," feeling abandoned. They listened with wide eyes, and welcomed me to their breakfast table. I had come to the true Koinonia at last.

After my outburst, Nashua expressed his relief to find out who I was. Before that, he said, he had thought I was "The Mystery Woman Who Came to Walk the Land." I liked that image. I thought that's who I was, too. But apparently I am more than that.

As I follow my serpentine path, I never seem to know what's around the next curve. But I'm always happy when it's not a pit viper. I am realizing that sometimes you really need to leave all, leave everything behind, have your own personal exodus, in order to get to the genesis that's waiting for you. Isaac, miraculous son of Abraham and Sarah, had to leave his home and head for the land of the Philistines in order to find the fresh water of his father's old wells. And like my own father, I had to leave behind my job, which had served as my identity as well as my sense of security and autonomy for many years, in order to find what was waiting for me in the fog. In order to reach genesis, we have to be willing to face some wilderness. And while we're in the wilderness, there can be comfort in reliving our genesis stories. Even when our mothers no longer remember them.

Sometimes, as for my father, there's only wilderness. Like all the other places, Koinonia was not the Great New Thing he hoped it would be. Though he went back two years after we left Koinonia to help dig Clarence's grave, the farm turned out to be yet another place for my father to leave behind, again with a bitter taste in his mouth.

But our family *did* find genesis at Koinonia: me. I have never understood why I was born at that particular time in that particular place. The family was unraveling, the violence beginning, and nobody knew where we were headed next. In many ways, it was the wrong time and the wrong place for new life. But maybe, just maybe, there's never a wrong time or place for new beginnings. Maybe there was a reason I needed to be.

5

Tornado

We left Koinonia with gale wind force. With mounting feelings of frustration about being stuck out in the sticks under Clarence's large thumb, Dad was the cork in a champagne bottle. He was ready to go, and the power of his departure sucked the rest of us tumbling out right behind him. As with every other move of the Henry family, the destination was almost beside the point.

During our time at Koinonia, Dad had gotten to know a wonderful character in the Georgia civil rights scene, Frances Pauley, Director of the Georgia Council on Human Relations. The council, based in Atlanta, helped to organize local councils across Georgia that consisted of biracial groups working to improve relationships and communication in towns large and small. Mrs. Pauley was a long-time activist, a spitfire old lady with boundless energy and conviction to go with it. She had been the one white woman in the room when SNCC leaders made the controversial decision to call Martin Luther King, Jr., and the SCLC to invite them to Albany, Georgia, for the campaign that ended in a nearly disastrous conflict between the two groups. With a laugh, Mrs. Pauley proudly proclaimed that the best compliment she'd ever received was from Georgia governor Herman Talmadge. He said he would have been able to make the county unit system part of the Georgia constitution, effectively creating all-white primaries, "if it hadn't been for that god-damned Frances Pauley." Julian Bond once called her "everybody's grandmother and nobody's fool." When she strode into the Georgia legislature, they woke up and took notice. My daddy thought she was the cat's pajamas.

When Dad reached his limit at Koinonia toward the end of 1966, his mind settled on Mrs. Pauley and the possibilities up in Atlanta,

Martin Luther King's hometown. Shortly before Christmas he went up to Atlanta to talk to Frances and check out the scene. The whole family went up to go house-hunting on Christmas day, and by the end of January we were all packed up and back in the VW bus. Dad had a job at the Georgia Council and we were moving to the city.

In many ways, it seemed like our family was rejoining the real world. Professional movers, paid for by Dad's new job, came to load up our few belongings. Though we had no money after living at Koinonia, Mrs. Pauley had agreed that the Georgia Council would pay the rent and utilities for the house we were moving into, with the understanding that the home would become a community center for the inner-city work that Dad would do. It was a nice house, standing on a tree-lined street in a middle-class neighborhood not far from Piedmont Park, with a generous front porch and a good yard for playing. With six in the family and only three bedrooms, we all had to share, but it felt like a palace compared to the backwards little farmhouse at Koinonia. There was even a real bathtub!

Though my sisters would miss the farm (I was too little at the time to care), there was no doubt they were happy to return to civilization, especially when it was time to go to school. Being the new kid was always a challenge, but now, in the big, integrated Atlanta city schools, they no longer stood out. Nobody knew where they lived, and even if they found out, there was no stigma to living on Sixth Street like there was to living at Koinonia. They could make friends again, play with their classmates after school, and even visit their friends' houses and have sleepovers. It was the end of isolation, the end of silence, the end of cold shoulders. They could breathe easy and skip down the street.

It wasn't a completely seamless transition, though—such moves rarely are. For Linda in particular, the academic gulf between Americus High School and Grady High School in Atlanta was huge. While she had studied the basic parts of a flower in biology for the first half of the school year in Americus, the Atlanta kids were already well into DNA and RNA. It was quite a shock when she walked into her first biology class at Grady High in February and saw a half-dissected fetal pig. She had some catching up to do. But with friends to help and nobody pointing or sneering, somehow her schoolbooks felt lighter and more manageable.

In addition to friends and her own music and songwriting, Linda also enjoyed sports. That first spring, she was on both the track and softball teams, leaping over hurdles and stopping the ball at first base time and time again. She played softball two years in a row, both of them at first base, with Yolanda, daughter of Coretta and Martin Luther King, Jr., on second. Linda remembers that they lost every game the first year, and won every game the second.

Though Mama rolled with the punches, I imagine that she, too, was relieved to be back in a regular routine. Daddy and the three big girls went off every morning to school and work, and then it was the two of us, Mama with her little blonde lap baby in a quiet house, walking to the park, going to the grocery store, fixing supper, doing all the normal things she had always done before moving to the wilderness.

For Dad, getting started at his new job with the Georgia Council was a time of learning and excitement. Frances Pauley was a wonderful mentor, with years of experience in community organizing and a clear sense of justice. Dad truly admired her, saying she was "one of the few committed persons who take and keep a moral position with integrity and determination." He saw her as a person who truly worked for the people rather than for money or power, his two greatest evils. Frances was one of the few people in his life, including every member of our own family, who didn't somehow let him down in the end. She was a remarkable woman.

After his experience in Birmingham, it was great for Dad to have a job where he was actually hired to bring black and white people together. He didn't have to pretend that he was doing something else. His job was primarily to strengthen the council's presence with inner-city groups working for civil rights in Atlanta (this was to take about two-thirds of his time), but he was also to work on starting local councils across the state, beginning in the little town of Fitzgerald, Georgia.

As Mrs. Pauley emphasized, the Georgia Council's role was never to go in and tell a local community what to do or even to give them advice; it was simply to find the local leaders and ask what they needed, thereby helping to build bridges between interested parties in the black and white communities. The role of the council was to be supportive, not directive, in nurturing biracial conversation and cooperation. As far as Frances Pauley was concerned, the wisdom was already in the community. It just needed some encouragement to be able to make a difference.

True to his nature, Dad jumped right in. His calendar was packed from the outset. During the first few months, he reached out to many groups (most of them religious) who were doing civil rights and poverty work in the inner city: Mennonite House, staffed with young Conscientious Objectors doing their alternative service during the Vietnam War; Emmaus House and its founder Austin Ford; Quaker House, where our family occasionally attended Friends Meeting on Sunday; and Vine City Council, a group in a black neighborhood where Dad's good (white) friend Hector Black lived and was quite active.

In the course of this early outreach, Dad felt an immediate kinship with the young folks at Mennonite House: Don Bender, Dave Shields, Waldie Unger, and Tim and Mary Yoder. Several of them had brought a group of kids down to Koinonia when we lived there, so Dad had met them before and understood their goals and ambitions. They liked what they saw in him, too—he was older, grew up in the South (unlike most of them), had been around the civil rights block a few times, and spoke with authority in his preacher-like voice. He introduced them to other fascinating people. The friendships quickly expanded beyond professional connections, and our family got to know the Mennonite House folks well—sharing meals, going camping, having picnics, singing freedom songs.

One weekend, Dad took a road trip to Mississippi and back with Don Bender to visit Don's family, the two of them spending long hours in the car in deep conversation. Dad also became the big brother that Dave Shields always wanted. Dave, who had been taking courses to become a minister, felt sure that his calling lay in that direction. After hearing my father's perspectives on the matter, Dave's life path quickly took a radically different turn.

It was a time of new connections and energy. After the closed-in feeling of the waning Koinonia community, this open, young, active fellowship was fresh air to Dad's lungs. He sucked it in.

Since our house was to become a Georgia Council integrated community center on Sixth Street, Dad wanted to start by hosting a lunch there for all the folks who had welcomed him and helped him launch into his new job. Though I cannot know for sure, I imagine lots of people came: Frances Pauley, of course, and folks from Mennonite House and Vine City, and probably from Operation Breadbasket, since Martin Luther King, Sr., had recently nominated my father to be a member of that group, sponsored by Dr. King, Jr.'s Southern Christian Leadership Conference. Parked cars would have lined the street, and people were probably spilling out onto the porch, enjoying the friendly occasion to share a meal and swap stories. But the neighbors didn't like it. Atlanta was changing as white people moved out to the suburbs and black people moved into the city, and a group of hippies had relocated to the neighborhood a few blocks away. The residents were already nervous, and our huge lunchtime gathering—particularly the black guests and questionable-looking young people—didn't help. Some of the neighbors started a petition to get us to move, and our phone rang at all hours with prank phone calls, some of them downright threatening. The atmosphere was dangerously reminiscent of our Birmingham days, when the hearse had driven slowly up the street toward the house, on a mission of grim warning. After the lunch, the idea of an integrated community center never really took off.

One night at about eleven o'clock, long after everybody in our family was sound asleep, the phone rang. Mom got out of bed, trying to wake up enough to sound coherent on the phone.

"Hello?"

"Hello, Mrs. Henry, this is Coretta Scott King calling, and I'm calling to invite you to a party."

Here we go again. Mom, whose patience was usually longer than anybody's, simply ran out of it. "Let me just stop you right there. We get these calls every night. It is the middle of the night, my family is asleep, and I do not believe for one second that this is the wife of Dr. Martin Luther King, Jr. Do not call this house again." And she hung up.

My parents were friends with the Kings' chauffeur, and he was at our house a few days later. "You know, Carol," he said, "Miz King was pretty upset that you hung up on her the other night."

Mom's jaw dropped and her face turned several shades of red. "You mean that really was her? And I...and I...oh, my goodness."

When Mama got up the nerve to call Mrs. King back and apologize, the person who answered said, "Just a minute—she's in the kitchen talking to Harry Belafonte. I'll go get her." Mrs. King, who had received her share of unwanted phone calls, was gracious and understanding, forgiving Mama immediately. But the party she had called about was already past, and as far as I know, the two of them never had another opportunity to socialize.

As for me, I was busy learning to walk at that time, following my big sisters around everywhere I could. Daddy's parents lived in Atlanta then, too, and Grandmama and Granddaddy Moore were a short drive away in Macon. Both sets of grandparents spoiled me on a pretty regular basis, even though my dad and Granddaddy Moore had a strained relationship.

Granddaddy worried about us, but he continued to be gracious to Dad when their paths crossed. Dad made sure that didn't happen much. He worked during the day and attended meetings many evenings, so he usually wasn't home when the Moores came to visit. As always, Mama made excuses for his absences: important meetings, busy time, charitable work. Grandmama took these explanations at face value; she never wanted to see the darker side of life if she could help it. But Granddaddy was known for his uncanny ability to read human nature. I imagine he recognized the strain beneath Mama's smile.

Though we saw both sets of grandparents now and then, they were never there at the same time, and didn't know one another well. My first birthday was an exception. All four grandparents came for the festivities, and Daddy was home, too (he had written *"Cindy's birthday"* twice in his calendar on that day, making sure not to forget). I imagine that my mama dressed me in my prettiest dress, shined up my little white leather toddler shoes, and brushed my hair till it shone. I must've been quite the sassy sight, tottering from one lap to the next, the reason for the party, bringing all these unlikely people together.

There were other happy times—visits from out-of-town friends, picnics with the Mennonite House folks, and always music, lots of music. That summer we took a family vacation and drove to the mountains of North Carolina, singing all the way. *"Gonna lay down my sword and shield, down by the riverside, down by the riverside...."* We went to Celo, a little place we had visited for the first time the summer before: a tiny, green community on the South Toe River. Dad loved to swim in the river with his long, lazy, comfortable stroke. My sisters went to summer camp for three weeks there; it was a welcome relief from Atlanta's July heat.

The summer of 1967 was a hot one indeed, and not just in Atlanta. Tornadoes had raged through the Midwest earlier that year, killing sixty-five people and injuring nearly fourteen hundred others. Throughout June and July there were tornadoes of a different kind: race-related riots all across the country: cities like Detroit, Newark, Milwaukee, Tampa, Buffalo, and Memphis. Forty-three people died in Detroit alone. Closer to home, Willie Ross, a young onlooker, was shot and killed by police during a riot in the Dixie Hills neighborhood in northwest Atlanta. Three others were wounded by police gunfire, one critically. Dad's contacts in the black community in tiny little Fitzgerald, Georgia, even heard rumors of riots there. Martin Luther King, Jr., and the SCLC had largely turned their attention away from race issues to focus on the broader issue of poverty as well as the war in Vietnam, but racism was still rampant. The Black Power movement was gaining momentum. People were angry.

When the riots broke out in Atlanta, Frances Pauley immediately focused the Georgia Council on community-building in Dixie Hills, and the staff worked with other organizations to pressure the Atlanta Aldermanic Police Committee to change police riot control procedures. But it seemed that white people could do little to help. In the council's annual report that year, Mrs. Pauley expressed her discouragement with police brutality: "It is our belief that Atlanta's government must truly be completely overhauled before there can be substantial change in police practices. In the meantime, we will continue to sit on top of a powder keg, wondering where and how large the next outbreak will be." She had other concerns as well. At the end of June, ten days after the rioting in Dixie Hills, she wrote to a friend,

> Do you have any ideas about jobs that are open for fat old ladies who want to do civil rights or welfare rights and who do not want to raise the total budget for the operation?
>
> I have decided to find another job. SRC [Southern Regional Council, the umbrella organization of all the State Councils on Human Relations] is cutting us off—no grant in aid after 1968. I'd like to get the present finances in shape and leave. In fact the whole philosophy of SRC has gone chamber of commerce. It is more than I can take. I'm too old to be in an organization where the top thinking is basically false.

Frances's conflict with the SRC leadership continued to build, and by the end of the summer, she was finished. She took a week's vacation in August, and on September 3 fired off a letter of resignation to Joe Hendricks, member of the Georgia Council's Board of Directors. She gave the board one month's notice. With their heads still spinning, the board scrambled to rebuild.

In solidarity with Frances, Dad felt called to quit his job as well. On September 29, with the help of Don and Dave from Mennonite House, he moved out of his office and came home with no further income from the Georgia Council and no job prospects. Part of Dad's recent work with the council had involved welfare rights, but now it looked like *we* would need welfare assistance. The next day, he went camping with Don and a group of slum kids from the Mennonite House after-school study center.

I was too small then to be aware of the larger situation, but when I think of it now, my heart goes out to my mama. Once again, her life was turned upside down as a result of my father's rash decision. Though she had no choice or voice, she had four children to feed, and her husband was more likely to stomp and rant than stop and assess the best steps for the family. Her own father, just eighty miles away, had plenty of resources he could have offered. But Walter Moore hadn't raised his daughter to ask for help, and maybe she was too proud for him to know the reality of our situation. Besides, my daddy would never have accepted a penny from the Moores, and he was still in charge.

After three weeks with no work, Dad decided he needed to get out of town again. Though Mama was probably gripped with fear about our family's future, I imagine her breathing a quiet sigh of relief. A weekend with the girls might allow the clouds to lift a little.

Dad had heard about a big march planned in Washington, a protest of the war in Vietnam. His concern about the war had grown in recent months. The United States had been deploying troops for two years and had lost 13,000 Americans, with 86,000 wounded. Vietnamese casualties—military and civilian—could only be estimated. Dad viewed it as a senseless war: the men who wielded the power were wasting human lives for no apparent reason. And he couldn't help remembering the exhilaration of his days in Selma, the crowds of people singing their hearts out, and Dr. King's rousing declaration: *His truth is marching on.* Here was another chance to take a stand, get inspired, and get away from the realities of his own dead-end situation. At six o' clock on Friday evening, October 20, Dad and his friend Dave boarded a Greyhound bus for the overnight ride to Washington.

The March on the Pentagon in Washington differed greatly from those in Alabama. Though there was some diversity in the crowd of more than fifty thousand, Dad saw far more white faces than black ones, and most of the black folks headed for their own rally near Howard University when the main march set out across the Potomac toward the Pentagon. Most in the crowd were young hippies, with colorful garb, wild hats, tie-dye, long skirts, ponchos, and capes. Flower children danced in the golden October sun, inserting daisies into the tips of MP assault rifles. Abbie Hoffman pledged to ring the Pentagon with people, conduct an exorcism, and levitate the building. (He was denied permission to encircle the Pentagon, so the levitation failed. The building stayed put.)

Overall, the demonstration, though huge and historic, was haphazard. Multiple tables dotted the landscape of the mall, set up by groups from all perspectives trying to recruit new members with their mimeographed leaflets. There was a kickoff rally at the Lincoln Monument, but Dad and Dave could hardly hear the speeches, which were less than inspiring. The entire spectacle was a bit of a letdown after King's "I have a dream" speech on those same steps four years before. Once the long column of protestors arrived at the Pentagon, no one was clear on what came next. Some stormed the steps and were arrested (nearly seven hundred that day), but Dad and Dave missed that part. They milled around with everybody else, without a clear "Amen" to end the march. Like the war itself, the march lacked focus, and probably left Dad with a vague sense of disillusionment and bitterness. In his mind, the hippie theme, "turn on…tune in…drop out," was beginning to weave itself around the "Leave all to follow Jesus" mantra that still echoed from Koinonia days. He felt drawn to join this counter-culture movement, cut his remaining ties with what he called the "filthy rich, economic, political, religious masters of the world," and be free.

But when he came home, there we were—needing him, tying him down. He wasn't a fancy-free college student; he was a man about to turn forty-one, with a wife and four daughters, no job and the rent due.

We moved out of the house on Sixth Street; we simply couldn't afford it. Doing welfare rights work in the last month of his job, Dad had learned about a poverty-stricken part of Atlanta called Cabbagetown. Now he turned a different eye on the area. Yes, houses were in sad shape, and the residents dealt with shootings and car thefts. But it didn't cost much to live there, and we didn't have much to pay. He found a place to rent.

When it was originally built in the late 1800s, Cabbagetown housed mill workers from the Fulton Bag and Cotton Mill (or, as many of them called it when we lived there, "Filthy Bag"). The neighborhood still hosted a unique community of poor whites barely supported by the mill, an Appalachian village in the middle of the city.

The people in Cabbagetown were mountain people. They ate fatback and biscuits, made quilts, and had kids called names like "Pig" and "Big Eyes" who were double first cousins—their mamas were sisters and their daddies were brothers. Early on, the neighborhood was known as "Pearl Park," named after the daughter of the man who developed the area. But that poetic name didn't last. Nobody seems to agree on the origin of "Cabbagetown." Some say a boxcar overturned, spilling cabbages everywhere, and people came running from all directions to scoop them up. Some say a cab company started calling it Cabbagetown, and the name stuck. Others say it was just the pervasive smell of the place—mountain people's cuisine. Regardless, the name was appropriate. It captured the down-to-earth character of the place as well as the people who lived there.

First maintained by the Elsas family who owned the mill, Cabbagetown was put up for sale when the mill was sold in 1957. A few mill workers were able to buy their own houses; slumlords bought many of them and rented them out, doing precious little to keep them up. The houses were dilapidated by the time we arrived—shotgun shacks with peeling paint, gutters half off, and rusty gates on chain link fences, barely hanging on by a screw. But they all had front porches, and unlike on Sixth Street, everybody knew each other well. The old-timers still say the motto of the neighborhood was, "I may not have anything, but you're welcome to half of it." Folks made sure that their neighbors somehow got by.

Though this poor white neighborhood was an unlikely destination for an active civil rights worker and his family, rent was cheap, and community-organizing opportunities abounded. As the Black Power movement grew, Dad rationalized that it made sense to begin working from the other side of the color line, recognizing that poverty affects all people equally. He hoped to find new possibilities for building bridges across the lines, with everyone, black and white, working together to end poverty. He had come to believe that the only way to make real change was to live in the community you wanted to help—not swoop in with charitable intentions from somewhere else. Our family lived alongside everybody else, barely making it from day to day.

On Saturday, November 11, the family loaded up the VW bus and made a few trips across town. Now it was time for Mama to create a home in half of a duplex on Berean Avenue in Cabbagetown. With their daughters filling the two bedrooms on the tiny second floor, Mama and Daddy slept on a pullout couch downstairs in the living room.

Once again, we were starting over, even though we'd only moved across town. As far as Dad was concerned, it made sense for my sisters to change schools and begin mid-year in the elementary and high schools closest to Cabbagetown. For the second year in a row, they would have to be the new kids in the middle of the year, but he figured they were used to transitions and should go to school with kids from Cabbagetown. It would have been Linda's ninth school (she was a tenth grader), Nancy's fifth (seventh grader), and Janet's third (third grader).

But on this point, Mama held her ground. She had no choice about leaving the nice house on tree-lined Sixth Street to move to a poverty-stricken neighborhood, but the girls were settled in school. They had friends. They were doing well. She didn't want them uprooted, and she wouldn't back down. Daddy finally agreed. Linda had her driver's license by then and could drive them across town to school.

The next challenge was close on the horizon: Christmas. Though our mama had adjusted to simple living by this time, sewing our clothes and stretching every penny of her grocery budget, the prospect of making Christmas special on so little money was daunting. The previous year, we had been on the road from Koinonia to house-hunt in Atlanta. And now here we were on the other side of yet another move, with barely a penny in the bank. Determined to have Christmas for her daughters, Mama suggested a trip to Macon to spend the holiday with her parents.

Dad had other plans. There was no way he'd go crawling down to Macon and accept his in-laws' charity, open presents, go to church, participate in the materialistic Christmas farce, and feel the questioning in Walter Moore's eyes. He refused. Without telling anyone, he packed his sleeping bag and got on a Greyhound bus. He was gone. Mama took us girls to Macon. Forty years later, my sisters still refer to it as "that awful Christmas."

I don't know why Dad went to Chicago. He didn't know anybody there. He stayed in a room at the YMCA for a few days, and then slept under a bush when his money ran out. Temperatures were in the teens that week. Finally, after the rest of us had returned to Cabbagetown from Macon and Mama was racking her brain about what to do next, he called collect to let her know that he was safe and on his way home. Tears stained her face as she hung up the phone.

Mama sat us around the kitchen table. "Girls, your Daddy's coming home. But it looks like we're gonna have to choose between having Christmas and having a daddy in this family." Nobody spoke, and Mama continued. "I think we'd rather have a Daddy, don't you think?" And so it was decided. No more Christmases for the Henry family. At just a year and a half old, I squirmed on my big sister's lap, not understanding a word.

As soon as he got home, Dad found a job to support the family. He had to. Until now, all his work, even after he left the church, had been some form of ministry. Charitable work. When we moved to Cabbagetown, he quickly needed a *job*. Ministry could happen on his time off. Shortly after he came back from Chicago that Christmas, he was hired as an ambulance attendant for Grady Hospital. That job, which involved riding around responding to emergencies in a Chevy panel van with little equipment and even less medical training, opened his eyes to some harsh realities of the time.

Dad's boss from Grady, Bill Breyer, described for me the interesting dichotomy on the ambulances at that time: the attendants, like Dad, were almost all liberal guys, many of them Conscientious Objectors doing their alternative service, like his friends Dave and Tim had done when they lived at Mennonite House. But each attendant rode with a driver, and all the drivers were ex-police officers. The drivers were conservative, racist, and carried guns on the job. Dad saw their blatant prejudice firsthand, as well as the regular police brutality that happened right there in the hospital. As Bill Breyer told me,

> I loved your daddy—he was my best friend. But as an employee, he was a pain in the neck, always complaining. He had zero tolerance for intolerance. It was all black and white to him—there was no gray area. Every time anything like that happened, he'd come running to me, wanting to file a complaint. He'd get all angry, his face would get red, and he'd just blow up. He'd try to buffalo people. But he never scared me—I was bigger than he was. I'd say, "Well, Al, why don't you just write one of your big, long letters to me about it the way you always do....
>
> I felt sorry for him, I really did. He was the white man who was gonna save the world. And then he'd just get so depressed when he couldn't do it.

My own earliest memory is from our house in Cabbagetown. We were often out past dark, at community gatherings or visiting friends at Mennonite House. Since my toddler years, this mental snapshot has stuck with me: our family coming in and turning on the bare kitchen bulb to be greeted by a flood of roaches covering every stained white porcelain surface. I can still hear the percussion of my parents' and sisters' hands, pointlessly squashing as many roaches as they could outrace. The population never seemed to diminish.

On a more positive note, the idea for an inner-city community center finally blossomed under Mama's nurturing gaze at our house in Cabbagetown. After a while, the VISTA volunteer living in the left side of our duplex moved out, and we expanded to fill the whole building. Then, with four small bedrooms, two living rooms, and two kitchens, we had room for a rummage store upstairs and an after-school homework club in one of the front rooms downstairs. Mama joined a weekly quilting group and taught the neighbors how to make a healthy meal starting with a block of government cheese.

Folks were constantly in and out of our house. Tony Clack, who lived with his mother (our landlady) next door, often visited and talked for hours. Many nights, long after the sun sank below the old mill's smokestacks, Mama would get up and yawn. "Tony, we're gonna have to go on to bed. But don't feel like you have to leave. Just lock the door behind you on your way out." As I stood similarly trapped on his front walk forty years later, Tony asked me, "Now why would I want to stay there after they'd gone to bed? I never could understand it."

There was always music. Linda with her guitar and folk songs. Suppers with friends, and sing-alongs as the light faded. Saturday night "hootenannies" at the larger Cabbagetown community center. Fiddles, banjos, guitars, and autoharps—anybody who couldn't play an instrument could tap their feet or bang spoons together, and everybody sang: "Boil them cabbage down, boys, bake the hoecakes brown...."

By the time I could talk, I was singing with my sisters. Together we made a complete set: Linda with her chestnut brown hair, Janet with black hair, Nancy's red, and my blonde curls. All of us singing away. Mama was proud of her girls. We seemed like such a happy family, and most people thought we were.

But one person wasn't so sure. Mary and Tim Yoder had lived at Mennonite House, but when Tim finished his alternative service, they had no more savings than we did. They moved in next door, and Mary and Mom grew close. Mary noticed details about us that weren't obvious to other people. Having grown up in a turbulent family, she recognized the warning signs. She worried about the extent of Dad's power over the family and Mama's quiet attempts to keep the peace. Mary especially identified with my oldest sister Linda, noting the sadness that she hid beneath a talented, beautiful façade. When Mary walked into our living room after one of Dad's tornadoes and saw Linda's guitar case shattered on the floor, she felt a dangerous chill. She knew who was capable of such rage, likely to lash out at the one thing that Linda held most dear. Yet there was nothing Mary could do.

There were certainly bright lights in the dingy realities of that spring of 1968 in Cabbagetown. Though Dad dictated that we stop celebrating birthdays when we gave up Christmas, I would soon be two years old and was learning to express my strong will with words. Atlanta was in bloom, with azaleas and dogwoods everywhere. Even Cabbagetown took on a little extra color. The war still waged in Vietnam, with lives lost every day, but national leaders were beginning to speak out against it. Dr. King was delivering strong anti-war messages across the country, and in March, Bobby Kennedy announced his calling to run for president, a strong young voice for peace. "I do not run for the Presidency merely to oppose any man," he said in the Senate Caucus Room on March 16, "but to propose new policies. I run because I am convinced that this country is on a perilous course and because I have such strong feelings about what must be done, and I feel that I'm obliged to do all I can."

It seemed that there was room for hope after all.

But then, on the evening of April 3, Martin Luther King, Jr., spoke these words at the Bishop Charles Mason Temple in Memphis, Tennessee:

> We've got some difficult days ahead. But it really doesn't matter with me now, because I've been to the mountaintop.
> And I don't mind.
> Like anybody, I would like to live a long life. Longevity has its place. But I'm not concerned about that now. I just want to do God's will. And He's allowed me to go up to the mountain. And I've looked over. And I've seen the promised land. I may not get there with you. But I want you to know tonight, that we, as a people, will get to the promised land!
> And so I'm happy, tonight. I'm not worried about anything. I'm not fearing any man!
> Mine eyes have seen the glory of the coming of the Lord!

The next day, as the evening began to cool on April 4, 1968, Dr. King stood with friends on the balcony of his motel room as one shot rang out. One shot, and Dr. King fell dead. He had been to the mountaintop, but the winds of hatred were too strong to withstand.

On a campaign stop in Indianapolis that night, Bobby Kennedy offered the following words to a stunned crowd:

> I ask you tonight to return home, to say a prayer for the family of Martin Luther King, but more importantly to say a prayer for our own country, which all of us love—a prayer for understanding and that compassion of which I spoke. We can do well in this country. We will have difficult times. We've had difficult times in the past. And we will have difficult times in the future. It is not the end of violence, it is not the end of lawlessness, and it's not the end of disorder.
>
> But the vast majority of white people and the vast majority of black people in this country want to live together, want to improve the quality of our life, and want justice for all human beings that abide in our land.
>
> Let us dedicate ourselves to what the Greeks wrote so many years ago: to tame the savageness of man and make gentle the life of this world.
>
> Let us dedicate ourselves to that, and say a prayer for our country and for our people.

Indianapolis was quiet that night.

Atlanta, on the other hand, exploded. Dad saw the worst of the riots firsthand, riding the streets in an ambulance, caring for the wounded, staunching the flow of blood, listening to a torrent of racist rhetoric from the man behind the wheel.

The destruction wasn't yet complete. Two months later, at a Los Angeles celebration of his California primary victory, Bobby Kennedy was gunned down at point-blank range. Richard Nixon won the election. Surely hope was dead.

Time went on, and each day on the ambulance was sheer hell for Dad. His soft-spoken friend Tim Yoder described the experience as one gruesome encounter after another: an abdomen sliced open, a severed spine, a burned body that "smelled just like good barbecue." He told me, "Your dad saw that stuff, too." After some reflection, Tim added,

> It wasn't the "blood and guts" that were the real cause of the nightmares. Rather, it was the racism and the discrimination.

I could tell you many, many stories of how the poor and the blacks were treated. Of how the police would brag about planting a knife or other evidence on someone they had arrested. Of how they beat up people and then lied about it. Of how blacks were often given third class treatment at the scene of an accident or when they called to have an ambulance come because of a medical emergency.

And then there were the forgotten and neglected at many of the nursing homes. In those days, old folks were often tied to chairs with bedsheets during the day and put into their beds at night and forgotten until morning.

I saw people die in minutes. But in the nursing homes, it would take months, if not years.

Dad earned $1.60 an hour doing this horrific work, and he rarely worked overtime—not because it was too much for him or he wanted to come home to us, but because he wanted to make sure that he'd never earn enough to pay taxes. He was willing to be the breadwinner if he had to, but he refused to support the U.S. war machine in Vietnam.

It wasn't easy to sustain a family of six on $275 a month, even with the government surplus food that was available if you waited in line on Thursday afternoons. Dad wasn't making even two-thirds of his Georgia Council salary (and only half what he made at the church in Birmingham), and the council had also paid for our rent, utilities, and VW bus upkeep. These were lean times, a steady regression of income and comforts. Mama never complained. And for Dad, with the call to "leave all" echoing more and more loudly in his head, it was progress—moving away from the uphill rat race of capitalism, thumbing his nose at the establishment, living closer to the edge.

Meanwhile, my Granddaddy Moore's star continued to rise, though he managed to retain his humility and self-deprecating sense of humor. He was still the much-beloved pastor at Vineville Baptist Church in Macon, and accepted invitations to preach at churches, revivals, and conferences all across the South. After serving several terms as Trustee at Mercer University, and even after leading the stormy committee that pushed for Mercer's integration, Granddaddy was elected president of the powerful Georgia Baptist Convention in 1968, and reelected in 1969.

During those troubled times, he brought a message of hope to the convention, preaching the 1968 conference sermon titled, "Is There Room for Optimism Now?" After citing a litany of discouraging cultural problems, he ended on a note that acknowledged the difficulties while also celebrating his faith in the light of humankind:

"The watchman said, 'The morning cometh, and also the night.'"
A strange saying: "I see dawn coming. I see midnight coming."
Darkness and light together. Unnatural!
But if we have eyes to see, we see darkness. "Behold, darkness shall cover the earth, and gross darkness the people."
And if we have faith, we see also the light. For it is in the darkness that the light has its opportunity. If there isn't any separation of men from men and men from God, then there isn't any crying need for Christians. But if all the darkness is real, and all the hurt and wrong and abominations do exist, then somebody needs to be the light of the world.
Watchman, what of the night? I see darkness, but I see light. Ye are the light. Let your light shine.

Grandmama couldn't have been more proud. Dad couldn't have been more scornful. The gulf continued to widen. Our family could have used some of the light Granddaddy preached about.

And still, we pressed on. The big girls went to school. Mama kept house, helped the neighborhood kids with their homework, and planted a few flowers in the corner of our tiny yard, next to the rusty chain link fence. In July 1969, men landed on the moon, with our family clustered around our little black-and-white television. Daddy went off to work every day, seeing the worst of the blood, poverty, and bigotry that the "city too busy to hate" (as Atlanta was known) had to offer. He often spent time with his Mennonite House friends, who had now moved to The Gladstone, a small apartment building not far away. He would stay late into the night, talking intently about the war, the awful state of the world, and his strong calling to leave all to follow Jesus—job, home, family, everything.

Then there came a moment when it seemed as if his youngest daughter left *him* instead, sucked violently out of his grasp. I'm not sure exactly when this happened, but I imagine it as early fall 1969, a day that started out much like every other day. Dad set out for work as usual, expected at eight o'clock sharp, and my sisters headed for school. But this day was special for my mama and me: we planned to go downtown for a fancy lunch with Nina, an old friend from Mama's younger days, truly a rare treat. I was three years old by this time, old enough to enjoy such an outing. We both dressed up, choosing the nicest things we had from the rummage room upstairs. Mama put a little extra spit on my patent leather shoes and brushed the tangles out of my hair.

One of the tallest buildings in downtown Atlanta was the new Hyatt Regency Hotel, designed by Atlanta architect John Portman and completed in 1967. It was famous as the first hotel constructed around a multi-story atrium, and the blue Plexiglas dome of its revolving restaurant, the Polaris, offered a stunning view of the city. Just the place for a ladies' lunch.

We had finished our gelatin desserts when we heard a loud noise from outside the hotel. We quickly left the restaurant and went to Nina's room in the hotel, heading for the balcony to see what the commotion was. As we stepped out, we faced an awful scene—an accidental explosion of fumes on an upper floor directly across the street had sent construction workers hurling out the windows, where they fell amid shattered glass on the pavement and the roofs of cars below. As we looked down on this scene, we heard sirens, and then an ambulance drove up. Amazed, we watched Daddy get out and run into the midst of the chaos. Mama knew that her three-year-old had seen enough. I had been standing on a lower railing of the balcony, peering over. When I turned to go, I pulled my foot back between the metal railings of the balcony, and my little patent leather shoe slipped off, falling many stories to the street below. "Oh, no, Mama!" She hustled me inside, saying we didn't need to worry about the shoe. It had come from the rummage, and we seldom went anywhere that required dressing up. But Nina wouldn't hear of it. "Y'all go on," she said, "and I'll go down and get the shoe and send it back to you."

After we left for home, Nina found my little shoe in the middle of the bloody scene below. Dad was still there, and she threaded her way through the confusion, stepping carefully in her high heels through the broken glass, peering around fire trucks and police cars, to find him. Though he had known her for years, Dad almost didn't recognize the well-dressed, carefully coiffed woman who matter-of-factly held out my white patent leather shoe. He panicked.

"Cindy? Here? And all you have is her shoe? *Where is my daughter?*"

When he got home that day, he slowly drew the little shoe from his pocket as he slumped into a chair. Even seeing my intact body and dancing eyes was not enough to erase that sense of utter panic. He held me close. I like to think that, for that moment at least, the gravitational pull of "leave all" lost a little of its strength. But in the end, it was just a moment.

Dad started looking for another job soon after that incident. October 14, 1969, was his last day on the Grady Hospital ambulance. I'm certain he was glad to slam the door behind him.

Two weeks later, Dad got a phone call. Clarence Jordan had died of a massive heart attack, sitting alone in his little writing shack at the edge of the pecan grove. Though they hadn't been in touch since our family left Koinonia, Dad got in the car at once to go help dig Clarence's grave in the sandy soil of Koinonia's Picnic Hill.

~ ~ ~ ~ ~ ~

In May 2006, when I finally got up my nerve to retrace our family's steps across the sprawling metropolis of Atlanta, my sister Janet (known as the bird dog of the family for her foolproof directional nose) agreed to come along as my navigator and perhaps my security blanket as well. Unfortunately, she realized that the journey would cause too much anxiety, so I had to go alone, following her careful directions.

Though this trip wasn't my first research foray to create my memoir, it felt like the biggest. Atlanta held some emotionally charged memories. I decided to follow the family chronology and go to Sixth Street first. My sisters didn't recall any details about our house, and I never figured out which one it was as I walked along, taking pictures. I even knocked on a couple of doors, trying to find someone older who might have lived on the street since the 1960s. No luck. It was as if the house didn't want to be found. So I respected its privacy and drove away.

Cabbagetown was a different story. Janet had seen our old house on Berean Avenue on Google Earth and described its location exactly. When I drove up, there it was, painted a coral color that reminded me of cut cantaloupe. A young woman sat on the porch, and when I introduced myself and explained my quest, she invited me in to see her house, the left side of the duplex.

I quickly noticed the transformation that had taken place in Cabbagetown. In 1977, the mill had closed and the neighborhood deteriorated further. Drugs, crime, and general decay got worse. And then, the 1996 Olympics in Atlanta brought a fresh change. White flight began to reverse its course across metropolitan Atlanta. Living in the inner city became cool. Houses were cheap in Cabbagetown, and artists moved in, making it hip. People with money started to notice.

A developer bought the mill and turned it into high-rent condos, winning awards for creative reuse. Arched ruins of the former mill now overlook the crystal-blue swimming pool. High-tech workout equipment has replaced textile machines in the basement. The "Filthy Bag" has gone upscale, and you'd be lucky to find a two-bedroom condo for $300,000. Cabbagetown has effectively become Arugulaville.

The gracious young woman told me that she had made some changes in the six months she had lived there—knocked out walls and redone the kitchen. None of it felt familiar to me. I saw beautiful skeins of yarn on a shelf upstairs. A big, friendly dog. Colorful art. Retro avocado-colored cabinets in the kitchen next to a side-by-side aluminum refrigerator. No roaches.

I was struck by how small it was. It seemed like perfect accommodations for one person—maybe two if they got along well. And there were six of us.

After getting no response at a house that the young woman said belonged to an old-timer, I decided to walk and explore the neighborhood. I first came to Cabbagetown Glass and Pottery Works—a gallery with a ceramics studio in the rear. I went in and learned that only one employee actually lived in Cabbagetown, but she knew none of her neighbors. At her suggestion, I headed to Little's Store on Carroll Street, but the red doors ("Since 1929," the sign said) were padlocked. Clearly, the store had been closed for months. Further down was the Carroll Street Cafe, with tables shaded by Bass Ale umbrellas on the sidewalk and a BMW parked out front. For better or worse (or perhaps both), this was not the Cabbagetown of my childhood.

Hand-painted signs in front of a ramshackle building caught my eye. "GO BACK TO FAUXHEMIA," one read. And another: "DON'T FORGET TO WASH THE GHOST."

The second one resonated. Is that what I was here to do? Just wash the old ghosts? Wring them out and hang them to dry in the sun? I kept walking, passing a few people who seemed to know as much as I did.

Finally I came across the mailman. Surely *he* would know who had been here a long time. I stopped him and told my story. Well, hmmm. He could only think of one house, down on Astoria Street. He pointed me that direction. I kept walking.

Unfortunately, few of the streets were labeled, and I couldn't figure out which one was Astoria. I came to a man and woman sweeping the street in front of their house. The house was old but tidy, built a few steps up from the street. I asked the woman if she could direct me to Astoria Street.

"Are you walking, or in the car?"

As soon as she asked, I knew she was from Cabbagetown. And I was right. She had lived in only three houses her entire life, and they were all right there on that same street. I stopped walking.

Her name was Karen, she told me, and she was my age. When I told her that my family had lived there when I was a toddler and I was trying to find somebody who might have known us, she exclaimed, "Well, you're an original Cabbage Patch Kid like me!" Her warmth engulfed me, and I sat basking in it on a church pew on the front porch, while she went inside to ask her mama (who was recovering from surgery) if it would be okay for me to come in and talk. "Bring her in!" was the response.

The room was dark when I entered, but when my eyes adjusted I was transported back in time—not to Cabbagetown but to the mountains of western North Carolina, where my family had lived later. Mama had developed close friendships with the mountain women around Celo, and this sitting room—dark, a little too warm, and crowded with overstuffed furniture—had the same mountain feeling. *This* was Cabbagetown.

Karen and her mother, Sarah, talked about the changes in Cabbagetown. "Used to be, nobody had anything, so we all shared what we had, just to get by. Now nobody knows each other, and everybody is about protecting what they have."

Neither of them remembered our family. "Do you know the name of *anybody* who lived on Berean Avenue when you were there?" Sarah asked. The only name I could think of popped out of my mouth—Tony Clack, the colorful character who had lived next door with his mother, our landlady. They both gasped and looked at each other. "Why, Tony still lives right there on Berean Avenue!"

Karen offered to walk me to Tony's house, warning me that he would talk my ear off. I assured her I was ready. Tony lived in one of the sagging houses that looked like it was being held up by the piles of junk inside. The yard, planted with what looked like all kinds of exotic plants, was completely overgrown, jungle-like. We made our way up the walk, and Karen opened the porch door and carefully tiptoed through the clutter to knock on the front door, before beating a hasty retreat back to the front steps to stand with me. We waited. No answer. Another knock. No answer.

Karen thought he was away, but then the door slowly opened and someone came out, wary and blinking in the sun. His gray hair stuck out in all directions, and several days' worth of stubble grew on his cheeks. A threadbare red plaid flannel shirt covered a ratty pink and blue New Orleans Jazz T-shirt, stretched tightly across his belly. He was missing some teeth, and the rest were angled in odd directions, filling up the

110

spaces. And then I saw the most beautiful, clear blue eyes I had ever seen. He looked relieved to recognize my guide.

"What is it, Karen?"

"Tony, I've brought somebody to meet you."

Pause.

"Actually, Tony," I said, "you know me already."

He looked confused.

"Do you remember Al and Carol Henry?"

Those blue eyes lit up, and he put his hands to his mouth. "You're Cindy!"

The last time he saw me I was four years old, and yet he knew me instantly.

We stood on the walk listening to him for an hour or more, Karen and I exchanging smiles occasionally, neither one of us saying more than three words the whole time. He talked about how much he admired my mama as she worked in the yard in her handmade dresses and worn Keds tennis shoes, or "played teacher" with the neighborhood kids at our house after school, always the lady. He thought it was remarkable, when he ate supper with us, that our family always drank water with meals. Only little Cindy had anything different, a glass of milk. Everybody else drank water. "Not even a glass of iced tea or Kool-Aid!" he marveled.

He mentioned that my parents took him to a march at the state capitol to see Martin Luther King speak. "I never did see Dr. King that day," he said, "but it was the first time I ever smelled marijuana." He also talked about Dad's liberal theology, saying, "Maybe that's where I got some of my ideas." Karen and I heard a long exposition on the many faces of God—Allah, Buddha, and the multitude of Hindu gods and goddesses.

When I finally managed to say good-bye to Tony and offered Karen my heartfelt thanks, I drove away with much to think about. The winds of change have certainly blown through Cabbagetown since we lived there. But as I came to the end of writing this piece of my story, nearly two years after I visited, much more violent winds blew through the spruced-up neighborhood. On Saturday night, March 15, 2008, a tornado roared through Atlanta, exploding windows in skyscrapers, stopping basketball players in their tracks as it ripped part of the roof off the Georgia Dome during overtime play, and wreaking havoc on homes in Vine City and Cabbagetown. Upper-floor condos at the former Fulton Bag and Cotton Mill were completely exposed, dollhouse-style, when the storm peeled away roof and wall. Hundred-year-old oak trees were left sprawling across smashed cars and houses, their roots buckling the sidewalks. Dozens were injured in Atlanta, but thankfully no one there was killed. I watched a YouTube video of the aftermath and saw an interview with my friend and guide Karen, who told the frightening story but ended with a smile, saying, "Praise God, everybody's okay, all in all, everything is good. Praise God."

When I think of tornadoes, of course I think of my dad. The human tornado. His roar could be as loud as those freight-train winds people talk about, and our fear was just as real. When Dad was angry, destruction ensued—splintered furniture, an obliterated guitar case, black eyes, sometimes blood. We got more second-hand furniture or sat on the floor. Linda got a new guitar case. Mom's wounds healed, though some scars remain. Some days her memories of those times return: "Remember when your dad used to get so angry, and you and I would have to go sleep in the car, or stay in the attic at our friends' house...your flute teacher...what were their names?"

Yes, Mom, I remember. The longest-lasting fear is of my own internal tornadoes—my personal feelings. What happens if I unleash them? Who will be hurt?

This fear keeps me from living life to the fullest. It keeps me from embracing the emotions of my children. When I hold back my feelings, I can't tell the story that I desperately need to tell. I must remember the faith of my grandfather. There is light in the darkness. The winds will pass. I will come out into the sunshine and rebuild, feeling grateful that I have survived.

I will tell my story of survival with tears in my eyes and a smile on my face.

I have survived.

Sunny

Carol and Sunny

Carol, Martha, Walter, and Miriam after Sunny's death

Walter L. Moore

Miriam McCall Moore

Albert L. Henry, III

Henry family at Koinonia Farm

Janet with the Koinonia cows

Moore grandparents' 50th anniversary celebration

Henry grandparents' 50th anniversary celebration

Cindy, four years old

Carol in Celo

Al at Virginia Beach

Cindy and John's wedding

The Henry siblings
Front: Nancy, Josh, Cindy *Back:* Janet, Linda

6

Scars

When my father quit his job on the ambulance, for once the Henry family didn't pick up and move. In his twenty-year career, this was the first time Al Henry's work and home were not financially connected: he'd lived in a parsonage as a minister, a in hospital-owned campus housing as a chaplain, in a Koinonia community house, and in a home whose rent was paid by the Georgia Council for Human Relations. Now he was just a guy with a job—when he quit, he went looking for another one and we stayed put. My sister Linda, midway through her senior year at Grady High School, must have been relieved.

Unlike Dad's precipitous departure from the Georgia Council (followed by several months of no work at all), when he left his job at Grady Hospital he had a new plan ready. Two days after his last day on the ambulance, he interviewed at a facility called the Georgia Retardation Center, located on the other side of Atlanta. He worked as a day laborer for Manpower while he waited to hear from the GRC, still bringing home a paycheck in the interim, with Mom still stretching every penny to make ends meet. Fortunately, as long as we lived in Cabbagetown, the ends weren't far apart. By the end of November, Dad had started full-time work in the GRC warehouse. He was promoted to Program Specialist when the first cottage (a residential building for the developmentally disabled) opened in January.

The GRC was a fairly new outfit at the time, a state-owned 350-bed facility for adults and youth with profound developmental disabilities. Dad had little experience with this population, but he felt some kinship with the residents there and they quickly became the next frontier for his social justice agenda. These people were locked up in a facility, and their only "crime" was being born different. Dad was determined to do what he could to make their lives better.

Life at the GRC was not particularly easy for anyone. It was primarily a "custodial care" facility: the staff was expected to ensure that the residents were safe, clean, dressed, fed, and occupied in the hours between morning and night. Families sent relatives here when they couldn't care for them at home. They needed a place to be, and that was all they got. To Dad, it didn't seem like enough.

As he had at Grady Hospital, Dad looked for kindred spirits among his coworkers at the GRC. He immediately connected with Alan Hoskins. Despite the twenty-year age difference (Alan was twenty-four and Dad was forty-four), they were both, as Alan described them, "social outsiders." Alan's long ponytail proved that he was willing to step outside the usual boundaries. He played guitar and sang his own folk songs to the GRC residents. As he told me later, he and Dad soon found that they "shared a perspective on life and faith." Dad introduced Alan to other close friends, and soon they went backpacking together on the Appalachian Trail. Alan and his girlfriend (later his wife) Karen also went on weekend trips with our family to Koinonia, Celo, and other places we considered special.

According to Mary Yoder, our old Mennonite House friend who also worked in the first cottage opened at GRC, Dad was generally well regarded:

> He and I worked in the same cottage for a short period of time. My perception was that he was very, very well respected there. And that it ate him up, too. Because it was very hard, even though you tried very, very hard to be good to people, and take care of them, those settings don't work. But "amazingly patient" was his reputation, and yet I often times saw him just literally walk away, and he probably got to the point where he knew he wasn't able to cope with it. So from my perspective, I could understand him walking away, but it was a little bit frustrating, because when one person walked away, the rest of us were still there.

In May, Linda graduated from Grady High School at the Atlanta City Auditorium. It was a festive family occasion, with both sets of grandparents present, posed photographs in our postage-stamp-sized front yard, and a big turkey for dinner. Even Dad was there this time— the white-bordered pictures show him clean shaven and dressed in a suit, standing between two unlikely men: his dad on one side and Walter Moore on the other. For this occasion, for Linda's sake, everybody could play the part. Even Dad.

With school out and Dad tiring of the long commute to GRC, it made sense to consider moving across town. Dad found Cambridge Square, a federally subsidized apartment complex in Doraville, on the north side of Atlanta a few miles away from the GRC. In July, we moved into a three-bedroom townhouse with a basement. Compared to slum life in Cabbagetown, it felt like the Ritz. The apartment was clean and freshly painted, none of the gutters in the neighborhood were falling off, we had central heat (with a thermostat!), and we never heard gunshots in the night. It was still hot in Atlanta, though, and Nancy and Linda were happy to head for the North Carolina mountains to spend the summer in tents at Camp Celo. Though we were packed in with other people at Cambridge Square, sharing walls with our neighbors on either side, it was a lonely after the hootenannies and quilting group camaraderie of our Cabbagetown days.

As the summer of 1970 drew to a close, it was once again a time of new beginnings for the Henry family. Janet and Nancy started at new schools: Janet at Oakcliff Elementary, a half-mile walk from Cambridge Square, and Nancy at Sequoyah High School. Linda got on a plane to head to Earlham College in Indiana. And Mama, Daddy, and I started on our own adventure: Montessori.

I don't know how my parents stumbled across Montessori, but it seemed to come at the right time for them. Dad wanted to do more for the residents at the GRC. He believed that they needed respect and true enrichment. I was four years old: too young to start elementary school but ready to do more than spend every day at home with Mama. Montessori was the answer for both Dad and me.

The Atlanta Montessori Institute had been founded two years prior, and Dad was drawn to its young, enthusiastic energy. He was accepted into the program to be certified as a teacher. He got an educational stipend from the GRC and permission to work split shifts: he would work evenings, and Mom would work the other half of his time during the day so that he could go to classes. The Children's House, a well-reputed Montessori school in an airy former church in Norcross, was only ten minutes from our home, so my parents enrolled me there. Our family was in no position to pay for private school, but Mama was able to trade her cleaning services to cover part of tuition. Soon, Marion Aland, the director and teacher of the school, realized that though Mama did a fine job scrubbing floors and child-sized toilets, she would be much more useful as a teacher's aide. Mama got her first promotion and still somehow found time to work at the GRC for Daddy, too.

A picture of me from Montessori used to hang on the wall in Mom's house. My hair was long and getting straighter, and my body had lost its baby shape. In the photo I was digging, working hard, taking the effort seriously. As the youngest member of the family, I loved that aspect of Montessori school—we weren't just playing. We had fun, but we called it *work*. The teachers took me seriously, and I felt like I mattered. I thrived on the combination of structure, with materials meant for specific and orderly use, and freedom to choose my own work. I learned to read early, writing lots of stories with my own invented but phonetic spelling. Life was predictable and safe at Children's House, the tall church windows let in lots of sunshine, and I could hang upside down on the geodesic dome jungle gym outside. I loved it.

While Mama and I built a pink tower, measured with red rods, traced the cursive lines of sandpaper letters, and counted with golden beads, Dad sat in classes of his own, learning the philosophy behind this method invented in Italy by Maria Montessori forty years before. He committed to memory the steps of a three-period lesson while sitting in a classroom with other adults; Mama learned it from watching Marion Aland, surrounded by the happy hubbub of preschool children. When Daddy came home with complicated assignments and projects to

116

complete, Mama did them with him, infusing life and love into the process. The colorful Montessori albums that he finally handed in, filled with photographs and descriptions of the different materials and the careful way to introduce and use each one, were a joint creation of both of my parents. And they were beautiful.

But once again, though Mama doggedly focused on the positive, our newest way of life began to wear thin again by springtime. Dad was losing his patience with Montessori training—he was a man of action and eager to get started with the new method at the GRC, where he knew the residents were thirsty for it. Continuing to cross the t's and dot the i's in the dictated Montessori way was beginning to feel like nitpicking. He wanted to get out of class and start *teaching* them.

There was strain in other areas as well. Dad had a jealous streak that was entirely unfounded, and it was getting worse. One Saturday morning that spring, Mom and Dad drove to Sandy Springs to pick up Janet from her friend Mae's house. Mae's parents had been friends of my parents since college days; though Jack and Gene were still married, they lived at opposite ends of the state. Somehow Dad decided that Mama was having an affair with Mae's daddy, Jack. As they drove back home in a beat-up Chevy II Nova station wagon, tempers flared and then exploded. Janet remembers it clearly:

> Mom and Dad were yelling at each other about Jack and Gene. Dad was driving, faster and faster, punching her in the face with his fist. I grabbed his arm from the back seat, shouting, "Don't hit her! Don't hit my mom!" I thought he would annihilate me. He said in a deep, slow, growling voice, "If you don't be quiet, I'll hit you, too."
>
> I remember sitting on my hands in my orange polyester shorts, the backs of my fingers getting bumpy marks from the vinyl seat.
>
> Mom's lip was busted, bleeding. I started screaming again, and he reached back and slapped right across my thigh with his open hand. We went flying from the left lane to the edge of the road, and he got out of the car, left the car door open, and walked into trees, away.
>
> I screamed again, "Shut the door, Mama, lock the door!"
>
> "Don't worry," she said, "he won't come back."

I sat there sobbing. She got it together in a little while, slid over behind the steering wheel, and drove us home.

We got back to the apartment, and Nancy was coming out the door with you [Cindy]. Nancy was in front. I remember pushing Mom so that Nancy would be between you and Mom, so that you wouldn't see that her face was bleeding. I remember how our bodies shifted. You were behind Nancy, so we were both between you and Mom. And we walked her in. And that's where the scar above her lip came from.

That's the first violence I remember. And the most vivid.

Janet's long pants covered the hand-shaped bruise across her thigh until it finally faded. Mom's lip eventually healed—I don't know how she explained it to her friends. But the scar remains, a thin white line of memory. Nancy doesn't remember that event. We all have our own ways of surviving.

Dad finished the Montessori training at the end of May 1971. Other interests appeared on the horizon. His friend Alan spotted a copy of a book in a bookstore remainder bin: *Edgar Cayce: Mystery Man of Miracles*. This book, authored by Joseph Millard and Cayce himself, told the story of a psychic. It fascinated Alan. When he shared it with Dad, it changed my father's life. The book threw wide the doors of alternative ways of thinking about the world: the unconscious mind, spirituality, diet, reincarnation, and more. When Mom was diagnosed with large fibroid tumors that summer and needed surgery (especially daunting since we had no savings or health insurance), Dad insisted that she take monstrous doses of vitamin E, and he invited friends over for a prayer vigil. Miraculously, it seemed, the tumors disappeared. Dad became even more confident in these alternative, new-age practices. Mom went along with the idea.

Since the GRC had made it possible for him to get Montessori training and his intention all along was to create a Montessori program for the residents, that fall Dad put together a formal proposal for the GRC leadership. He wore his only suit to make the presentation to the committee. It was the evening of October 27, 1971, the day after his forty-fifth birthday. Dad gave an impassioned speech about the need for

118

the program and the opportunities it would offer to the residents. The committee turned him down. The materials were too expensive; it wasn't the direction they had in mind; it wasn't going to happen. Dad's spirits plummeted, and two weeks later he submitted his resignation, giving the required thirty-day notice. His last day at the Georgia Retardation Center was December 15, 1971. Once again, he had no job prospects and no plans for the future. He was done. Empty.

Mom still had her part-time job at The Children's House, but most of that was in trade for my tuition. Her pay didn't cover the rent, food for our family, and the expenses to keep our beat-up cars on the road. It was another crisis. We squeaked by for another two months, but then it was time to move again.

Back when we lived at Koinonia, a family named the Blacks had come to visit. The parents, Hector and Susie, had met in the 1950s at the Bruderhof, a religious community in Pennsylvania. Susie, who had grown up in the strict Hutterite community of Forest River in North Dakota, was confined to a wheelchair by rheumatoid arthritis. She was a strong woman nonetheless. Hector, who had grown up in New York City, was a tall, fun-loving, charismatic man. In the late 1960s, when they visited us at Koinonia with their three daughters, they were the only white people living in Vine City, an infamous black slum in Atlanta. When we moved to Atlanta for Dad's job at the Georgia Council for Human Relations, Hector had been a key contact for Dad in establishing his inner-city network of civil rights activists.

By 1972, when Dad left the GRC and was casting about for a new place to live, Hector and Susie had left Vine City. Hector, like Dad, had become embittered by the slow rate of change he saw in the South's profound prejudice and discrimination. The Black family briefly returned to the North, but found the thinly veiled prejudice there just as insidious, though less honest. They decided, like Clarence Jordan of Koinonia, to live their values without fighting for them, and bought a large farm in the country outside of Atlanta, where Hector could finally pursue his lifelong love of horticulture. They started a nursery, growing fuchsias and other plants. They built a bakery where Susie and her Hutterite sisters, who often came to stay, baked bread and sweet rolls to sell to Atlanta restaurants. They felt that they had come home at last.

Though Hector and Susie had no intention of forming an organized community (the Bruderhof was another source of bitterness for Hector), their farm, Hidden Springs, was a natural gathering place for seekers and hippies. News of Hidden Springs traveled, and young people looking for an alternative lifestyle were drawn there, often camping on the property for weeks or months at a time, helping in the nursery or bakery and joining the family at the long table for dinners of fresh vegetables from the farm. Under Susie's watchful eye, everybody took a turn with the dishes.

To Dad, Hidden Springs looked like another oasis as he labored at the Georgia Retardation Center, witnessing the daily suffering of the residents, always wanting more for them, never satisfied with what he could achieve. Our family went to the Blacks' farm regularly on weekends or just for the day. The openness and isolation of Hidden Springs drew Dad like a hummingbird to the fuchsias that grew with such abandon in the large greenhouse. When it was time to leave Doraville, Hidden Springs seemed like the natural place to go. There was a small extra house on the farm, and we moved into it on March 4, 1972. The next week, Nancy and Janet were enrolled in new schools, starting over yet again in the wilderness. Nancy remembers walking into school from the big yellow bus on the first day to be greeted by the smell of sauerkraut, permeating the entire building from the lunchroom. Though she had brought her own lunch and wouldn't have to eat it, the smell alone was enough to set her opinion about the whole place. She quickly decided that this was the worst first impression she'd ever had of a new school. For the first time, she didn't even bother to try to find a best friend—calls to Doraville weren't long distance, and it was easier to keep in touch with her friends from Sequoyah than to find new ones. She wrote copious letters to camp friends. For once, Janet had a friend already when she started the new school: Aggie Black. They had all their classes together.

Linda, meanwhile, was facing her own crisis in her sophomore year of college. She had chosen Earlham, a small Quaker liberal arts college, partly because her first true love, Dan Fuson, whom she had met at Camp Celo when she was fifteen, would be there, too. We all loved Dan. He was beautiful to look at, gentle, fun, and loved kids. Linda told me that when Dan learned about the birds and the bees he was heartbroken: he had always looked forward to being pregnant and having a baby himself. By early 1972, Linda and Dan had been together for four years, but as the bleak Indiana winter stretched on, their relationship began to crumble. They made a difficult decision, breaking both their hearts, and decided they needed to go their separate ways. Linda, who knew that Mom was doing all she could to hold it together herself, felt that she couldn't call home to get the solace she desperately needed. Two weeks after our family moved to Hidden Springs, Linda took a leave of absence from Earlham and left mid-semester, heading back south for a taste of spring. Dan dropped out of school for good at that time, with only one trimester left before graduation, and drove her to Hidden Springs. He stayed for months.

My parents worked hard on the farm. Mama tended plants in the nursery, and Daddy got up early to bake dozens of loaves of bread each day, then headed out to the mower in his straw hat as the afternoon sunshine poured over him. They both tended our new cow. Janet played with the Black sisters, and I tagged along after them, dabbling with my multi-hued, long-haired troll dolls along the shores of the mud puddle in the farm driveway. When it was warm enough, the big girls swung screaming off the rope into the swimming hole at the creek and crawled through the brambles to the rose-covered garden house, an old chicken shed at the back of the farm that served as a fine clubhouse. I scrambled behind, always hoping to be included, too. And sometimes I was.

But as it had at Koinonia, the romance of agrarian life soon faded. Nancy and Janet had to ride the school bus more than two hours a day to get back and forth to Paulding County High School and Junior High. And after the rigors of metropolitan Atlanta schools, they found their classes easy to the point of utter boredom. Nancy, always looking for the best in the situation, took the opportunity to double up on her classes, taking two sections of English at once. Though Janet enjoyed being with her dear friend Aggie at school, Aggie had worked hard to keep her school life and her home life, which many would have viewed as hippie and strange, completely separate. It was almost impossible for Aggie to maintain those boundaries and be a good friend to Janet at the same time.

Dad began to clench his teeth, as he had with Clarence, when Hector called the shots on his farm. He resented working so hard for no pay. Mama dealt with her own questions, such as why there was always enough money for wine but never enough for orange juice. Though finances on the farm were combined, our family had meals at our own house, only joining the communal table at the big house for special occasions. My sisters and I heard our parents argue in the night. The tension grew.

Finally, twelve-year-old Janet was tired of it all. It was nearly midnight one night, and the yelling had gone on long enough. Janet decided to run away. She put a few clothes into a paper bag and stomped down the dark gravel road. She was going back to Atlanta.

Janet stomped a long way before she began to feel the rocks under her tennis shoes, hear the night noises, and realize what she had committed herself to do. But Janet had always been stubborn. After a few more steps, she began to hear footsteps on the gravel behind her. She sped up, not daring to turn around. On came the footsteps, getting faster behind her. She tried not to panic and looked for places to hide, but it was too dark and the footsteps too close.

Finally, someone said, "*Janet?*"

It was Dan—wonderful, safe Dan, personal Prince Charming to each of us. Janet's relief quickly turned to sobs, buried deep in Dan's broad shoulder. He respected her anguish and got her safely home without forcing her to concede her point. After all, she was right. It was too much for any kid to bear. But what choice did we have?

Towards the end of May that year, even I started to sense the strain. I was used to being the tagalong kid, often teased, tolerated though not necessarily invited. But it seemed that things were getting worse. Janet and the Black sisters, Rosemarie, Aggie, and Annie, spent more and more time in the Black girls' bedroom in the big house, firmly shutting the door and making it clear that I was not to set foot across the threshold. They whispered and giggled, and I knew that I was missing out. Squatting at the edge of the big mud puddle with my trolls wasn't as fun as it used to be. They wouldn't even let me into the room when they weren't there. I hated being the little one.

Soon, though, I forgave them all. On May 28, 1972, the day before my sixth birthday, we spotted cars started driving down the rutted road toward the big house. I recognized the Dodge Dart and the long, blue Ford. *Both* sets of grandparents were here! Mama made sure I was clean behind the ears and told me to put on my pretty light blue dress. Linda brushed my hair back into a grown-up looking bun. When we got to the big house, "SURPRISE!" A party for me! We hadn't celebrated my birthday since I was a baby, and I could hardly believe it. Guests, a table piled high with food (Mama made a cake shaped like a giraffe), and even presents! It took my breath away. My two grandmamas sat in straight-backed wooden chairs next to each other, eating lunch on their laps, both in blue polyester dresses, one striped, one plaid. And then, out of the Black sisters' darkened bedroom came the most beautiful thing I had ever seen: a dollhouse constructed out of cardboard and painted dark blue, inside and out. It wasn't that they didn't want to play with me—all that time they were making an amazing dollhouse just for me! I was loved after all.

Three days later, the entire Children's House Montessori school came to the farm on a field trip and to celebrate my birthday all over again, sitting cross-legged in a big circle on the grass. The sun had never shone more brightly in my little life.

One week later, the sun came crashing out of the sky.

It started as another argument. Dad growled about Hector, the unending work on the farm, the injustice of one thing or another. Mom tried a new tactic: she had never particularly wanted to live on the farm, anyway, so maybe they could move the family back to Atlanta. He could get another job, maybe in Montessori this time, and we could start over again. He snapped.

"Don't you understand?" he roared.

Maybe she didn't. He told Mama that he would never have another regular job, would never support the family again, would find a new path to follow in life. He could no longer be the breadwinner of this family. He felt a call far beyond the limits of what she could imagine. The tears rolled down her confused face.

He started packing that night. In big penciled letters, he wrote in his week-at-a-glance calendar, "FATHER NO MORE."

The next morning, though, Dad was still home. As a family, we rode with my oldest sister Linda to the bus station in Yorkville. She would fly from Atlanta to Mexico the next morning, setting off on an Earlham-sponsored summer trip. Linda had worked hard to earn a spot in the program, studying Spanish, applying, filing for scholarships, saving money, and making her own travel arrangements without asking our parents for help. As she climbed the steps of the Greyhound bus, paisley canvas suitcase in hand, Mom reached out her arms. "Travel safely. Don't forget to write! We love you so much."

Dad, silent for the whole morning until that moment, slowly growled, "No, we don't."

Linda climbed on the bus and rode away, his words etched into her memory forever.

The next day, he was gone. We didn't know where. We didn't understand why. We didn't know if we would ever see him again. He was just gone.

In the midst of our family turmoil, the news of the burglary at the Watergate Hotel in Washington must have seemed hardly notable to my mother. It simply confirmed what Dad tended to rant about: the extent to which power and money corrupts everybody and everything. The Vietnam War raged on in spite of Nixon's empty promises to end it. The war on poverty had fallen flat. There was nothing to hope for anymore. The break-in at the Democratic Headquarters seemed like just more of the same. There was an eerie resonance between the unraveling in our family and the unraveling in our nation.

A week after Dad disappeared, Nancy left, too, riding with friends back to Celo to be a camp counselor for the summer. Two weeks later, Mama put twelve-year-old Janet on a Greyhound bus by herself to Montgomery, Alabama. Uncle Buddy and his family were on their way from Tallahassee on a trip out west for the month of July, and Janet would join them. Then it was just Mama and me, together in the house on the farm. It was time for her to figure out what to do next.

This was not the life she had imagined for herself. How had this happened? What had she done wrong? Mama had always envisioned her life following a path similar to her own mama's. While she went to college and got a good education, she made it no secret that she was really at Mercer to "marry the handsomest ministerial student I could find." And as soon as she graduated, she did marry that man.

Al Henry was handsome, with a strong chin, an excellent physique, and an irresistible twinkle in his eye. Though Mama's father always had doubts about this dashing young man, her mother was tickled pink. The marriage was promising at first, but then Mama followed Daddy through one traumatic disappointment after another. He always had a strong calling—he saw so clearly everything that was wrong in the world, all the people who were oppressed and needed to be uplifted. But his attempts always seemed to fail. None of them worked out the way he hoped.

My mother loved him. However, she couldn't rely on him anymore, couldn't be the housewife, couldn't wait for him to decide the next chapter. She would have to take charge. She decided to move us back to town where she could earn money to support us, whether Dad believed in it or not. Somebody had to be the responsible one.

Mama called Marion Aland at Children's House, who had become a close friend by this time, and explained our circumstances.

Marion called back the next day and said, "Paul and I have talked about it. We've looked over the books, and we think we can afford to pay you to come back full time. We would love to have you back in the classroom." Mama offered up a brief prayer of thanksgiving. She called the Cambridge Square rental office and was relieved to learn that they had a three-bedroom opening up in August, number 258. Two weeks after Janet returned from the great trek across the West, we packed up and moved back to town.

We learned later that Dad had lived in a tent in the woods in Carrollton, Georgia, all summer, just thirty miles south of Hidden Springs. He had made friends with a man named Jim Boyd, who owned some land there, where Jim and others experimented with building geodesic domes. Dad camped next to a waterfall, did yoga, learned about the Humanistic Psychology program at West Georgia College, and read books about new age topics: astrology, tarot, massage, alternative health care, diet, the Kabbalah, and anything else he could find. When he got word that we were moving back to Doraville, he came out of the woods.

That fall of 1972 we began to learn what it was like to have this new kind of Daddy in the family. His hair and beard grew long. We saw him for brief periods, but he was mostly on the road with his thumb out, ping-ponging up and down the eastern seaboard. That fall he went from Carrollton to Virginia Beach (former home of the psychic Edgar Cayce, where the Cayce foundation, the Association for Research and Enlightenment, was a magnet for new age ideas and people); to Atlanta; back to Virginia Beach; back to Atlanta; to Rural Retreat (in the mountains of southwest Virginia, where there was an ARE summer camp and others with similar interests); back to Virginia Beach; to Atlanta; to Rural Retreat; and back to Atlanta—all in the course of about three months. Linda, who chose to not return to Earlham in the fall, traveled with Dad some, also hitchhiking, working terribly hard to understand where he was coming from and gain his approval by being with him.

Though much younger than Linda, I, too, was trying to come to terms with how to relate to my father. A letter to him from that time, which I wrote when I was learning to write and spell, was forwarded multiple times from "General Delivery" at one post office to another and then another. It conveys my confusion and sense of loss:

Dear Daddy
i just fixed my room.
Daddy will you come home
because I love you very much.
the end
maybe I can come to you
love
cindy Henry

The national news made no more sense than Dad did. In November that year, despite ongoing reports in the media about follow-up to the Watergate break-in and the endless, pointless loss of lives in Vietnam, Richard Nixon enjoyed a landslide victory for reelection over George McGovern. One of the few times I remember Mama yelling at me was when I came home from my friend's house wearing a Nixon campaign button. The McGovern loss was a blow. It was also a safe focus for Mama's anger at a time when she doggedly showed a smiling face to the world in spite of the blows she was taking at home.

That December, thanks to the extra classes she'd taken at Paulding County High, Nancy graduated early from Sequoyah High School in Doraville. There was no graduation ceremony midyear, but Nancy was more than ready to move on.

For Christmas, Dad hitchiked back to Atlanta, and we drove to Virginia Beach, where we camped in the wintry cold and Mom, Dad, Nancy, and Linda attended a conference at the ARE in Virginia Beach. Janet and I entertained ourselves, playing outside the building. To help keep me occupied during those long days, Mama bought me some simple toys: a big balloon with a rubber band tied to it, to bounce over and over again against my hand, and a Sesame Street town with all the characters. Since we didn't celebrate holidays, I rarely got new toys. I was in awe, and heartbroken when a boy came along to play with us and stole my big red balloon.

Nights were cold, and some evenings my sisters and I huddled together in the cement block campground bathhouse, the only place with heat, until it was time to climb into our sleeping bags in the tent. It never occurred to me that in other families, people were gathered around fireplaces, singing Christmas carols, enjoying the holiday season in an entirely different way. I was six years old, and this was what our family did.

Linda decided to go back to Earlham in January 1973. Nancy, determined to get her first real non-camp job, walked up and down the four-lane Buford Highway near Cambridge Square, filling out job applications. Ironically, she landed a job as a waitress at Sambo's restaurant, cheerfully delivering plates of steaming pancakes while a white-skinned, turbaned "Li'l Black Sambo" cavorted with tigers around the illustrated walls. Dad returned to Virginia Beach and set up his tent in the swamp behind the ARE, Mama and I went back to school at the Children's House, and Janet returned to Oakcliff Elementary, where she was in seventh grade. That winter and spring, while top-level Republicans came tumbling down as they desperately scrambled to cover up Watergate mistakes, our family conspired to cover up our own problems as we learned what it was like to live without a father at home.

Cambridge Square was a fun place for an elementary school kid to live. The playground behind our apartment had monkey bars, swings, and a long metal slide. Our unit was in the "model building" at the corner of the complex, which offered one of each available apartment style and was built in a wide U shape around a circular sidewalk, with grass in the middle. It was the natural gathering place for kids in the neighboring buildings as well. We played endless games of spud, kick the can, and monkey in the middle, skated, or rode tricycles and bicycles. Sometimes I flipped over my trike and it became an imaginary ice cream machine that made imaginary treats, which I sold for imaginary money. When we heard the tinkling notes of the real ice cream truck, though, and kids came yelling from all directions, Janet and I would wander the other way, our hearts sinking. We knew better than to ask for money for a red, white, and blue ice pop. They were for other kids.

Through Dad's letters, we learned that he was camping in the swamp, walking on the beach, fasting, and studying in the ARE library. His life seemed far away and hard to understand. One he wrote to tell us that his belongings were stolen, though they were actually impounded by the state park rangers since he was camping illegally. Another time he wrote that he was sleeping on the beach under catamarans, listening to the waves, swimming with the dolphins. I longed for him to call and ask us to come pick him up. I wanted our family to be okay. In every one of my letters to him, I asked the same question, in my scrawly invented spelling: "Do you still love me?"

The nation, though peopled by adults who cloaked their basic questions in more complex language, was wondering the same thing. Does anybody care about the real people in this country, those of us who go to work every day to keep our way of life running? It seemed not.

When summer arrived, headlines screamed that Nixon was refusing to hand over presidential tape recordings to the Senate Watergate Committee. Somehow he managed to argue that the intangible "future of the presidency" mattered more than the truth that the American public was so hungry to hear.

In our family, Nancy and Linda headed back to Camp Celo, and the rest of us got a taste of Dad's life. We drove our beat-up Chevy station wagon up I-85 to Virginia Beach and slept on the floor of a community center so we could volunteer at a Friends International Work Camp in Seatack, the black ghetto there. Next we traveled to Rural Retreat, where Dad's friend Charlie Stevens owned a huge farm. Charlie leased part of his land to the ARE for their children's summer camp, and we camped in a cow field by a creek not far away. It was an adventure at first—playing in the creek, eating cherries up in the tree till my belly hurt, going to fiddlers' conventions, riding on top of the big trailer of hay while Dad and the other men threw the rectangular bales up beside me.

But the romance faded. When we were away one day, the cows came to our part of the field, trampling our tent and denting our cooking pots. Even though we were in the woods, living the life Dad wanted for us, it was never enough. As always, the tension built and I looked to Janet, waiting for the moment when it was time for us to crawl into the rhododendron thicket on the side of the steep hill and wrap ourselves around each other as we waited for the storm to pass.

After another violent episode, Janet heard the ARE camp bell echoing down the valley and made a decision. She walked to camp alone, introduced herself to the director (who knew Dad), explained that our family was camping by the creek, and asked if they had a scholarship and room in a cabin for her. They made room. When she packed up and went to camp, free at last, I stayed by the creek with our parents. There was nowhere else for me to go.

At the end of summer, Dad headed to an organic orchard in northern Virginia to pick apples for the season. Linda decided to try Earlham again, and Nancy started as a freshman there. Mom, Janet, and I went back to Doraville: Janet entered Sequoyah High School as an eighth grader, and I started elementary school. Though I was seven and old enough for second grade, the school insisted on testing me because they felt that "many children who come from Montessori schools are not at the academic level of the other children." The school was right—my academic level differed from my age. My test scores showed that I was close to the fourth grade level. So I started second grade and went up a grade for reading class. Mama politely abstained from gloating, but her smile gave her away.

In October, amid swirling charges of extortion, tax fraud, bribery, and conspiracy, Spiro Agnew resigned from his position as vice president, yet another scandal of epic proportions. Dad's response of withdrawing from the world seemed like the best choice. Though Mama loved him with all her heart, wished she could make him happy, and recognized that he was right about those with the most power, she refused to lead the rest of us over the cliff where he was dangling.

By Christmastime, Dad was back in Atlanta, making sure that we didn't celebrate the holidays. The big occasion that season was his parents' fiftieth wedding anniversary. Dad's younger brother Jordan, a successful businessman in airline catering, planned a huge party for them to be held in Macon, where Grandmama grew up in a prominent banking family, and where she had met and married Granddaddy. All of us were invited to the celebration.

Dad, who was no longer comfortable sleeping under a roof and not about to cut off his hair and put on a suit, made it known that he disapproved of the anniversary party. As far as he was concerned, it was another opportunity for people to spend money trying to impress each other. Mama felt that we ought to be there—after all, he was their only other son. Our family should be represented. As an attempt to keep the peace, though, she promised to stay home with him. The four girls dressed in our fanciest clothes, me in the blue dress I had worn for my birthday at Hidden Springs the year before. With Linda behind the wheel, we rode a hundred miles to Macon for the evening soiree. The pictures show us grouped awkwardly around Grandmama and Granddaddy Henry, white cake in hand, Grandmama throwing her head back to laugh hysterically, the rest of us less than comfortable. Now I wonder what Mom faced at home that night, withstanding the torrent of Dad's rage about the party for his parents' special day.

In Washington, mysterious gaps had appeared on the subpoenaed presidential tapes. No one, certainly not anyone in our liberal circle, believed that Nixon was free of guilt in the Watergate crimes and cover-up. We thought he would receive the discipline he deserved. But as we were all learning, life didn't work that way. In our house, as well as the White House, rules were broken and people were hurt. Things that should never have happened continued to happen. And we all kept the conspiracy of silence.

For almost a year, Dad was home. It was another chance for us to learn how to be a family with this new kind of daddy. Though he was at home with us instead of traveling from place to place and writing letters, he wasn't the same. He didn't go to work, didn't attend meetings, didn't try to find a way to change the world. Most days he didn't even get out of bed; he just lay in a darkened room in his sleeping bag or spent long hours in the bathtub. Daddy was home, but he was still far away from us. The twinkle in his eye had been snuffed out.

He was still deep into esoteric ideas and materials. The mysteries of the ancient Kabbalah held him rapt. He found an old Ouija board, and would get Mama to use it with him, asking questions, contacting whichever wayward souls happened to be hitchhiking through the nearby ether. Mama agreed in order to pacify him, but she admitted later that it always felt wrong to her.

Linda and Nancy's friend Dale Moody, who had lived at Hidden Springs for a time, remembers coming to visit us at Cambridge Square when Dad was with us. Dad asked what became his trademark sing-song opening question: "Dale, what's yo' sign?" and added, "Do you know what time, exactly, you were born?" Dad worked all night to create a complete astrological chart for Dale, and then he spent hours interpreting it for him. Dad was struck by the enormity of Dale's conception: Dale's parents had worked with refugees in the Middle East when he was conceived, but he was born in the United States. Dale was conceived in Bethlehem and born in Celo, North Carolina, and Dad found it fascinating. He spent months creating similar charts for all of us, and he talked about astrology interminably. I learned that Dad was a Scorpio and I was a Gemini, but I didn't understand.

Another late night, Dad wrote a thirteen-page letter to his elderly friend Charlie Stevens, who shared his interest in esoterica. Written in pencil, with dark erasures throughout, the words captured the twisting and turning of Dad's manic mind. He asked Charlie to think about the two Hebrew letters ח and ט, both of which indicate a "t" sound. Then, in a complex, mind-blowing series of paragraphs, Dad made connections between Jews, Christians, and adherents of new age beliefs and finally came to his main point:

So in our obsession with a ח [that is, suffering] cross-blood sacrifice system of atonement for guilt (we have continued to shed blood on mass scale in wars, etc.), we have completely lost our sensitivity to hear God. With no sensitivity we have no sense,—we can't sense the truth, we can't make sense out of life—we have "lost our sense"—of hearing—

Cents have been substituted for sense—Dollars have been substituted for our 6th sense in our values.

Working for & accruing material dollars has become all-important to the neglect of listening to our inner spiritual sensitivity with our inner

132

third-ear. We have become spiritually deaf and <u>dumb</u>. {to spiritual values—to the inner spiritual plane}

Sacrificing our life energy (our life blood) to gain dollars is sapping spiritual energy from our spleens, and killing our bodies (to say nothing of our souls).

At best, Christianity has acknowledged blend of "Son of Man and Suffering Servant," thereby subverting Son of Man's standing alone.

The scriptures have been tampered with going & coming by the historical economic-political-religious hierarchy to reinforce and justify economic-political-religious institutions of exploitation—the opiates of the suffering people.

Jesus Christ was killed by a Π-cross theology, —man-made traditions. This was man's plan & his doing—not God's. All Jesus' statements about the necessity of his dying on the cross indicate his awareness that Jesus' submission to this brutal man-made system of guilt and blood atonement was necessary in order for men to see through it,—that God did not devise it.—that God had another way—(See book of Hebrews).

Pauline theology completely perverts the meaning of this Π cross and wrongly attributes its source to God rather than man.

If the cross is an evidence of the love of God it is only because God submitted to it so mankind could discover it was not his plan.

Mankind devises the cross (Π) God overcomes it through his creative life energy, Ʊ.

Substituting Π for Ʊ is a grievous error.

An underground Christian faith based on Ʊ rather than Π is called for. Again it will result in persecution and crucifixion as the people center their faith in Ʊ rather than Π. Yet the sun of man Ʊ will rise victorious over the cross Π.

Other people's daddies didn't talk like this. To him, it made perfect, urgent sense. I tried to tune it out.

But there were things we couldn't tune out. Dad became convinced that it was critical to control our diets. No more meat, he said, and no more sugar. We must eat only natural foods. On the inside of a kitchen cabinet door, he posted a chart that outlined how we should or shouldn't combine different foods. No proteins and starches together. We should eat mostly fruits and vegetables. If we had to sweeten something, we could only use honey. No white rice, nothing refined—Mama had to buy wheat, grind it, and use the resulting flour for baking dark, heavy bread. No liquids with meals; we had to drink water either ten minutes ahead of suppertime or half an hour later. He counted as we chewed every bite one hundred times. By the end of the meal I felt like a horse in the field, chewing my own tongue. And Mom's coffee—oh, that was the worst kind of poison. Dad talked on and on, in his southern twang, about "acids and alkalahns [alkalines]." Before we ate, we all held hands in a certain way for the silent blessing: left palm up, right palm down, to ensure the energy flow in the circle.

Janet and I got energy boosts in other ways. We'd sneak to the 7-11 store up the street, where she bought Hostess cupcakes with one white squiggle of icing on top of the dark chocolate. Every crumb and smudge had to disappear by the time we got home. I've had a special relationship with chocolate ever since.

We ate a lot of beans, especially soybeans. One day when Linda and Nancy were home from college, we were hanging out in the kitchen while the pressure cooker swished away on the stove. All of a sudden there was a loud, explosive SMASH, and boiling soybean guts spewed everywhere. Was *this* THE COMING CRASH that Dad had been talking about all this time? We scattered. The others rushed through the open door into the living room and out the front, while I desperately tried to clamber over the multiple bikes stored between the sliding glass door and the kitchen table. I got hopelessly tangled in bicycles, and when the spewing stopped and the family returned, we all dissolved in laughter. We found the renegade pressure cooker valve, Mom mopped the ceiling, and we ate something else for supper. I, for one, was not disappointed by the menu change.

After sugar and white bread, furniture was the next comfort to go. Dad was determined that we live as simply as possible and wanted to eradicate all forms of materialism. We were allowed to keep the kitchen table and chairs, the piano, and the chests of drawers that held our clothes, but we gave everything else away. Our television was already long gone, since our tiny black and white set had had stopped working years before. No more couch or coffee tables; Mom got out her black Singer sewing machine and created big fuzzy cushions so we'd have something to sit on in the living room. No desk for doing homework; we could use the kitchen table or the floor. Our beds were foam mattresses on the floor. Somehow the bright orange butterfly chair was exempt from the purging, it was the one remaining chair outside the kitchen, probably because it folded and wasn't comfortable for anybody over ten years old. But I enjoyed it immensely, sitting in it as I watched Mama sew together my new navy blue down sleeping bag from a kit. Feathers were everywhere.

Other than chocolate, our biggest big guilty pleasure was Grandmama and Granddaddy Moore. We rarely saw them, but they stopped by once in a while, and occasionally we visited them at the house they'd retired to in Cedartown, where the store-bought, buttered, white bread toast melted in my mouth like the finest French delicacy. But they never saw my father, of course, and when he was in town they were off limits for all of us. By this time, Dad's bitterness towards Granddaddy was a bottomless well.

Dad was vigilant about enforcing all the restrictions. If he found evidence that one of us had strayed, or if he had a hunch or even imagined that someone had done something outside the rules, we all paid the price. Especially Mom. We walked on eggshells.

But the explosion was always inevitable. I knew when it was coming. The air thickened. A familiar metallic taste filled my mouth. He spoke louder, threatening. Mom's alto voice grew higher, panicky as she tried to hold her ground. I wanted to intervene, but I always knew better. Instead, Janet and I left together, if it was daytime. We sat on the monkey bars in the playground, silently waiting, or walked around the apartments, hand in hand, or just sat on the sidewalk somewhere, waiting for it to pass or for Mom to come find us, saying that it was time to take a ride in the car. There was no place to go. We just rode.

The worst, though, happened in the dark of night when Janet and I couldn't leave the apartment. Voices rose, and there was no way to sleep through it. I usually went to Janet's room, closed the door, and climbed in bed with her. Together we sang under the covers, our soprano voices blending in freedom songs of peace, trying to drown out the shouting and banging on the other side of the wall, trying not to picture what we could only hear.

"I ain't gonna study war no more, ain't gonna study war no more..."

In the morning, all was quiet.

Janet, firmly into her teenage years by this time, was angry at the world. Anytime Mama suggested something to her, Janet's invariable response was an impatient exhalation followed by, *"I know."* She had a couple of good friends at school, still kept in touch with her best friend Aggie Black at Hidden Springs, excelled in her classes without working hard, and spent every other waking moment listening to John Denver records on her blue record player with cubical speakers. *"Rocky mountain high, Colorado..."* She would have given anything to be out there on that mountain, leavin' on that jet plane, or anywhere, *anywhere*, besides stuck in our apartment in the middle of our family's mess. She wanted *out*.

Summers offered some opportunity for escape. Camp Celo was a refuge for my sisters, and each one survived adolescence living from summer to summer, anticipating the return to that cool, green valley with the river winding through it. Their true friends were from camp, people they wrote letters to throughout the school year, other people who shared our hippie lifestyle but had a lot of fun at the same time. By the time I was eight years old, both Linda and Nancy were counselors at camp, and Janet was a counselor in training (they called them "helpers") so she could spend the whole summer there without paying camp tuition. I was finally old enough to be a camper myself, and I spent three weeks there, sleeping in a tent, going for hikes, acting in silly skits, and singing around the campfire. Three weeks was a long time to be away from home and Mama, but with all three sisters nearby, I could hardly be homesick.

We spent the rest of the summer traveling around the Appalachians and camping, eating wild foods (Dad had discovered Euell Gibbons by this time), and "surviving on the land." I learned to recognize daylily buds, lamb's quarters, watercress, and other plants that grew wild by the sides of roads and creeks. I hoped Dad wouldn't see them. I hated eating weeds.

At one point we were camping by the river near Celo and went to the Celo Friends Meeting on Sunday morning. At the end of worship, an older couple who were self-proclaimed wild mushroom experts announced that they had seen a patch of delicious chanterelle mushrooms growing near the meetinghouse. They were on their way out of town and couldn't stay for a meal, but our parents picked a bunch of these mushrooms, and Mama cooked them with vegetables in butter over the fire. We loved them for an hour or so. But then we all started feeling strange.

At the swimming hole, Janet said thought she was going to throw up, but made me promise not to tell Mama and Daddy. But soon, everyone was sick, including camp counselors who had eaten the mushrooms. We climbed into the camp station wagon, a car full of retching people with buckets. At the emergency room, the mushrooms were identified as poisonous mushrooms commonly known as Jack-o'-Lanterns. We were all given Ipecac to empty our already emptied stomachs. The nausea eventually passed. I didn't eat another mushroom for years.

America continued to suffer its own form of illness, finally expelling Richard Nixon. He resigned on August 8, 1974, after more than two years of Watergate and amid other political scandals and the ongoing war in Vietnam. With no TV at home, we wouldn't have watched the speech anyway. But news of it it was everywhere when we returned to civilization. To my parents, Nixon's words once again echoed with empty politics:

> I have never been a quitter. To leave office before my term is completed is abhorrent to every instinct in my body. But as President, I must put the interest of America first. America needs a full-time President and a full-time Congress, particularly at this time with problems we face at home and abroad.
>
> To continue to fight through the months ahead for my personal vindication would almost totally absorb the time and attention of both the President and the Congress in a period when our entire focus should

be on the great issues of peace abroad and prosperity without inflation at home.

Therefore, I shall resign the Presidency effective at noon tomorrow.

Hooray for a quitter, and better late than never. Gerald Ford, who had been appointed vice president just ten months earlier, became the leader of our country.

That fall of 1974, Linda returned to Earlham, while Nancy decided to take a leave of absence and go backpacking out West with three friends. Dad was always proud when his daughters chose counter-cultural paths, especially when the paths led to the great open road and sleeping under the stars. Linda and Nancy had both developed an interest in Transcendental Meditation (they called it "TM") as well, which I resented because it meant there was a lot of tiptoeing around the house whenever they were upstairs doing whatever they did. Again, Dad thought it was great and helped them explore new planes of existence, get in touch with the deeper side of life. He wrote to a friend during that time, "I have made it a point to get as much into the periphery of American life as possible, though that is not easy to do.... I have been an iconoclast all along, but in more recent years I have centered more into revolution of spirit, rather than an economic or political revolution.... This kabbalah trek is leading me along inner paths I never dreamed existed." Dad's inner paths were gradually becoming more real and important to him than anything in the physical world. Including his family.

When Nancy returned to Earlham in January, she and her backpacking friends moved into the "TM House" off campus where Linda was already living with others. Nancy ditched her former interest in literature and enrolled in a cosmology class, co-taught by astronomy and philosophy professors. She was ready to "go deep" and leave superficial things behind.

But seven weeks into the ten-week trimester, with a battery of deadlines and final exams looming, Nancy had a revelation. She sat in a hot lecture hall, wearing a sweater that was too warm for the room and knitting a poncho out of wool yarn. The room was oppressive, the course was oppressive, school was oppressive—the whole system felt wrong. She knew she had to get out. In the next few days, she went to her advisor and each one of her professors in turn, telling them her decision. All but one responded, "Well, it sounds like you've thought it through. Maybe you don't need to be here." Her astronomy professor was the only one to challenge her: "You won't get anywhere without a college education. You need to stay here and train your mind. This is no time to leave."

Nancy left anyway.

Unlike Linda, though, she didn't come home. She called to let Mom and Dad know she was dropping out, and she stuck out her thumb to travel across the country with a guy from school. She didn't call home again for another week and a half; Mama had no idea where she was. Later we learned that the two of them hitchhiked from Indiana to the Outer Banks, to Poughkeepsie and then to Baltimore before their relationship began to fray and she turned up back at Cambridge Square. She had no idea where to head next, but she was clear that she wouldn't return to Camp Celo that summer—she was ready to explore new horizons. When she got back to Doraville, Dad was there as well, and the two of them spent long days at home while the rest of us were at school. He loved the idea of new horizons, so they cooked up a plan to hitchhike to Nevada and see the Native American medicine man, Rolling Thunder. Dad had been plagued by phlebitis in his leg since he was a young man, and he was convinced that Rolling Thunder could heal him. Together, he and his second daughter would find enlightenment. Nancy still remembers her second revelation:

It was May, and we were just a few days shy of going. We had been making lots of preparations for the trip. All of a sudden I just choked, and really felt like I was going over the edge with him. Somebody we knew was driving to Tallahassee. I called Uncle Buddy and said, "I know this is short notice, but I gotta get out of here. Can I come down there?" He answered, "We're waiting for you."

She felt like she had narrowly avoided going down Dad's rabbit hole into a land of no return.

After a few days with family in Florida, the world came back into focus for Nancy. She called Dot Barrus, director of Camp Celo and asked if there was room for her. She got the same response: "We're waiting for you." When she needed them most, Nancy found open arms. But not at home.

Linda finished her long years at Earlham in May, walking down the aisle in her cap and gown for the second time, gratefully receiving her diploma. Aunt Martha, Mama's younger sister who lived in Cincinnati, was the only family member there to celebrate with Linda.

That summer, Linda and Nancy were both at Camp Celo again, and Mama worked a session in the camp kitchen in trade for my tuition. Janet was there, too, but Dad was in Virginia. In the fall, Linda stayed in Celo to work at the Arthur Morgan School, an alternative junior high school across the field from camp. Nancy spent an unhappy season picking apples at Golden Acres, the same orchard where Dad had picked apples two years before, and then she hitchhiked north with another friend, finally ending up back in Celo in January 1976, where she lived in Camp Celo's tiny octagonal "meditation hut" in the woods, worked for the Barruses in return for room and board, and gave herself time and space to regroup. Dot Barrus listened empathetically to Nancy's anguish, and Bob had more faith in her than she had in herself. She learned how to drive the camp's stick-shift truck, worked hard outside, breathed deeply, and found some peace.

The rest of us, though, still lived in the war zone. I was in the fourth grade and Janet was in the eleventh. Mom continued to teach at Children's House. Dad was mostly there in Doraville, too, though he traveled occasionally, often bringing home friends he had met on the trail or on the road, men who stayed with us for weeks at a time, sleeping on the living room floor. One of them nonchalantly exposed himself to me as I played in the living room, and asked questions about my private parts. I quickly packed up my Play-Doh and headed upstairs to my room, utterly confused by what I had seen. I told no one.

School was a welcome relief from the tensions of home. In the afternoons, Janet and I spent as much time as possible outside playing with friends. On the rare weekends that our family wasn't hiking or backpacking, Janet and I desperately invited friends to spend the night; somehow our father's blow-ups never happened when people outside the family were around. When summertime came, it was a repeat of the ones before—we were thrilled for the weeks at camp (that year I got to go to ARE camp as well as Camp Celo), and we dreaded every other moment of the season, when the four of us camped in the woods with no escape from the heat of the family.

During my camp session, Mama cooked again to pay for my tuition. She stayed in the little one-room meditation hut in the woods where Nancy had lived during the school year. Though she worked hard, six days a week, with only one hour off for herself each day, the time at camp was precious for her, too. Solitude was a rare gift, and even one hour a day in the hut gave her the opportunity to think about her life in a new way. She still loved Dad with all her heart. He was the one and only man she had ever loved. He wasn't the same as he used to be, but he clearly wasn't well, and she had promised to love him and care for him "in sickness and in health." But life was difficult in Doraville. She loved her job but had no other support system—she had lost touch with most of her friends. And my father was angry with nearly everyone they had been close to in the past. It was hard to know who to turn to, and she didn't want to make the situation any worse.

One day after lunch cleanup, Mom returned to the meditation hut for a quick afternoon nap during her hour off. Camp was quiet, as all the campers had gone to their tents for rest hour as well. There were no happy shouts to silence the conversation of the birds in the woods around her. She settled down quickly in the tiny sleeping loft and fell into a deep sleep. When she awoke a few minutes later, a thought had formed in the pool of her mind—the circles were still rippling out towards the edges.

"We could move to Celo before the year is out."

It was clear to her, in that moment, what needed to happen. Over the years of coming to Celo—camping, attending Friends Meeting, and serving at camp—Mom had made many close friends in the Celo community. Linda was working at the Arthur Morgan School, and

Nancy was making plans to start working there in the coming school year, too. Living there would bring our family closer together.

But it made no sense. How would she support us? There was no way to make money in Celo. There was no federally subsidized housing. The idea seemed impossible, but Mom knew deep down that it was the thing to do. And this time she, not Dad, was the one to announce it to the family: "We're going to move."

~ ~ ~ ~ ~ ~

The early 1970s were a fractured, painful time for my family, echoing the bitter struggles of our country as a whole. I had a lot of traveling to do in order to put this part of the story together—geographically, virtually, and through other people's memories as well as my own. I found, not surprisingly, that as my family moved further towards the periphery of society, we left fainter footprints. No books have been written about this part of my family's history. There are no archives. No church histories. The last calendar that Dad saved, documenting his daily thoughts, plans, and activities, was from 1972. After that, we went over the edge of a cliff.

One place remains: Cambridge Square Apartments. Going there was my scariest foray of all. It holds so many long-buried memories. So many scars. It was a hard place to go alone, but I did it. And what I found surprised me.

There were a few changes. The playground behind our apartment was gone. There were bushes in the middle of the sidewalk circle out front. A wrought-iron fence encircled the entire complex, blocking the driveway entrance near our apartment building. Most everybody living there appeared to be from Asia—mostly Korea and Vietnam. When I knocked on the door of number 258, our second apartment, a young boy answered the door. I peeked around him and saw his brother, sitting on the floor directly in front of a huge TV screen. The room was filled with furniture. Yes, some things have changed.

But the buildings were in good repair, still red brick at the first floor and white siding above. Flowers bloomed everywhere. People came and went. It was lunchtime, and delicious smells wafted out of open windows. As I walked, a thought cycled over and over through my head— "It's just a place. It can't hurt me now." Bricks, wood, concrete, a few flowers, and nobody I know. There's nothing scary about Cambridge Square anymore.

I found the Georgia Retardation Center online. Named "Brook Run" in 1991 and then shut down in 1997, the GRC buildings had fallen into disrepair. Almost all the references I found to the GRC or Brook Run were on ghost-hunting websites. I watched a YouTube video of teenagers in the dark, looking for ghosts but mostly swearing, breaking glass, and acting tough. Through further Internet searches, I learned that the building has since been torn down. The property is now a public park with a skateboarding feature. Plenty of teenagers but no more ghosts.

The original Hidden Springs Farm near Yorkville, Georgia, is no longer there. I haven't been to see the place myself, but I've heard that the bakery and greenhouse are caving in and kudzu vines have claimed our old house. The spirit of Hidden Springs is very much alive outside Cookeville, Tennessee, though, where the Blacks moved the farm in 1977.

I visited Hector and Susie in the springtime and got the loving, open-arms welcome that has become so familiar on my journey. I went there looking for two things. First, I wanted to be with the Blacks and remember the feeling—the smells, sounds, and emotions—of being in the company of their unique communal family. The other was to find out what they remembered about our time with them in 1972, especially Dad's departure, which had been a pivotal moment for my family.

When I made my way to the farm, Hector greeted me with delight. "Come in! Come see the daffodils that your mother gave me years ago! They came from her mother's garden. And I brought them here from Georgia." As it turned out, the daffodils were finished blooming. The blossoms' brown, curled-up remains dotted the hillside.

Hector and Susie's home and family felt familiar. Big, communal meals around the long table that dominated the main room. Meal prep and cleanup under Susie's stern but loving eye. Social justice and laughter in the air. Though the fondness remained, they remembered few details of my family's time at Hidden Springs. Neither of them seemed to know why we left or to remember any tension, either within our family or outside it. Loving feelings remained from that time, but there were few concrete details. I filled my emotional tank with waterfalls and wildflowers instead.

The one real surprise from my travels on this leg of the story came on a trip to Celo, where I found Waldie Unger, a member of the old Mennonite House crowd who often spent time at Hidden Springs. Our family has kept in touch with Waldie over the years; he and his wife eventually moved to Celo as well. He's an auto-body man by trade, though he recently retired. He was the one car salesman I could always trust. He'd buy wrecks at auction and completely rebuild them. Every car I've ever owned, save one, came from Waldie. I went to Waldie's house to ask about his memories, not expecting to hear much from this reticent man. But as we sat in the sunshine on his back patio, Waldie poured out his heart. We both cried. I was stunned.

Waldie was born in Germany, and his father left the family when Waldie was young, leaving his mother to raise the kids on her own. Unlike my dad, though, Waldie's father left to join the Nazi army (he had no choice, apparently) and never returned. The family didn't know what became of him. Waldie heard of others who used the war as an opportunity to cut old ties and start a new family, and he always wondered if his father did the same. His mother moved the family to Canada, and Waldie grew up there.

When Dad left us at Hidden Springs and went to Carrollton, Waldie took it hard. He wondered how it could happen to a family he cared so much about. He told me that he went out to Carrollton in the summer of 1972 and found Dad. "You have a wonderful wife and four beautiful daughters," he said to my father. "Why in the world would you leave them?" And Dad answered him. Waldie told me,

I wanted to know what was going on in his life, and he spoke with words that were foreign to me. You know, I'm not college educated and they just didn't mean anything. I mean I can pick up and read a book and understand it, and I can pick up a real intellectual book and get zero. I'm just reading a word at a time, not knowing what I'm reading. And that was sort of how it felt like basically my week went with Al....

It sounded like an explanation, and I really felt he dealt with a lot of guilt about doing it. I didn't feel like it was an easy decision for him. But I still felt he abandoned the children, just like my father abandoned his children.

He talked a lot about his spiritual journey, and I was thinking, "Well, you know, you can take your whole family on a spiritual journey."

For me as for Waldie, there was no real answer to why Dad behaved the way he did. But I was elated. In this case, I didn't need an answer. What I needed, without even knowing I needed it, was the story of the question. Somebody cared enough to ask. As far as I knew, nobody—not Mom, not Granddaddy, not Clarence, not anyone—had ever held Dad responsible for his actions. I thought nobody had the guts to ask, "Al, why are you doing this?" Now I knew that Waldie had asked. Dad's manic answer was irrelevant.

Many of Dad's old friends were confused by the direction his life took, most shaking their heads, some trying to explain it in a way that made sense. His friend Alan Hoskins, who once felt like Dad was his spiritual brother and had introduced him to Edgar Cayce and the ARE, interpreted Dad's journey this way: "Al felt the world's pain too personally. I think his sensitivity left him less capable of caring about and looking out for those closest to him." It was hard to live through and even harder to understand when you're one of "those closest to him." But it rang true.

The research for this book gave me insights into Dad's own traumas and how deeply they must have affected him. In childhood, Dad and his younger brother were passed back and forth between their grandparents when their mother, diagnosed as a manic depressive, was in various mental hospitals. Early in his career, Dad saw such psychiatric treatment firsthand, when he served as chaplain at the Mississippi State Hospital in the 1950s. The staff at this mental hospital performed many of the same primitive procedures that his own mother had undergone. Just a few years later, he experienced his own first serious bout of depression, spending weeks lying in bed beside infant Janet, who was born two months premature and barely survived. Then, as later, Mama held the family together.

When life got especially harrowing in our family, Mama always reminded me, in her typical cheerful way, that "what doesn't kill us makes us stronger." But what I have goes beyond mere strength. My daddy never hit me, not once. Unlike Mom, I have no visible scars to show for the scary things I lived through as a child. But I have scars nevertheless, and they go clear to the bone.

For me, though, each scar is a gift. Though the pain still crops up sometimes, catching me when I least expect it, I don't need to blame anybody for it. There's another side to old wounds. The scar tissue is still there, a part of who I am, but it enables me to celebrate my life like nobody else I know. To me, a bite of chocolate is a party in my mouth. A birthday cake is as good as a sky full of fireworks. Sitting on a comfortable couch to watch a goofy TV show in my own living room is a miracle. The magic of a decorated Christmas tree, twinkling in a dark room, takes my breath away. And a gentle husband who enjoys life but doesn't need to save the world or escape from it, who goes away and comes home again exactly when he says he's going to, with a paycheck in his pocket and a warm smile on his face, is one of the most amazing things on God's green earth.

I feel lucky to be here. Scars and all.

7

Bridge

Do you see a bridge as an obstacle—or just another set of steps to climb to get from one side of a canal to the other? We Venetians do not see bridges as obstacles. To us bridges are transitions. We go over them very slowly. They are a part of a rhythm. They are the links between two parts of a theater, like changes in scenery, or like the progression from Act One of a play to Act Two. Our role changes as we go over bridges. We cross from one reality ... to another reality. —Count Marcello in *The City of Falling Angels* by John Berendt

With Mama behind the wheel, moving was an entirely new proposition. Gradual. Systematic. Planned. She wrote lists and letters and even made the occasional long-distance phone call, always keeping it short to save money. Though she knew it was a risk, Mama intended for this move to Celo to go off without a hitch. She had determined that it would be her last big move, and she wanted to be sure we did it right.

After her epiphany in the meditation hut, we came home at the end of the summer, back to real life, to see if the decision still felt right. It did.

Mom had learned that public school jobs were hard to get in Celo, especially if you were an outsider. She started researching in earnest and found a fledgling Montessori school in Spruce Pine, just about fifteen miles from Celo. She contacted the two young mothers who had started the school (neither one with any Montessori training), and they agreed to meet her, being clear that they had no openings for teachers. Mom planned a trip for that October, piled us in the car, and we went to check it out.

Up to that time, Celo had been our special summer place. The girls went to Camp Celo for a session or a summer, Mama cooked in the camp kitchen to pay for tuition, our family camped for weeks at the Carolina Hemlocks campground by the river, and we got to know a few members of the community by attending the Celo Friends Meeting when we were there. But it was always a lush, green escape from Atlanta's hot pavement—we had never looked at it as a place where a person might actually live. It was time to look at it with a new perspective.

Celo Community was founded in 1937, when Arthur E. Morgan, then the founding Chairman of the Board of the Tennessee Valley Authority, learned that a wealthy Chicago friend wanted to dispose of some extra money in a charitable fashion. Morgan, former president of Antioch College, had noticed a trend of young people coming to him in those lean Depression years, "wanting to work out their own economic patterns." He wished to find ways to help them "make a virtue of necessity, and get a footing in self employment when otherwise they might be wasting their time in unemployment." He proposed a rural community, similar to the ones that the New Deal had strongly supported earlier in Ohio, West Virginia, and across Appalachia, where these young men might "get a foothold for themselves."

Unlike Koinonia Farm, which was founded by people who wanted to live communally and get their hands dirty together, Celo's founders were absentee leaders. Arthur Morgan deputized his son Griscom to scout out potential property, and Arthur and his wealthy friend, William H. Regnery, recruited Clarence Pickett, Executive Secretary of the American Friends Service Committee, as a third member of the Board of Directors. After Griscom found the twelve hundred acres in the South Toe Valley and Regnery provided the money to purchase the land, the directors hired a succession of managers, each with the assignment of recruiting community members, finding sustainable ways that the members could become financially self-sufficient, and establishing a workable infrastructure for the community. It was a tall order, and none of the managers was particularly up to the task. Celo limped along until about 1945. According to at least one history of the community, it took the organizing efforts of several community wives for the community to finally become self-governing.

By the time we were planning our move to Celo, the community was thriving. In addition to Camp Celo, in operation since 1948, Celo held the Arthur Morgan School, a small alternative junior high boarding school founded by Arthur's son and daughter-in-law; the active Celo Friends Meeting, housed in a converted goat barn; the Celo Health Center, with two full-time doctors and a nursing staff; Ten Thousand Things, a health food co-op; and Toe River Craftsmen, a store owned and staffed cooperatively by a group of glassblowers, potters, weavers, and other craftspeople in the valley (they later shortened the name to Toe River Crafts to reflect the gender diversity of the members). A new bed and breakfast, the Celo Inn, was under construction.

Legally, Celo Community Incorporated (CCI) was a land trust. The seventy-five members owned the land communally, but each family had a holding, a piece of the property where they could build a house, plant a garden, and call home. Though the community did not operate as a tight commune like Koinonia—there were no regular communal meals, for instance, and family finances were never pooled—the community membership made decisions by consensus about what buildings to build, which trees to cut down, and other changes that could affect the long-term health of the land. There was an involved trial membership period. For various reasons, not everyone was accepted into the community when they applied.

One of the many beauties of Celo, though, was that you didn't have to go through the rigmarole of joining CCI in order to experience the benefits of living in the area. If you found a place to live nearby, you were welcome to be a part of the Friends Meeting, join the health food co-op, and participate in the folk dances, potluck suppers, and other social occasions at Celo Community. You could feel a part of the community without having to sit through the interminable Meetings for Business. That suited Mom just fine (and Dad, too, to the extent that he was a part of the decision).

When we visited that fall, there were two orders of business on Mom's list: find a job (or jobs) to support the family, and arrange a place to live. She refused to move without both pieces in place. Once they were, then she could figure out the time line. She was determined to move before the year was out. Remarkably, everything fell into place on our visit. We heard of a nearby three-bedroom house by the river with reasonable rent; it would be available in a few months. Mom went to Spruce Pine to meet with the Montessori moms and blew them away. Though they realized it made no business sense, they also recognized that Mom had the magic their new little school needed—she could take it to the next level and they could step back. They all shook hands to seal the agreement. She wouldn't make enough money to support our family, but it was a start, and since it was part-time, Mom could bake bread to sell to community members and find other odd jobs to fill the gaps. We drove back to the city to finish out the school term and prepare for the move.

As we got ready for a new life in a different place, Dad, still unemployed, spiraled lower into paranoia and depression. Janet had transferred to an alternative high school, riding the city bus across town and doubling up on her coursework so she could graduate by the time we moved. Her last day was Monday, October 11, and then she stayed home baking bread to sell at the Norcross Montessori school, saving money so she could move away as soon as possible, though she had no idea where to go or what to do. She grimly watched Dad's mental and emotional descent while firmly maintaining her own grasp of reality. Her memories of that time are dark:

> He was off the wall. He kept telling me that Mom was trying to poison him—that I needed to be watching her to see if she was poisoning him. He was depressed and delusional, very strange. He would lie in his sleeping bag on the floor between the bed and the wall for weeks at a time. I was finally old enough to see vividly that it wasn't just anger, it was crazy. It was so vivid to me.
>
> I was relieved that you and Mom were gone. He was calmer when Mom wasn't there. But he was always trying to convince me—he would

go on for hours and hours. I was stuck there, sitting at the kitchen table, waiting for the bread to rise. I'd remind myself: "I have to not punch it down too hard, doggone it." I was trapped by the bread. Nowhere to go. No car. I just about wore out my shoes, walking around and around the apartments.

One Saturday morning, Dad realized that when Mom left home to go to the Children's House, she began each work day by going to the cozy basement office and pouring herself a cup of instant coffee, a warm cup to wrap her hands around as she planned the day's lessons for the day, a little pick-me-up that was just for her, when everything else she did was for others. But to Dad, mired in the rigid dogma of acid-alkaline diets, coffee was the greatest of evils. He was convinced she was poisoning herself. We felt the familiar tension begin to build.

By this time, especially when the storm clouds gathered during daylight hours, Mom knew better than to wait for the lightning to strike. She hustled Janet and me out of the apartment and into the car, and we drove around Atlanta for hours with nowhere to go.

Finally, when she felt sure the storm had passed, Mom drove back to Cambridge Square and pulled into a parking space. We didn't know what we might find: the storm still raging or Dad hibernating in his sleeping bag in a dark room. Or perhaps he was gone altogether, somewhere out on the interstate with his backpack on and his thumb out. It was often that way after one of his raging spells: we'd run from a blazing wildfire and then come back to find it completely out. Not smoldering. Not quenched. Just gone. But the charred remains were always still there. Us.

This time was different. We walked across the sidewalk circle to the front door, and Mom opened it, with Janet and me right behind her. There was Dad, sitting cross-legged on the floor of the mostly bare living room. What was left of the dining room chairs, splintered into tiny pieces, surrounded him. Dust from the ceiling, where he had jammed a chair into the drywall before slamming it to the floor, powdered the room. As we walked in, he turned a confused, tear-stained face in our direction. He was still sobbing as he began to speak.

"What happened here? Why is all this furniture broken? Why did you leave me?"

Mom fell to her knees and wrapped her arms around him. Janet and I silently went upstairs to our bedrooms, closing the doors behind us. When we came down, supper was ready, the splintered wood was swept up and thrown away, and Daddy was napping. The incident was never mentioned again, but we carried it in our hearts.

And then came bad news from Macon: Granddaddy Moore had been diagnosed with multiple myeloma, an incurable cancer of the bone marrow. We didn't know how long he'd live, but it looked bad. Mama finally realized that she'd never have to choose between the two men she loved the most. Circumstances were choosing for her.

Finally, moving day arrived: December 20, 1976. I was out of school for the Christmas holidays. Mom had said the last good-byes to her beloved Montessori kids. The apartment was painted, the U-Haul rented, and the boxes packed. Linda had driven down from Celo in a pickup truck with Ben Geouge, a family friend, to help with the move. The last details were checked off Mom's list. We piled into the vehicles: Ben driving the U-Haul with Dad beside him to talk about astrology all the way to North Carolina; Linda in the pick-up truck; and Mom in the old station wagon packed to the gills, with Janet and me squeezed into the front seat next to her.

There's one thing you can count on with the best-laid plans, and we got it. Somewhere around the state line, the steady rains began. As Janet and I peered between the raindrops to count the "squiggly line" road signs, the windshield wipers slapped a rhythm: "movin' away, movin' away, movin' away."

It took about six hours for our caravan to make it across the mountains to Celo, including stops to adjust the tarps on the pick-up, eat our lunch of peanut butter on dark homemade bread, and use the restroom. But we made it, with the rain still pouring down. All three vehicles parked across the river from the house, and the drivers huddled under ponchos for a soggy powwow about what should happen next. Unfortunately, there was no way to drive all the way to the house. To reach it, you had to park at the gravel pull-off by the road, walk down a short, steep trail to a suspension footbridge (called a swinging bridge, though its motion was more bouncy than swinging), make your way across the undulating bridge over the river, and then walk the hundred yards up the hill to the house.

Ben, the mountain man among us, mentioned a ford up the river, and though we still wouldn't be able to drive all the way to the house, he could at least get the truck across the river and we could carry everything up the hill. He drove the truck up the road toward the ford, then down the rocky lane to the river. Dad put his feet up on the dashboard. They shook their heads at each other and grinned broadly as the truck plowed into the river. The water was higher than they realized, coming up above the bottoms of the doors, but they were in the middle of the torrent by that time, and Ben kept his foot on the gas. The wheels spun against the slick river rocks as they climbed up toward the bank on the other side. As the truck pulled onto solid ground, they both realized they'd been holding their breath all the way across, and let it out with the great big laugh of men who had dared and made it. Mama, standing in the rain to watch the truck's progress from the swinging bridge downriver, breathed a quiet "Amen." That afternoon and evening, everybody pitched in to carry boxes up the hill. I carried a few, but then I was happy to be the youngest and exempt from the hard labor. I perched on the window seat in my new bedroom, watching the cloaked and dripping figures slowly trudging over the brink of the hill and across the yard to the house, clouds hanging low above.

After a simple supper and many rounds of thanks, Ben went home. The rest of us fell into bed (the house was *furnished*—we had real beds!), relieved to have the trucks empty at last, the boxes piled everywhere in the small house.

As we slept, the weather changed again. The temperature dropped, and we woke shivering in the morning, feeling the wind blowing through the rattling windowpanes. It was our first introduction to the bitter cold of mountain winters, and we weren't prepared.

The house had one small electric wall heater in the living room at the rear, a fireplace which sucked up as much heat as it put out, and an old woodstove in Mama and Daddy's room at the front of the house. Ben had kindly supplied a few sticks of wood to get us started, and Daddy piled it in the stove for a big, roaring fire. Though he'd built many campfires, Dad wasn't used to woodstoves and didn't know which way to turn the damper. The room began to fill with smoke. "Open the windows! Open the door! I can't see anything!" Freezing winds swept through the house. I put my warm down sleeping bag on the couch at the other end of the house and climbed into it, but then someone shouted, "The house is on fire! Get everything out!" I jumped out of my sleeping bag and threw it out in the yard first—if we had no place to sleep tonight, I'd need it. Thanks to Mama's good planning, the phone was already connected and she called the volunteer fire department. Janet and I shivered in the yard, wondering what could possibly happen next.

The fire truck plowed through the weeds over the brink of the hill. Ben Geouge, who had driven the moving truck through the ford the day before, was also a volunteer fireman and was behind the wheel again. It struck him as funny, somehow, to see all the stuff we had carefully put inside the house now lying helter-skelter in the yard, as if the house had spit it right back out.

While the firemen swarmed, Janet and I were hustled across the swinging bridge to the road and into a fireman's warm, idling car. I leaned back into the leather seat and wondered what it would feel like to have a car that wasn't dented and old, one that never broke down and left you stranded.

Then my eyes were drawn to the house. It was still early morning, but through the gray light I had a clear view across the narrow valley to our cabin on the hill. I could see smoke pouring out around the eaves all the way around. Would the roof fall in? Or burst into flames? It all felt surreal. We had left everything we knew in Atlanta to live in this cabin by the river, and now it was going up in smoke. But somehow I wasn't worried. Maybe because I was only ten years old. Or maybe because we'd already survived so much. Somehow I knew everything would work out.

And it did. There was actually far more smoke than fire. It had started as a chimney fire; the ceramic thimble (which connected the stovepipe inside the house to the chimney outside) was cracked, and fire had shot through to the wall. But the firemen were quick and skillful. They extinguished the flames promptly with minimal damage. The house was cold when Janet and I walked back across the bridge and up the hill, but intact. As always, so were we.

A month later, the four of us—Mama, Daddy, Janet, and I—gathered around the radio beside the woodstove in the same room where the fire started, this time to listen to Jimmy Carter's inaugural speech. "This inauguration ceremony," our new president told us, "marks a new beginning, a new dedication within our Government, and a new spirit among us all." Our president was not only a Democrat but also from Georgia like us. Plains was in Sumter County, Georgia, right next to Americus and Koinonia Farm. What I didn't know at the time, cozy there by the fire in our little cabin deep in the mountains, was that the architect of Carter's campaign, now becoming White House Chief of Staff, was none other than Hamilton Jordan, Dad's first cousin. There we were, hippies in the woods on the Edge of Nowhere, and my daddy was on a first-name basis with one of the most powerful men in the world. If somebody had told me, I wouldn't have believed it.

But at that point, all that was relevant to me was figuring out how to make the transition to my new life. I was in the middle of fifth grade, and, unlike my sisters, I was moving for the first time since I started school. But I wasn't worried—I had never had trouble making friends.

I was in for a rude surprise.

On my first day at South Toe Elementary, I learned quickly what it was like to stand out. In this little school, there was only one fifth grade class. I knew one boy (his parents were the Camp Celo directors, and I had gone to camp with him for years), but he was busy fitting in himself and didn't want to associate with me. I talked differently; after hearing my sisters talk after returning from college, I had recognized my southern twang and was studiously trying to eliminate it. I dressed differently from the other kids, wearing long denim skirts that my mama had converted from blue jeans by adding a colorful fabric triangle in the front and back, topped off with homemade hippie blouses. I brought health food for lunches while everyone else ate lunches on trays from the school lunchroom. My hand was always the first one to shoot up when the teacher, Mr. Deyton, asked a question of the class. He quickly noticed my facility with numbers, and appointed me Loan Officer of the school bank in a hallway booth. Having the other students in my debt didn't help my case. They hated me. I had one friend, a girl who lived in the community, but she was a year older, so we could only play outside of school. For me, the entire school day, especially the bus ride each way when I was teased and criticized unmercifully, was miserable.

It was a frigid winter. Our water pipes froze, so we had to use the outhouse in the yard, a relic from the home's pre-bathroom days. Dad would go down to the river to get water to do the dishes, lowering a bucket on a rope from the bridge, hauling it back up as the bucket and bridge swayed in the wind, and then lugging it up the hill to the house. But then the river froze over, and he'd have to hack holes in the ice to get water. The roof blew off the outhouse, and the seat was an icy ring first thing in the morning, especially on the days when I had to brush the snow off before I sat down. And the windows of our house still rattled in the wind. Mama's side of the bed was right next to the window, and some mornings she woke with snow on her face.

Janet, who slept in the coldest room of all and felt that every minute in this god-forsaken place was sheer torture, contacted friends from ARE Camp who lived outside Washington, DC, and their family helped her find a nanny job with someone they knew. Two weeks after the fire, she stood at the foot of the bed as Mama lay there doing a crossword puzzle.

"I'm leaving here," she said. "I just need somebody to take me to the bus station."

Within a few days, she was gone. And then there were three of us. Mama. Daddy. And me. Now, when the air began to thicken and the familiar metallic taste of fear came into my mouth, there was no Janet to turn to. There was only me.

One day, Dad found a box of Mom's old keepsakes while she was working at the school. By the time she and I came home, he had flung everything out of the box and was poring over an old scrapbook she'd kept at Mercer before she met him. It had pictures of her friends, and notes and souvenirs from outings and dates. Dad was livid with jealousy, his long hair wild as he shook the pages of the thirty-year-old scrapbook in her face. As their voices rose, I turned on my heel, ran down the front porch steps, and hurried down the hill to sit on the rocks beside the river. As the water splashed and giggled next to me, I grimly watched it, still able to hear every shouted word in the house.

Another day, Mama was in bed, reading an article in *Reader's Digest*, a gift subscription from her parents. Dad walked in and saw her reading that conservative publication sent by her father, whom he despised, and immediately flew into a rage. There was no buildup, no time to get away. He grabbed her around the neck, choking her and slamming her head against the pillow as he screamed profanities about *Reader's Digest*, my grandparents, and her. When he relaxed his grip briefly, she scrambled away, terrified. She came into my room, said, "Get your sleeping bag— we're leaving," and hurried me out into the icy darkness. That night, as we slept in the back of our station wagon on a back road in the woods, I was grateful for the warmth of the goose feathers around me. My world was small and warm: my mama and a sleeping bag. Maybe that was all I needed. At least we were safe.

It was a rough spring. Dad continued to rant and rage, ever more paranoid, ever more delusional. He needed to leave, for everybody's sake, and go back to Virginia Beach, or Rural Retreat, or somewhere. Anywhere. But he wouldn't go, and Mama wouldn't ask him to. Linda and Nancy, living next door to each other as houseparents just over the ridge at the Arthur Morgan School, were unaware of our nightmare. I fantasized about my big sisters rescuing me, swooping in to take me to live with them. I buried myself in my books, finding solace and escape in *Harriet the Spy*, *Anne of Green Gables*, *A Wrinkle in Time*. My friends were largely fictional, and my imagined parents were mainstream and reliable.

When summer came, I once again had the real escape of summer camp. I went to both camps again that summer: two weeks at ARE Camp in Virginia, where Linda was a summer counselor, and three weeks at Camp Celo. It was my first summer as a senior camper at Camp Celo, and I carried a heavy backpack high up into the Black Mountains and sang at the top of my lungs.

Mom suffered terribly while I was gone. Without my innocent presence in the house, nothing stopped Dad from going over the edge into one blind rage after another. In desperation, Mom finally approached Judi McGahey, a friend from Quaker Meeting who also happened to be one of the two doctors at the Celo Health Center. Until that point, Mom had told almost no one about our home situation—all her energy went into creating a happy, functional façade. But she was beyond that now. She was too frightened.

As a doctor, Judi had consulted with many women over the years who faced threats at home, and she had no trouble accepting that Dad needed psychological help. But the first priority, as far as she was concerned, was Mom's safety, and mine when I got home from camp. "You can't face this alone," she said, "and you need to let Nancy know what's going on."

During a long walk in the Celo woods, Mom finally told my sister Nancy what was happening. The raging. The broken furniture. The screaming. Though she always looked for the best in every situation and even called herself a "Pollyanna," Nancy finally understood the true danger. "We have to do something. We have to get him out of there."

Nancy went back to Judi, who was also a houseparent at the Arthur Morgan School, to devise a plan. "If he won't leave, we need to get him committed. Can you do that?" she asked.

Judi, visibly pregnant at the time, agreed to lead an intervention, but she knew it wouldn't be wise to do it alone. Nor should another family member be there; Judi wanted to make the meeting with Dad as neutral and non-threatening as possible. Nancy's friend Anne, who worked at Camp Celo, was trained in co-counseling, so Nancy asked if she was willing to be the other person in the room; Anne agreed. The meeting took place at Woodside, the house at AMS where Nancy lived with her co-houseparent, Randy Raskin. Since school was out, the house was empty of students at the time.

Like some other critical family stories, the details of this one are hazy. Though Mom wasn't there and her dementia would likely have swept away the memory regardless, several people remember clearly that the event happened. Judi remembers being there, and Nancy remembers crouching at the base of a big tree in the woods above the house, waiting for the intervention to end, fervently hoping it would improve our lives. Randy stepped onto the front stoop, not knowing the meeting was still underway, and overheard an earful of Dad's ranting about what a "no-good snake" Randy was. He quickly retreated before being seen. Judi did her job, remaining calm and rational, letting Dad know that she understood the situation and that Mom and I needed to be safe. She presented him with two options: leave Celo or get psychological help. He finally agreed to leave, and by the time I got home from camp, the house was peaceful. But Mama was worn thin.

That August brought a family celebration for the Moore family: Grandmama and Granddaddy's fiftieth wedding anniversary. Unlike Dad's parents, who had celebrated with a splashy fancy party, the Moores planned a small family affair. Granddaddy's health continued to decline, and most of his loved ones knew that this would probably be his last family gathering with us.

We gathered at what we called "The Lake" in north Georgia. Grandmama and Granddaddy had owned a cabin on this small private lake since Mama was a girl, and we shared many fond memories of diving off the dock, floating on inner tubes, playing games with cousins, hiking to the waterfall, and eating supper at the long wooden table on the porch overlooking the green water. Granddaddy had spent long hours with his fishing rod, his fly dancing across the surface to haul in bass after bass. He cleaned the fish on the dock, patiently identifying all the guts for me before tossing them into the shallows. The lake was a special, happy place for all of us, and since Daddy refused to go there, it was also the one place that always felt safe.

But this was a bittersweet gathering. Uncle Buddy and Aunt Marian had worked hard on the cabin all summer—painting, insulating, laying new floors, sprucing it up. Aunt Martha had created and framed a Moore family tree with all of our names and pictures of each of us. Mama felt lucky just to be there, and the photos of the event show her looking thin and weary, no longer able to maintain her usual cheerful exterior. With her marriage in tatters and her father fading away, Mama wondered how she would keep going.

A family friend came to photograph us, first lined up stair-step fashion on a path through the woods (that was about as formal as it got), and then lounging on the dock by the lake. We were a motley crew, but we sure did love each other.

That fall of 1977, Dad landed back in Virginia Beach and Janet enrolled at Warren Wilson College, a small school a short hour away from Celo. She rarely came home to visit, though, so it was just Mama and me. We finally felt secure in our house by the river with the woodstove to keep us warm, books to read and games to play, and a fluffy blonde kitten to curl up with on the front porch swing.

I loved that house. My room had two closets on either side of the window seat, and I pretended they were elevators. After shoving the junk to the side (I was not an organized child) I got in, sliding the door closed behind me. After a brief pause—one, two, three, four—I slid the door back open and *voila*! I was in a whole different place! Though I complained about it, I loved the bare bulb in the old-fashioned bead board ceiling, and my own whirling darkness dance to find the long string hanging in the center of the room. I loved the texture of the braided rug and then the bumpy linoleum on the floor under my cold feet as I ran through Mama's room and across the hall to get to the bathroom on an icy night. I loved climbing back into my big bed to put my cold feet against the hot water bottle, nestled under the heavy quilts.

And then, of course, there was the river. I spent hours wading in the freezing-cold water, baking on the rocks, and playing on the bridge above. I became a master of the bridge, climbing the steel of its upright supports, dancing and marching on the waves of its boards, compelling its flexible structure to do my bidding. I could dash across its narrow length without ever touching the cables on either side, my feet knowing just when to come down, as the bridge rose up to meet me. We were one, spanning the clear green water beneath.

I knew the curves and crevices of every rock in the river—one was my desk when I pretended to go to work; one was my house, with the swirling bathtub in the middle; and one beneath the water was slippery, but it offered a fine ride into the deeper water under the bridge. I made friends with the minnows who nibbled at my toes, and warily watched for the snake that lived in its water cave just up from the beach.

My life in the mountains was very different from the one we'd left behind in Atlanta, and I had plenty of news to share when Mama reminded me it was time to send a letter to Daddy:

Sat. Nov. 5 (77)
Guess what—
On Halloween, Mr. Zullinger took us to Mt. Mitchell! He drove us in a bus, up to the mountain, and then we hiked across Mt. Craig to Big Tom. We saw the place where a plane crashed 3 years ago. It was kind of creepy. When the guy hit the mountain he was killed instantly. (Only one man was in it.) Ugh! When we got back, it was time to go home!

It has rained so much this week that the river is so high it looks almost like an ocean!

Yesterday we got our pictures made. The photographer was very weird. He called all the girls dolls and all the boys names like Sam and Harvey. Anyway, if you're not back by the time we get the pictures I'll send you one.

I've got new magic markers. (If you can't tell already.) I got them so I can draw mandalas and pictures, and write multi-colored letters.

Well, Mom wants to take this to the mailbox.
Much love,
Cindy

It was the last time Mama walked across that particular bridge to the mailbox by the road. All night, the rain continued to pour down. Mama woke me up early with dancing eyes, saying, "Cindy! Listen to the river! Let's go see how high it got!" As we squelched down the path, the roar of the river grew louder, and we could see its muddy whitecaps well above the usual banks. Yahoo! Then, where the path took a turn at a rock, Mama stopped. I nearly crashed into her back, and then my own mouth fell open. The bridge was washed out, most of the planks gone, their support boards swinging loose from the cables above. We could see the mailbox over there and our car on the other side, but we had no way to get across.

The logical thing for Mama to do was panic. First fire, now flood. Here we were, stranded. We had barely any money and no physical connection to the outside world, with winter on its way. It would have been an obvious time to give up.

But my mama's response? "What an adventure!" We had wood for the woodstove and food in the cupboards. There were bridges a mile away both up and downstream, so we could decide on our route: does it feel like an upriver or downriver kind of day? We'd have to carry our laundry and groceries, but we had backpacks and strong legs. Mama didn't see any problem at all. I took her cue and enjoyed it.

According to local reports, others in the county had a harder time:

> Flood waters receded rapidly from the November 6 flash flooding that was called the worst to hit this area in 67 years, but it will take Yancey County a long time to recover from the destruction left behind.
>
> Eleven inches of rain that began on Friday, November 4 and continued through Sunday, resulted in the pre-dawn rage that forced usually calm creeks and rivers over their banks. Homes, automobiles, bridges, roads and hundreds of acres of farmland were swept away by the water. At one point sixty-five percent of the 14,000 residents of Yancey County were isolated by washed out bridges and roads. Being cut off from family and friends in other parts of the county by inaccessibility and lack of communication caused much concern.

The car bridge across the river into the heart of Celo Community was declared impassable, and the bridge on Highway 19 at Cane River was completely washed out, cutting the county seat of Burnsville off from

162

Asheville, the nearest city, for three full days. A helicopter flew over our house and we heard a bullhorn, calling to make sure we were okay and had enough to eat. We ran out into the yard and waved it on, with cheerful shouts of "we're fine!" The adventure continued.

It didn't take long for word to get out that we'd lost our bridge, and within a week, Bob Barrus showed up in the light blue Camp Celo truck, with a canoe and paddles in the bed. Now Mama and I could pile everything we'd need for the day into the boat, paddle across, and secure the canoe on the opposite bank.

One day after work and school, we approached the river and saw that the boat was on the opposite bank. We called until we were practically hoarse, and finally a strange figure came hurrying down the hill from the house. He had helped himself to our boat and our home. From across the river, he raised his hand in greeting and yelled, "Giturinon." After exchanging a confused glance, Mom and I both decided that this must be "hello" in his language. Cupping our hands around our mouths, we shouted back, "Giturinon to you, too!"

At that point, he hopped lightly into the boat and paddled in our direction. We were sure he was some faraway land; he didn't even know how to hold a paddle. But it turned out that he was merely a friend of Dad's from Virginia Beach. Dad had sent this man, Giturinon, to us, assuring him that he'd get a friendly welcome. And good old Giturinon probably thought he did. But Mama and I were both happy to send him on when the time came a few days later.

My letter to Dad from that time was longer and newsier than earlier ones. He was "Dad" instead of "Daddy" now, and I worked hard to connect with the little I understood of his astrological studies. I was learning to fake it, to act as if everything were okay between us.

Dec. 4, 1977

Dear Dad,

Mom called this guy up about the bridge last week and he said that he'd send a crew in this week! Isn't that neat? I think so.

Oh, and guess what, the McGaheys have a new baby boy! He was born at two o'clock on Sunday morning. I don't know what his name is.

Is he a saggitarius snake? Also, the Perrys have a new baby girl. Her name is Mary Elisabeth but they call her Mary Beth. She was born on Nov. 29th at six o'clock in the morning. Is she also a saggitarius snake? Anyway, she's really cute.

I was out of school for three whole weeks because of the flood! But, the catch is, we only get three days for Christmas holidays. I think that's terrible. Ugh!! Oh, well I guess I'll live through it. No use crying over spilt holidays. Huh?

Not much more room.

Love ya' muchly,

Your little bear

Honestly, I was disappointed when the state finally came to fix the bridge. I liked it when it was just Mom and me, two survivors living on our own little island.

~ ~ ~ ~ ~ ~

When people ask me where I grew up (as they often do, because I live in the South but don't talk like it), I tell them about Celo. Depending on the person and how much time I have, I either go into detail, or simply explain that it's "a hippie community way back in the mountains." Mom lived in Celo until she moved to a rest home a few years ago, so it felt more like home to me than any other place our family lived. Groovy though it may have been, it was a solid foundation. And like the rest of the world, it's not nearly as groovy as it used to be. People in Celo have televisions now, and reliable cars, and retirement accounts. Celo has grown up a little. As have I.

In adulthood, I've drifted from my Celo roots. When I got married, I eagerly took my new husband's last name. My rationale was that I had the opportunity to choose between the names of two men: Dad's or my fiancé's. The decision was obvious. I was still angry and therefore eager to cut that tie.

But then I was no longer Cindy Henry, the name everyone in Celo knew me by. My kids came along, I worked full-time, and weekends filled up with soccer games and birthday parties. We had few opportunities to go up the mountain for community brunches and potlucks. Family gatherings still called us back to the lush, green valley, but I rarely saw community folks anymore, and began to wonder if they remembered me. Though Nancy was still in Celo, my home wasn't. I always feel welcome at the Celo Inn, where Nancy and Randy (who eventually got married) have been innkeepers for two decades, and I can drop in any time. But it isn't home. At forty years old, I finally realized that my home is the one where my name is on the mortgage check every month. I'm grown up. And there's no going back.

Or is there?

To write this story, I needed the help of people in Celo. I had tea with Bob and Judi (now called Geeta) McGahey, and they sent me home with blueberries from their bushes. I sat on Ben Geouge's back porch in Secluded Hollow as he cracked black walnuts with a hammer beside the whirring fan, and the hummingbirds buzzed around the feeders. And I went back to our old house by the river, just me, and listened to the silence. No matter my name, Celo still knows me.

From the outside, the house looks much the same. It's still red, with a swing on the front porch and the rain-friendly tin roof. The old Crow's Egg apple tree, which once bore my tire swing as if it were a feather, still stands, scrawny but determined. But the smokehouse is gone, a flowerbed in its place. The hemlock hedge outgrew its usefulness and got hacked. And the hill down to the river, which was open enough to be my sled run in that cold winter of 1977, is completely grown over with trees and underbrush. You can barely see the house from the road anymore, and trees block the view of the mountains from my bedroom window seat.

The house is available for vacation rentals, and the owners have updated the inside. They replaced the brown geometric 1970s linoleum with a nondescript white, guaranteed not to offend, except that it shows every speck of dirt that anybody tracks in. The buckling bead board ceiling, the first thing I saw when I woke up every morning, is gone from my bedroom, replaced by uninteresting tiles. A new window lets light pour into the big living/dining room on the back of the house, and a new deck extends off the screened side porch. There's no woodstove in Mama's old room—they've put sheetrock over the chimney hole, and decorative metal peacocks, their bodies facing each other but their heads looking away, now grace that wall.

I went out the front door from Mama's room and onto the porch, where I sat for a while on the porch swing, remembering the hours I spent there, lost in a book or a reverie. I recalled my old fantasies, back when I imagined the handsome boy from school riding up on a horse, sweeping me up and carrying me away, declaring his undying love as we galloped off. Now, I realized, that same boy was living in a trailer up a holler nearby, an alcoholic, his kids gone with his ex-wife. And what am I? Blessed. Charmed. Loved.

Would I have been satisfied back then, I wondered, if I could have seen this moment in a crystal ball? Would it have been enough to know that someday I would have my true love? Hard to say.

It was too chilly to put on the swimsuit I'd brought, but I walked down to the river, now low with drought, to sit on my old familiar rocks. It was like looking at the back of my hand, every bit of it still so familiar. I realized that, no matter how far I may go, that river will always flow through my heart. Drought or flood, it's a part of me.

I looked up at the bridge and realized the obvious: it's still there. The original got washed out by torrential waters, but the same steel supports hold up a new, strong bridge that still dances to my footstep. And unlike a boat, the bridge stays where it is, always open to both sides, always ready to be crossed.

I don't have to be Cindy Henry or Cindy McMahon. I don't have to lose touch with my old self to be an adult. I can be all of who I am, loved in the past, loved in the present. Cindy Henry McMahon. I can always go back, and I can always come home again. Because it's all inside me, and I'm right here.

8

Tadpole & Chrysalis

Right here. That's where my mama always seemed to be. And no matter how bad things got, she managed to keep her sense of humor, noticing and remembering all the funny things around her.

The preschool kids at her Montessori school in Spruce Pine were an endless source of chuckles, and I recently found a folder where she collected notes of her favorites.

> Adam: I'm going over to Jamie's house this afternoon to play. They're Christians, you know.
> Carol: And you're not?
> Adam: Oh, no. We're Democrats.

> Roanna: I know how we can have no more hitting at our school.
> Everybody: How?
> Roanna: When you see Mark coming—RUN!

And then I found a story that our family never forgot:

> Andy was watching the newts and tadpoles in the pond aquarium. All the other kids were out on the playground. Now and then a newt would eat a little tadpole.
> "Why don't you go out and play with the rest of the kids?"
> "I'm watching the tadpoles. They don't know what to do."
> "Are you telling them what to do?"
> "Yes," turning back to the aquarium: "just be brave, little tadpole."

We needed reminders to be brave that winter of 1977 and 1978. We hadn't seen Dad since August. We had survived the flood and its aftermath, even enjoyed the adventure, but at the same time we knew that Granddaddy was fading in Macon—his cancer was progressing and the reports didn't sound good. I never saw Mom's grief at losing her daddy (or don't remember if I did), but it must have been deep. Though the years and circumstances had made it difficult for her to be near him and she never shared with him the truths of her marriage, the bond between them held fast. He was always the man she admired most in the world. Soon after she learned of his illness, she sent a special letter to her parents, putting into words the depth of her gratitude:

Dear Folks,

I feel like writing a little thank you note today—for some things I think I've neglected to thank you for—it was a long time ago. They've been going around in my mind today.

The first one was a sense of humor. Since I was tiny you've always laughed a lot—with me, not at me—and helped me see the humor in many a situation that might otherwise be a little grim—or at least, boring. This gift has helped make many an otherwise dull situation actually fun.

Another thing is a sense of worth. I've always been able to feel that you really like me, respect me & believe in me. This can make the difference between futility & joy—a mighty big difference!

Along with that is a feeling of self-reliance. You always helped me to help myself—or stood by patiently until I did. I remember a time that I thought that a fish was much too big for me to pull in, but you thought I could do it, Daddy—and sure 'nuff I did. And there were many times I wanted you to tell me the answer to a math problem or at least how to get the answer, but you just kept asking questions until I figured out how to do it myself. This has been one of the greatest gifts of all.

But one of the most joyous has been the sense of wonder—a way of looking at a mountain, the "dew on the rose," a baby's smile—sometimes just very ordinary things—with delight & awe at God's hand in creation.

There are so many others—music, a basic integrity, enjoyment of people & appreciation of each one as a unique, worthwhile individual,...I could go on forever, but I'll just say they all add up to love, and not a day goes by without my realizing it in one way or another.

I wish I had been able to express it more often & more adequately, but then I guess there are ways other than verbal to express things. It's a good thing!

One thing I can do is try to be a good steward of these gifts & pass them on. They can keep on making people happier, stronger, & on a higher plane from now on.

…Another thought just occurred to me—that it wasn't just a long time ago that you were giving these special gifts to me. It's still happening now—to me and to everybody who knows you—just simply because you are who you are.

Knowing that they knew how much she loved them must have given Mom some peace, and as Granddaddy used to say, it was "mutual on both sides."

We were all looking forward to the next Moore family gathering: on December 27, Mom's younger sister Martha, up to now always our elegant unmarried aunt, would marry her fiancé, Phil Crabtree. They planned a small wedding at Grandmama and Granddaddy Moore's house in Macon, and Martha hoped that Granddaddy would be well enough to perform the ceremony, as he had for Mom and Dad in Waycross twenty-seven years before.

But by Christmastime, it was clear that Granddaddy could not be there. He was in the hospital, and his cancer had progressed to the point where he could no longer get out of bed: in the act of simply turning him over, a nurse accidentally broke every one of his ribs. We all knew he was near the end.

The wedding became a time of good-byes. I didn't get to see my Granddaddy—I guess Mama thought it would be too upsetting for me—but I remember sitting wide-eyed with my cousin Martha in the hospital waiting room as Mama went up to visit him.

The visit stayed in her memory well past the point when all her other memories were gone. She held his hand, fragile now, no longer the strong hand of her childhood, as he described the angelic music he was hearing. Finally he turned and looked straight into her eyes. "I won't love you if you don't let me go." I know the tears must have been flowing as she assured him, "You can go, Daddy. You can go."

We drove back to Celo after the wedding. On the following Friday, January 6, before I went down the hill to wait for the school bus, Mama said, "You have a dentist appointment today, so you'll get picked up from school instead of riding the bus home. I'll pick you up unless Granddaddy dies—if he does, Nancy will take you." That afternoon, when I stepped out from the brick building into the sunshine of the gravel parking lot and saw Nancy waiting for me in Randy's Mercury Comet, I knew Granddaddy was gone. Mama had left for the funeral.

And more than our family grieved his loss. Granddaddy was widely known and beloved, and newspapers and Baptist publications across the South carried his obituary. Rufus Harris, president of Mercer University, sent his condolences to Grandmama, writing, "Walter Moore was a paradox—he was at once the gentlest, sweetest of persons, and the stoutest fellow and the most positive Christian I have known. He had boundless compassion for people, but when the chips were down he stood taller than most men are willing to extend themselves." Another friend described him as an "unusual combination of Christian scholar, and reg'lar fellow."

Somebody sent Grandmama a copy of a eulogy from "The Messenger," the newsletter of the First Baptist Church in Carrollton, Georgia:

A Great Man
Scholar, outdoorsman, writer, wit, compassionate friend, teacher, superb preacher—Walter Moore was all of these. When he died last week, the Carters, Wests, and Brantley and I lost a beloved pastor.

Most of you didn't personally know this former president of our convention. I wish you had known him for he was a rare human being—a gentle giant.

Although this is not ordinarily a eulogy column, I have to say some things about Dr. Moore because perhaps you like me are encouraged by news of one who has fought the good fight and won.

"Silent rivers run deep"—Dr. Moore could be so quiet in a meeting that you would almost forget he was present. Then at the right moment he would have something to say. When he spoke people listened. He chose his words wisely; there was real authority in his words.

However, when an occasion arose where someone or something needed defending, he fought like a tiger. Better than anyone I know, Walter Moore knew what he believed and stood on it regardless of the crossfire.

He was physically weak from the time we first met him in Macon, Georgia. Yet he was strong. His character and integrity were impeccable. The hardships he faced as a missionary in Cuba, disappointments of smashed dreams, pain of one illness after another—none of these destroyed the beautiful uniqueness of his spirit.

Each of us would like to know a really "great" person. Dr. Moore was one.

For me, he was "Granddaddy"—huge, gentle, and loving, patient with my questions about fish guts, never eating peaches with the fuzz still on, smiling as he set the camera and then ran around it to be included in a family picture. And I was always fascinated by his big earlobes. He was my safe place, and I loved him for it.

He never really left us. He showed up regularly in my dreams for months after he died—always tall, always comforting, letting me know that it was going to be okay. We were all going to be all right. I believed him.

And actually, it wasn't a bad year. It was my last year at South Toe Elementary School. Two girls my age had moved into the community, and several Celo friends regularly came over to play or spend the night. I danced on the school clogging team and loved it. No longer was I the new kid in my class. Mr. Zullinger, my teacher, was also principal of the little school, and he took pleasure in giving me challenging work to do and interesting books to read. His eyes lit up when I asked probing questions. I won the Multiple Sclerosis read-a-thon for the whole school and was presented with a $25 savings bond, more money than I'd ever had. Life was good. And Mom was getting by, too, as she wrote in her journal at the end of winter:

3/5/78

A quiet morning on our Windy Hill—not an appropriate name for it today. The only sounds are the soft whisper of a gentle fire in the wood stove here beside me, the call of a crow passing overhead, and the occasional rustle of the sheets in the next room, as Janet and Cindy stir peacefully in their last moments of sleep.

Cindy is so happy to have Janet home for a few days (spring break from Warren Wilson College). Janet seems content to be here, receptive to our warm welcome, and comfortable about being a helpful part of the family. Almost as soon as she got home yesterday, she was in the kitchen, starting some good spaghetti sauce. Then later she taught Cindy a "new" dance named "The Hustle." Such fun watching the two of them go through it. Dancing is one of Cindy's favorite things right now, and she doesn't get much opportunity to learn new steps or to dance with such a good dancer.

The rest of the family is scattered all over. Nancy, on an AMS field trip, will be getting to the Meeting School in N.H. about tomorrow, and Linda plans to meet her there—going by bus from Boston. Linda is doing some traveling—visiting friends and seeing places. She expects to go back to Va. Beach in a couple of weeks for the Easter conference and then come to Celo and spend the month of April, hopefully earning a little money working at the Song Book Co. and Propst pottery studio.

Al is at the Beach and has been since he finished picking apples in Ontario before Thanksgiving. He's staying at some friends' house on 80th St. where he keeps a tent up in the yard—and is washing dishes at the Bosom of Abraham (natural foods restaurant). We haven't heard from him much lately, but that's not surprising. Christmas, Martha's wedding, Daddy's death, & Grandma Henry's illness are events and circumstances he's better off staying far away from.

It hasn't exactly been an easy winter for me, but it certainly could've been worse. We've had the beauty of the mountains, a warm house (even running water except for a couple of days), enough income from school and baking (about 20-25 loaves a week now) to keep us going, our health, and many good friends. I don't mention God directly in this list, because I see all these things as manifestations of His loving support.

The future, in some ways, looks a little uncertain, but it's an interesting challenge. School will be out (except for making up snow days) in another 8 wks. or so. I'm planning to have a summer program here, but plans aren't too definite yet. There's much to do.

We'll lose most of our children to public school kindergarten in the fall, so we need to do quite a bit of recruiting to keep things going. I'm not exactly worrying, but I can't take things for granted as much as I did in the Norcross situation. More of it is up to me.

That's the way things look to me these days—days characterized by joy, satisfying hard work, moments of loneliness and frustration, times of inspiration and determination to walk more completely in the Light, hope, sadness, fun, exhaustion, pain, rewards. We might ask for an easier life but never a more challenging one. To really do justice to the opportunities of the day would take more than I am or have.

Somehow, Mom managed to be everything to all of us, even to her older, mostly grown daughters. When Nancy returned a week and a half later from leading Arthur Morgan School kids on a three-week field trip up north, she was very ill and soon diagnosed with pneumonia. Mom wrote Dad a letter, telling him not to worry but wishing to keep him informed. I moved into the spare room so Nancy could use mine to convalesce, and Nancy still remembers the feeling of comfort as she lay under the quilt in my iron-framed double bed, Mom lovingly washing her long hair in a basin of warm water.

That spring, Dad's friend Charlie Stevens, who lived at Mountain Valley Farm in the Virginia mountains, invited Dad to drive with him out west to see Rolling Thunder, the medicine man that Dad had long wanted to see. Dad climbed into Charlie's old van, and off they went. Mom had heard that the trip might happen but didn't know the details, and as the spring blossomed, she felt that he had been gone long enough. She and I sent letters to Dad, mailing them to Charlie's house at Mountain Valley. Mom invited him to "come play" during her school break, and added, "I want to see you, my beloved husband." I started my note with "Long time no see!" Our message got through to him, because he came home a couple of weeks later. He had been gone and mostly out of touch for eight months.

After a good sixth grade year at South Toe and a fun summer going to both Camp Celo and ARE Camp, starting middle school was a shock to my early adolescent system. As it turns out, "be brave, little tadpole" does nothing for you when you see the newt coming at you, its big jaws gaping. Suddenly I was in the world of cheerleaders and makeup, "dressing out" for gym, and a principal who carried a paddle with him as he walked around at the end of the day, watching the yellow buses swallowing their daily loads. My body developed in slow motion compared to the other girls, my friends from elementary school had moved away or gone to other schools, and once again I learned that it's not always good to be the smart kid. The popular girls teased me unmercifully as they applied their makeup on the bus. "You're so ugly!" "What is that thing you're *wearing*, anyway?" "We hate you!"

Getting off the bus brought no relief. In those days, high school students drove the county school buses, and the guy who drove my bus acted as if I didn't exist. Every afternoon, as the bus approached the swinging bridge, I mentally willed him to lift his foot from the gas pedal, slow down, prepare to stop. But every day he forgot. As the bus sailed past the bridge, I squealed, "Stop, Ricky!" He slammed on the brakes and grumbled at me as I got off the bus, my face flaming red as I walked back up the road toward the path to the bridge. Somehow it was my fault that I was forgettable. What was wrong with me?

And then I had to step into a house where Dad lived once again. Walking those hundred yards up the hill was my only chance to prepare myself. He could be happy, friendly, sleeping, silent, or gone. I never knew what to expect.

One day I found him and my fluffy blonde cat, Spumsy, staring at each other. Like all cats, Spumsy could be mysterious, sometimes aloof.

"He's in there," Dad said.

"Who's in where?"

"Your grandfather. He's in there."

What?

"I knew he wouldn't leave me alone! Even after he's dead! Your Granddaddy Moore has taken over this cat, and he's watching me. I can't stand it. I'm gonna have to kill the cat."

He didn't kill Spumsy, but I finally began to understand that something was wrong with my daddy. Normal people didn't say the things he said. Feeling guilty about it, I began to wish that he would go away again. Though the pipes froze when the temperature fell, the car broke down all the time, and we had to work hard to have enough wood to heat the house, life was easier when it was just Mom and me.

In December, I got my wish. The rest of us planned a trip to Macon for the holidays, wishing to take part in a dedication ceremony for the new Walter L. Moore Education Building at Vineville Baptist Church. Dad wanted no part of it, of course, so he headed to Virginia Beach. We could actually celebrate Christmas. It was a gift indeed.

While he was in Celo, Dad had often talked to his friend Bob McGahey about the restrictions of family. He argued that family is a social invention that traps people like him in a net. Everybody would be better off without it. That winter and spring, Mom, too, thought about what it means to be family. She thought back to her hot August wedding day in 1950, when her mother's hard work and sacrifices finally came to fruition. The heavy satin dress her mama had made by hand, the fancy wedding breakfast, Buddy's beautiful young tenor voice soaring over the flower-filled sanctuary. Walking down the aisle with her uncle, while her daddy waited at the altar to join her in holy matrimony to Albert Lafayette Henry III.

"In sickness and health…for richer, for poorer…." She and Dad had endured both ends of the spectrum and everything in between. "What God has joined together, let no man put asunder." That verse and then her father's signature, right there on their marriage certificate. She had never wanted to let her daddy down. But now he was gone.

For years she had thought of Dad as a ship captain who spent most of his time at sea but always came back to his family. For years her friends, who didn't even know about the violence, had asked, "Why don't you divorce him?" but she loved him too much. She saw his sickness and remembered her promise. That spring, as she finally began to consider her options, she was haunted by the question, "How can a true Christian get a divorce?" After everything our family had lived through, her faith was the last hurdle.

That summer, after Dad had been gone for seven months, Mom drove me to Virginia for the first session of ARE camp. Dad was there, and she saw him briefly at a new age "happening" in the woods. But she didn't demand anything. Didn't ask him to come home. Didn't offer to stay with him. Instead, she climbed into the car and drove back to Celo. Alone.

Since I was too old for Camp Celo, I returned to ARE Camp for another session later that summer, and Dad showed up in Celo shortly before I left. At first, he seemed happy to be there and even took Mama, Nancy, and me out to lunch at a salad bar in Spruce Pine. Then, a few days before I was to leave for camp, he grew restless and said he was leaving. Mom offered to give him a ride, but he figured he could catch a ride to town and then continue on to Virginia. He stuffed his sleeping bag in its sack, packed his books in his heavy backpack, and set out. Mom and I figured he was gone.

In a couple of hours, though, he was back. He hadn't been able to get a ride after all, so he'd have to stay. It didn't bode well. And when Mom stepped into the kitchen to start supper, the situation went from bad to worse: no water came from the tap. The well was dry. Knowing that Dad would stay self-controlled with another person in the house, I invited a friend over the next night, water or no.

And then I went off to camp, never happier to be away from home.

Mom was not so lucky. With me gone and Dad feeling like a trapped animal, she had no protection. Finally, she felt scared enough to seek Nancy's help. This time Nancy knew she had to get Mom *out*. Celo wasn't safe anymore.

Nancy and Mom went to the lake in Georgia, Mom's sanctuary since she was a little girl. It was a Moore stronghold, and the one place they knew Dad would never show up. After a couple of days, Buddy and his family came, bringing cheerful games of Scrabble on the porch and family meals around the big wooden table. A little normalcy. A chance to breathe. A time to feel protected and cry some private tears. Mama knew it was finally time for a change. And she had to be the one to do it.

After a week of August heat and laps across the lake in the cool, green water, Mom had the strength she needed. She came home on August 15 and went to Burnsville to meet with the lawyer the next day. Though Dad was still staying at our house in Celo, a legal separation was established, effective August 10. Mom camped out by herself that night.

Still immersed in the world of ARE Camp, I was blissfully unaware of the family drama and expected Mom to pick me up on the last day of camp. But I was informed that I would be flying home and camp staff would take me to the airport. Flying? By myself? I'd never even been on a plane before! Where would my family get money for a plane ticket? I was sure there was some mistake, but my counselor assured me that this was the plan.

When I checked in at the airport desk, I was given a round pasteboard sign with a piece of elastic attached and told to wear it around my neck until I arrived in Asheville. In large print on the sign were the words "UNACCOMPANIED CHILD." "Me? A child?" I thought. "But I'm thirteen!" And it was strange to be "unaccompanied." Mom had always been there for me. I knew something had happened, but all I could do was get on the airplane and hope for the best. And of course, when the plane landed in Asheville and I walked across the asphalt to the little terminal, Mom was there. I was glad to take off the sign and just be me.

When Dad found out about Mom's steps toward divorce, he was livid. Even after years of talk about "leaving all" and discussions with friends about the concept of family as an artificial construct and his need to be free of it, he had a different response when faced with the reality of the end of the marriage: "How could you do this to me?" Though he now spent nights in his sleeping bag in the old smokehouse, he didn't leave, and our household was tenser than ever. Mom responded by filling up her days: participating in sacred harp sings, eating potluck meals at friends' houses, inviting friends over for supper at our house, doing chores, going to town for errands. I did likewise, inviting friends over as often as possible, babysitting, staying in motion. Now and then, though, we could feel the inevitable coming. Mom wouldn't wait for the explosion. "Get your sleeping bag," she would say, and we'd be gone.

In the middle of the family chaos, I started the year in a new school. Mom knew that I was miserable at East Yancey Middle School, and Nancy and I had both tried to convince her to let me go to the Arthur Morgan School, where Nancy worked as cook and houseparent. Though AMS was a junior high boarding school, they accepted day students. Mom finally relented partway through my year at East Yancey and let me apply for the next year, with one caveat: "I know kids cuss over there at AMS. If I ever hear of you cussing, I'll take you right out." I kept my end of the deal—she never heard me cuss.

The idea of private school, with our precarious financial situation, seemed crazy. But since Nancy was on the staff, the AMS clerk agreed that Mom could pay for my lunches, and tuition would be free. I went through the interview process and was accepted. I couldn't wait to start.

AMS was established in 1962 by Celo founder Arthur Morgan's son Ernest and his wife Elizabeth, based on Montessori principles as well as the educational philosophies espoused by Arthur Morgan when he was president of Antioch College in Ohio. The school was run as a close-knit community, with lots of meetings and music, backpacking and other expeditions, and service work as an important component. In my first year, there were only twelve students and at least that many staff. It's amazing that the school stayed afloat.

When I think back on that time, it's hard to say whether I enjoyed it or not. Home life was so complicated. I was still struggling with the awkward tadpole stage of my adolescence—self-conscious, wanting boys to notice me, feeling ugly and out of place in my body. I certainly didn't like myself very much. And the small-school intensity of AMS, boiled down to twelve students, seemed to sharpen the focus.

In the boiling, anger bubbled up in me. On a regular basis that fall, I would feel it building inside me, lash out at someone else in the group, and stomp outside. I can remember the crunch of the leaves as I ran through the woods, ducking under rhododendrons, away from all of it, to climb a tree and let the steam rise. Though it must have seemed to everyone else that I was angry and needed solitude to cool off, the opposite was true.

What I craved more than anything was for someone—anyone—to follow me, find me, listen and understand. Give me comfort. No one did. Instead, when we had "switcheroo" day and the staff and students dressed up as each other, the redheaded staff member who became Cindy for the day threw her chair back and stomped loudly out of the dining room at lunch, causing a big scene in the midst of raucous laughter. I laughed, too, letting no one see how much it hurt.

Mom continued to face her own challenges. She kept expecting Dad to leave, but he stayed put, even going so far as to find work nearby to help support the family, something he hadn't done in years. After putting it off for several months, Mom sat down and made herself do the one thing she had dreaded: she wrote a letter to her mama, finally letting her know that the marriage was coming to an end.

10/20/79

Dear Mom,

This is a letter I've been waiting a long time to write—too long, probably—but I kept thinking things would become definite sooner than they have. Anyway, I want you to know what's happening.... I have finally decided that divorce is the best solution for Al & me & have taken steps in that direction. Naturally it has come as a great surprise to him after all these years, and he hasn't fully accepted the fact.

We'll always care about each other, of course, & will always be in touch—because of the girls, if nothing else—but our paths are so different that it seems to me there's not a real marriage anyway, and we're much better off to face it and be free of the struggle to make it one.

According to N.C. law, if a couple lives apart for one year, they can sign papers to that effect, & that's it. I have established Aug. 10 as the beginning of that year.

Please don't worry. In many ways you're relieved, I'm sure, because these past few years especially have had many difficult times. But don't forget the positive things. He's still a mighty fine person in many ways.

I've talked this over with all four girls and with Buddy & Martha. The girls love their daddy very much but have accepted my decision, & not one has tried to talk me out of it. I'm so thankful for this loving, supportive family—including my Mama and the daddy of my daughters!...

Our good friend from Atlanta, David Shields was here a couple of days this week. As much as Dave loves Al, his surprise was not that we're getting a divorce but that I've stayed with him this long. I've been asked about that before, of course—and the reason is pretty obvious to me. It's the same as why I married him in the first place.

Well, enough of that for now.

Thanks for your last phone call. It's always mighty good to hear your voice.

> I love you—
> Carol

By the end of October 1979, we needed a new car, and Mom was able to pay cash for a used Honda Civic that our friend Waldie Unger found. This was a big step for her, and she wrote in her journal from that day, "It was a satisfying feeling to be able to pay cash for it, but that's not something to be proud of—just thankful for." My journal from that time shows that I was excited about the car too—and other new things as well—but concern for my parents grew. Several entries reveal the progression of my thoughts:

11/1/79—I'm getting worried about Mom and Dad. Mom said if Dad didn't leave she might have to move and then I would be a boarding student. Oh, gosh, if that happens I will be so sad! I hope it doesn't.

11/4/79—Mom and I will probl'y move into Sally and John's for a while. Maybe until Thanksgiving! I don't really want to, but if that's what needs to happen, I guess it's a good thing to do. I really feel like anything that can be done to help Daddy see that it could work better another way, needs to be done. I really love Dad a lot, but I really love Mom a lot, too and it's pretty obvious that something has to happen in the situation.

11/6/79—Yesterday Dad blew up at Mom. He was yelling at the top of his lungs, throwing her around and telling her to go _____ Ben! Mom

180

and I left and went to Mary Dart's house. We had a good cry and got some sympathy.... Mom said that she might have to call the law to get Daddy! Oh, what can I do? What can anybody do? Why does all this have to happen to me? Why, why, why?

When Dad "blew up," I felt some responsibility for the first time—it was sparked by something I had said. While Dad had been away much of the previous two years, our family friend Ben Geouge had gotten wood for us, fixed the car many times, helped get the water running when the pipes froze, and been a friend and confidante to Mom. Sometimes he was there late and slept in the spare room instead of going home. One day, in front of Ben, Dad, and Mom, I made the mistake of referring to the spare room as "Ben's room."

As Dad started screaming at Mom, Ben, in his quiet way, reckoned it was time to leave, and started heading down the hill. Not knowing what else to do, I ran after him and apologized for Dad and for what I had said. Dad was out of control when I got back to the house. That night, Mom and I moved in with John and Sally Burrowes. Good friends of Mom who lived a few miles away, they offered us two twin mattresses on their attic floor. For the first time, I felt like we were truly hiding as we climbed up the pull-down stairs and then retracted them behind us. Though it felt safe in the little attic, just the two of us tucked away, I was afraid.

Mom had a significant dream while we slept in that attic: a tooth fell out of her mouth, "an enormous jaw tooth," she wrote in her journal, "as wide as 3 or 4 normal teeth—it was bloody, & I was washing it off." Somebody in her dream suggested that she try putting it back in her mouth, that she might need it. She responded that it would be impossible to put back. "The roots are totally disintegrated." Like the marriage.

Just when hope seemed lost—the "new" car was already falling apart, and Mom was struggling to figure out our next step—Dad packed his backpack again and set up his tent in the National Forest. He wasn't gone completely, but he was out of the house. Mom and I moved back home.

Changes were brewing in the rest of the family as well. Nancy, who had worked at AMS for the last several years, was now living by herself for the first time, no longer a houseparent with Randy. Though she and Randy were still romantically involved, she was frustrated with their relationship. She resigned from her job at AMS and decided to move away. Where hardly mattered to her. She just wanted to get *away*. Linda was moving in the other direction. After traveling for the last year or so, she and her boyfriend Michael felt ready to settle down and planned to move into the house that Nancy was vacating. Janet had decided to take a leave of absence from Warren Wilson College, not sure if she'd ever go back.

"What next?" Mom wrote in her journal. "As long as we can keep our vision—keep in touch with that of God within us—our possibilities are unlimited—for service, growth, love happiness—all the things we know life can be—and really want it to be." Somehow, amid the swirling changes and heartbreak, she managed to hang on to her center. And she kept us all grounded in the process.

Christmas was a bright spot, full of gatherings with family and dear friends. The days leading up to the second anniversary of Granddaddy's death were hard for Mom, but once again she chose to find the beauty in her life:

1/6/80
After several days of dark negative feelings—weakness, sadness, loneliness—a change was overdue. And it began to come when I first woke up. Decided to read something from Dad's meditation book—for the first time in quite a while. Turned to Jan. 6 & found—"adversity can be your ladder to success"—mention of Homer, Milton, Helen Keller, who in spite of her handicaps, lived victoriously—prayer—not that our burdens be lifted, but that we be given the strength to bear the burdens we're given. Jan. 6—two years ago today Dad died. It's as if he dropped in to say—"Perk up, kid. You can make it." *I* can't—but *we* can.

By the middle of February, Nancy (who had moved to Boston and gotten a job as a courier, hustling through the cold winter winds with architectural plans under her arm) decided it was time to head back south to her support system. Running away hadn't solved her problem. Three weeks later, Linda and Michael went to Friends Meeting with Mom on Sunday and announced their engagement. Joy filled the room. When I was away for three weeks on an AMS field trip, Mom cleaned out the smokehouse, going through boxes and burning her old letters and keepsakes from Dad. When Easter arrived, she opened herself to the feeling of rebirth, filling that day "with enough memories stored up to keep us smiling for the whole week."

That spring and summer, Dad stayed away. Mom felt stronger, writing, "Today I feel, for the first time in many months, that if Al were to come, it would be all right. I could handle it. I hope he is well and feeling strength and peace." Though she didn't see him that summer, I did. I got a ride to ARE Camp with friends to go on a camp-led week-long hike on the Appalachian Trail. I had done plenty of backpacking by that time but nothing that far, for that length of time, or that strenuous. I was nervous. I didn't even have good hiking boots. But for the first time in my life, Dad took me shopping. We went to a Redwing store and bought boots that looked more like farmer's boots, lacing halfway up my calf. He showed me a quick and easy way to lace the shoestrings through the hooks by holding both strings in one hand and weaving back and forth, back and forth.

The boots didn't look suitable for the trail and I didn't have time to break them in, but my daddy had bought them for me and shown me how to lace them up, and I was determined to wear them. After a week of fifteen-mile days with a full pack on the tallest mountains in Virginia, I was the only person in the group who didn't have blisters. It was a sweet time.

As the summer drew to a close, divorce loomed large on Mom's horizon. She wrote in her journal, "Less than a week now 'til the divorce is final. What will that be like? I dread it. Life is not fair."

Two days later at her birthday dinner, Linda and Michael announced that they were indefinitely "postponing" their wedding, which at that point was only three weeks away. Everything was planned, our dresses were made, and the final stitches had been sewn in the wedding quilt. But it turned out that Michael wasn't ready for monogamy, and Linda finally realized that she didn't have to put up with it. The wedding was off.

Shortly after that, Michael felt that Mom was less than happy with him, and he called her to see if they could talk about it. Coming from my mother, whose most scathing criticism of anybody up to that point had been "poor thing, he has an unfortunate personality," her response to Michael was an atomic bomb: "There's nothing to talk about—you're a dirty rotten skunk." She promptly hung up the phone.

The next hurdle was the divorce itself. John and Sally Burrowes had agreed to come to court as Mom's witnesses. I was at school that day, and Linda filled in for Mom at the Montessori school. By the time the divorce was final, it felt to Mom like a bit of an anticlimax. It was done. She later wrote that she had taken the necessary legal step, but she felt "more like a widow than a divorcee." The man she had married no longer existed.

When she came home that afternoon, she found a card from Linda on the dining room table. The monarch chrysalis in the terrarium at Mom's school, which all the kids had been watching since its caterpillar days, had gone through its final transformation while Mom was in court. Linda's card, with a beautiful drawing of the orange and black butterfly, read, "Today is the day the Monarch was born into flight." As Mom reflected later, "It was a meaningful symbol."

Not long afterward, Mom got a call from her high school friend John Garner, who had also been a hunting and fishing buddy of Granddaddy's. A devout Baptist himself, he had heard about the divorce and called to reassure Mom. "I just want you to know that if you're having any feelings of guilt about getting this divorce, you need not feel bad about it, 'cause it's what your daddy would have wanted." He made her day.

My day was a little more complicated. Right about that time I got a letter from Dad, who had been thinking about the divorce himself. The envelope was addressed to me and contained two separate letters. The first basically said, "I know this divorce is all your fault, I don't love you anymore, and I never want to see you again." The second read, "Well, I've changed my mind and I think maybe I do still love you. But I don't want to see you for a long, long time."

I was devastated. Was this the same man who had lovingly shown me how to lace my boots before sending me off on the trail just two months before? I remember standing on the cold, hard concrete floor of the laundry room at AMS, those two letters in my hand, trying to figure out what to do. I was in shock, completely empty.

Finally, I made a mature choice for my young years—I threw both letters in the rusty trash can and walked out. I carried the pain with me, but I didn't have to carry the letters, too. I didn't tell Mom what he had done.

That autumn, Linda wrote a song that captured what we all felt:

> I watched your colors growing,
> Growing oh, so strong.
> Now I watch your colors fading,
> And it won't be long.
> It's time to let go of all that you know
> And give yourself to the wind.
> Come to the earth, who gave you your birth,
> It's time to start over again.

I sang Linda's song as I walked to school through the reds, yellows, and oranges of the maples and oaks, fervently hoping that it was possible to start over.

~ ~ ~ ~ ~ ~

When Grandaddy Moore died, Mama made the choice to shield me from the loss of him. I waited downstairs that day in the hospital when she said her good-byes, and she went to the funeral without me. The closest I got to his death came much later as I went through the family archives at the lake in 2006. I wrote about it while I was there:

The cabin wasn't quite so full of family this trip—just the four of us for a good chunk of the time. And I had some time to go through the keepsakes still in Grandmama's chest of drawers. Her college scrapbook from the twenties is there, along with her wedding dress, her oldest daughter Sunny's baby books, and a picture of the flower-piled cemetery the day after little Sunny died. I've been to that cemetery now, so I recognize it when I see it.

It's different being there now—I have a new lens for looking closely. I know more, understand more, ask different questions, feel through it in a different way.

This time, I even went through the drawer of Granddaddy's slides. The phrase "gold mine" is over-used, but it fits. When you first open the drawer, you notice that it's tumbled-up and disorganized, though most all the slides are in boxes. Some are labeled correctly, some are mislabeled, and many have no notations at all. So when you pull out a box and start popping slides in the viewer, there's no telling what you'll find.

But, oh, goodness, once you really dig in, the *life* that streams out of that drawer!

Granddaddy loved photography—he had lots of equipment, and even developed his own pictures (though not the slides, of course). And looking at the slides, just me and that lit-up 2x2 square of color, is about the closest I can come to being inside his head, seeing what he saw. Loving what he loved.

There are photos from their travels all around the world: Cuba, Panama, Chile, Ecuador, Rome, France, Luxembourg, Scotland, England, California, New York City, Mt. Ranier, The Lake. And there are pictures of people, mostly family. Us. Some posed, some not. Pictures of us swimming, playing, concentrating, eating, talking, smiling at him. Loving him back.

And he's in a lot of the pictures, too. I have lots of memories of waiting, posing while he got it all set up, then all of us counting together, eager with anticipation as he ran around and joined us just in time for the shutter to capture the moment with him in it.

But there's one roll of pictures that's completely different. No people, no exotic places. Just the lake, the changing fall trees, their house in Macon. A few simple images. It's from October of 1977, just three months before Granddaddy died of cancer. He knew he was going, and through the lens of his camera, he said goodbye.

Goodbye again, Granddaddy.

After writing this piece at the lake, I came home and learned that my Aunt Martha, my mom's younger sister, had drifted peacefully away in her sleep in the wee hours at the hospice facility in Cincinnati. More good-byes.

A few days later, Nancy, Janet, and I took Mom up to Cincinnati for Martha's funeral. My sisters and I were taken aback at Mom's lack of grief over losing Martha, her only sister. I could only imagine how I'd feel if it were one of my sisters—such incredible sadness! But Mom kept insisting, "I'm happy for her. If I were at that point, I'd be ready to go. Homeward bound." Just a month away from moving into an assisted living facility herself, it was as if the dementia had stripped away Mom's capacity for feeling grief. Our grief was multiplied.

But now I wonder.

If it's a survivor, the wriggly tadpole grows legs and climbs out of the water, hopping away from the hungry newt. The caterpillar attaches itself, upside down, to the milkweed stalk, miraculously becoming the iridescent green chrysalis. Finally it emerges to fly away.

"I won't love you if you don't let me go," my granddaddy had said when it was time for him to die.

Our lives are natural cycles. Loving, changing, letting go. As I write now, my own mama no longer knows who I am. She knows I'm a daughter, but which one? All those years of the two of us are completely gone from her memory. She's in the chrysalis again. And when it comes time for her to fly, I need to let her go.

You can go, Mama. You can go.

9

Patchwork

It seemed that life should have finally been simpler for us.

Mom was now the breadwinner (partly by baking and selling bread), and we were firmly settled into our little house by the river. Linda and Nancy lived nearby, and we had the support of close friends in the community. Granddaddy had passed gently away, so she could let go of her fear of disappointing him.

And Mom had taken that monumental step. The divorce was final, and Dad was out of the house and gone from Celo. Surely, I thought, the drama was over. Surely we could take some deep breaths and start to move on.

But not yet.

In late November, a letter arrived to all of us from Dad. We hadn't heard from him in several months. Even though I dealt with some complicated feelings about his letter that blamed me for the divorce, he was still my daddy and I wanted to know that he was okay. I was surprised to see that the return address was Santa Cruz, California. We thought he was in Virginia. I carried the letter across the bridge and up the hill, picturing Dad's bearded face.

When I got up the hill to my room and settled in the window seat looking out to the dark November mountains, I saw that the contents of the envelope were even more unexpected. Dad revealed that he was living with a woman named Dana Smith—someone we'd never met—and they were expecting a baby.

The floor fell out from under me. Mom captured our experience in her journal the next day.

11/23/80

An unforgettable weekend. Al is going to be a father again. A letter from him to the girls tells of his happiness that he & Dana Smith are expecting in June & that they are living together in Santa Cruz.

So many emotions. Numbness first, sadness—for the unborn baby, for Cindy, whose tears won't stop, for that young mother who has no idea what she's letting herself in for.

Anger—a hell of an example to set for your daughters—"just go meet up with somebody & in two months or less make a baby with them. Never consider marriage"—such irresponsible behavior—can't even wait 'til your divorce is final.

Sympathy—for a man so lonely, confused, desperate, helpless— reaching out for any caring available. After all, I can't really know what it's like to be so alone. I have these 4 wonderful daughters right here with me.

Cindy opened the letter, read a page or two, threw it down & ran outside sobbing deeply.

Nancy picked it up, read a little & looked at me with wide tear-filled eyes & in just about a whisper said, "He's going to have a baby."

We called Linda at McGaheys' & I walked over to meet her. She read a little, just shook her head & put her arm around me.

Janet doesn't know yet. We'll tell her Wednesday when she comes—or Thurs. I can't quite guess her reaction.

Last night was very restless, but today I've gone thru' the gamut of emotions. Maybe tonight will be more restful for us all.

It is the task of the adolescent to differentiate herself from her parents; my dad was doing that work for me. I felt utterly rejected—I would no longer be the youngest, the apple of his eye. In his letter a week later, addressed to me personally, he compared his current situation to his memories of Koinonia, where I was conceived.

At present, Dana & I are living cooperatively with 12 other people in a large Victorian house on a cliff overlooking the water here at Santa Cruz. We share housekeeping & food preparation, etc. It is a lot like it was at Koinonia.

From our windows, we can see the mountains meet the sea on both sides of the huge bay. Also we can see the Boardwalk with concessions, ferris wheels, etc. We can see the large local fishing pier or wharf. In the other direction is the lighthouse. Beyond that are the beautiful monarch butterflies....

Dana and I love each other very much. Our days and nights are filled with anticipation about our baby, —another Gemini, we expect. Of course we are occupied with all the things new couples give attention to, —getting to know each other in our unfolding relationship.

The fact that this baby would share my astrological sign, when astrology was Dad's main focus, was not lost on me. There was no place for me in his new, "unfolding relationship." Though we learned only a few weeks later that Dana had left Dad and he was back in Virginia Beach, that didn't make a difference for me. He was gone. My mama was all I had left.

Mom and I held each other close and slowly began to enjoy all the delights that Dad had denied us. Mom openly drank a cup of coffee in the morning, and by the time I woke up the house was filled with its comforting aroma. I noticed that she stopped grinding flour for bread; sometimes she even bought unbleached white flour to mix in with the whole wheat. Brown sugar crept into the cabinets, and then even refined white sugar. The Spooners, our neighbors, invited us over for dinner one evening shortly after they'd butchered a pig. As we were leaving, they offered us fresh sausage and bacon to take home, and Mama accepted. I was delighted. Meat! At our house!

And then there was Christmas.

Since the awful Christmas in Cabbagetown when I was a year old and Mama had decided we needed to choose between having Christmas and having a daddy, there had been no Christmas tree, stockings, or other holiday rituals. But now Daddy was utterly gone. We no longer had to choose.

Since we lived on the edge of a forest full of evergreens, we cut down a little hemlock, brought it in the house, and set it up in a metal bucket. Mom decided we could afford one string of lights. She bought them in Spruce Pine when she went to work the next day, even splurging on a bag of shiny red plastic apples. Then we got creative, using what we found around the house. A small corduroy lion from under my bed happily hung from one of the stronger bottom branches. We wrapped toothpicks with colorful thread from Mom's sewing basket to make god's eye diamonds that dangled from the tree's fingertips. We strung popcorn on white thread and draped it across the branches. I crocheted and knitted ornaments out of yarn to add color.

And then we turned out the lights.

Mom and I sat in the darkness, arms wrapped around each other and tear-filled eyes reflecting the colorful lights of the tree. Christmas came to our house, and it was magical.

I started high school the next fall. With unhappy memories from my one year at East Yancey Middle School and then two years in Arthur Morgan School's complicated cocoon, I was nervous about returning to public school. My other Celo friends went to boarding school, while I began as a sophomore in a place where the rest of the students already knew their way around. I was the oddball again. Pushing myself away from home and family—even Mom and I began to have the occasional heated squabble, with sarcasm on my side and tears on hers—I wondered where I would find my place.

As it was for my sisters, Camp Celo was the answer to my growing sense of isolation. After two summers of being too old to be a camper and too young to be anything else, finally I was old enough to go back as a "helper," a counselor-in-training. This position provided free labor for the camp—the helpers did all the grunt work, washing the dishes, mopping the floors, cutting the grass, weeding the garden. I loved every bit of it. Camp Celo was the one place where I never felt like an oddball.

I slept in a two-person tent on a platform the entire summer, with just enough room for two metal cots. Two wooden cubbies between the cots held toothbrushes and flashlights. Nails along the boards by the beds held our shorts, T-shirts, and rain ponchos; we didn't need much else. We always went barefoot—by the end of the summer the soles of our feet were so tough we could race shoeless down the gravel road without wincing.

My tentmate was Carol Tenney, a girl I had met when I was a camper. The first summer we shared that tent, we quickly became best friends. She tolerated my piles of clothes on the tiny sliver of floor between our cots, and I was patient during the times when she was kissing a boy in the tent and I was ready to climb in bed. Even better, Carol loved me unconditionally. She held me accountable for the dark moods that sometimes hit me, but I knew she'd still love me when the mood passed. I could be myself. We requested to share the same tent the second summer—the best summer of all.

As a returning helper, I knew what to expect and felt comfortable with my duties. It was the perfect combination of responsibility and autonomy for my sixteen-year-old self. I was great with the kids. I loved that Bob and Dot, the camp directors, could say to me, "Cindy, we have a need," and trust that I would take care of it. The music of camp moved through my body, and my harmonies soared above the melody. The outdoors filled my lungs. I was in my element and purely happy. My teenaged self-consciousness fell away.

In the course of that summer, I started hanging out with Will, a lanky, scraggly-haired counselor who played guitar and entertained me with a sense of humor that veered well off the beaten path. It was widely known that several of the female counselors were on the prowl for a boyfriend, and Will was one of the few unattached candidates. I also knew that he was not interested, and possibly even frightened by the prospect of being found alone on a wooded path by one of these overfriendly counselors. In a joking moment, I decided to take on the job of protecting him. He didn't object.

Will and I became inseparable. We both loved music, and he taught me new songs that the two of us could sing as we strolled among the tents at dawn, gently waking the campers for the day. We traded obscure jokes and wrote silly letters to each other while supervising the long wooden tables of kids dutifully putting pencil to notebook paper to send letters home. I'd sit next to him on his bed in the tent full of kids during rest hour after lunch, reading a book while the campers slept or played quietly in their cots. At night Will and I stayed up late on the big porch of Bagski, the central gathering spot in the middle of camp. Nights were chilly, and he'd wrap his arms around me.

My friends started asking questions, but I brushed them off.

"We're just friends!" "He's way too old for me anyway." "Nothing's going on."

I said the same things to myself. Adamantly. After all, we had not kissed, and hugs were normal at camp. We simply liked to hang out. (Though I hated to admit it, I'd never kissed anybody. It seemed unlikely that Will would be the first.)

Then, entirely without meaning to and without ever admitting it, I fell in love. I hadn't planned it, hadn't even started out with my typical "crush." I was just entirely happy, not thinking or worrying. Just being.

I did finally kiss Will, late one night on Bagski, or maybe he kissed me. And I liked it. At the end of the summer, he taught me a new song:

> Come all ye fair and tender ladies,
> Take warning how you court young men.
> They're like a star on a summer morning,
> First they appear and then they're gone…

I loved the tune but never cared for the words. Soon enough, though, I understood that Will wasn't merely teaching me a pretty new song. It was another damn life lesson.

Going back to school for my junior year felt wrong. I sat in my classes feeling like I was wasting time—making good grades didn't matter anymore. Will stayed in Celo after camp was over and lived on the edge of a field in a tiny one-room house with a single chair and a woodstove. By then I had my driver's license and could easily visit him, but it wasn't the same. He acted first welcoming, then awkward, and eventually clearly not happy that I kept showing up. Mom's subtle questions indicated that she didn't like me spending time with Will and going to parties with him and his friends. What had felt right during the summer was now obviously wrong, but I couldn't let go. Wouldn't let go. Absolutely couldn't face the thought of being rejected again. I pined.

I had one friend left in Celo—Robin, who was much older than me. When Nancy and Randy moved to Pennsylvania after they finally married, Robin had promised to keep an eye on me, and he did a fine job of it. But I still felt alone, and Carol, my faraway best friend, continued to be a lifeline. I wrote letters to her almost daily, and we arranged visits as often as possible. It seemed that she was the only person who fully understood me, and I clung to our connection as I looked for a way out.

Since my Celo friends—other than Robin—had gone to boarding school, I figured I would follow them there. I applied to The Meeting School in New Hampshire, a Quaker school where several of my friends attended. Mom was not happy about it and didn't help with the application. When I got accepted, I started filling out the financial forms, stubbornly refusing to consider how I would pay thousands of dollars every semester for tuition. I just knew I needed to get out of Celo. Finances seemed irrelevant. Mom continued to apply firm, gentle pressure to get me to stay. I plowed ahead. It was the first time I had made a major decision without her support, but I was determined.

Finally, Mom resorted to the one mode of parenting she never used: bribery. "If you'll stay here next year," she said, "I'll help you buy a car." I was flabbergasted. She finally had my attention. We went to the used car lot in Burnsville and test-drove a few vehicles—I remember sitting behind the wheel of a tired-looking Mustang, thinking, "Wow, she must really want me to stay." We didn't find an affordable car we liked, but Janet offered to lend me a beat-up Toyota station wagon with loose steering, and somehow I managed to change my attitude about living in Celo. I was lonely and angry, but Celo was my home, and I would stay.

My senior year flew by in a series of unrequited crushes ("what's *wrong* with me?" was my internal mantra), no date for the prom, a nomination for "Class Clown" (Mom was truly proud), and new friends among the popular crowd when they finally tired of each other and cast around for somebody new and interesting. It turned out I was a lot more fun than they had thought. But I knew I was just a diversion. I didn't really belong.

When it was time to apply for colleges, Mom willingly assisted me. Carol Tenney and I took a Greyhound bus to visit friends at colleges across the Midwest; I decided that one such bus trip was plenty. I would choose a college closer to home. Guilford College, a Quaker school in Greensboro, had the size and values I wanted, was less than three hours from home, and no one I knew went there. Looking forward to a fresh start, I envisioned college as four years of the best of Camp Celo. Earning an Honors Scholarship made it financially possible. Finally, I would find my year-round place.

My favorite graduation gift came from Nancy: a hand-stitched log cabin quilt, just the right size for my twin dormitory bed. The colors formed diamond shapes, with a white muslin background and recurring dark green accents, so Nancy named it "emeralds in the snow," in honor of its beauty and my birthstone. I immediately recognized many of the scraps in the pattern—a dancing skirt Mom had made for me when I was an AMS student, a beloved blouse she had made, and various pieces of my sisters' clothes as well. It was a piece of home I could take with me out into the world. I knew I would need it.

With the doors to Guilford opening so smoothly, I thought it must be the right place for me. I got placed in Mary Hobbs, the dorm I requested, and eagerly wrote to the person I learned would be my roommate: Melantha Herman-Giddens, a girl from Chapel Hill.

No response.

Move-in day for freshmen arrived. I got there before Melantha and immediately loved my beautiful new room in the old building. It was a big corner room with shiny wooden floors, mahogany furniture, and huge windows on two walls, looking out to the tree-filled quad. I hung up sunny posters, put my clothes in the closet, and smoothed out the cheerful patchwork "emeralds in the snow" on my bed. And then I waited to meet Melantha.

She didn't show up for hours. When she came, there were no parents in sight. She was with a guy she called Tim—I couldn't tell whether he was her brother or boyfriend at first. They had matching hair, but it was clearly dyed an unnatural shade of red. I didn't have a sense of what she thought about my "Rebecca of Sunnybrook Farm" side of the room, since she hardly spoke to me, but she created a decidedly punk aesthetic on her side. No color, mostly black. Dark posters. Skulls. The life-sized poster of Humphrey Bogart, gazing at me from under his hat with smoke rising from his cigarette, was vaguely threatening. She left with Tim, and I didn't see her again until the next day.

As it turned out, my introduction to Melantha was a good indicator of how I would feel at Guilford, though I wouldn't admit it, even to myself. I made other friends but never felt entirely comfortable, never in my own element as I had at camp. I always felt different from everybody else; it seemed like they were all from the real world, while I was from Celo, a different planet.

On the first morning of exam week in December, I woke at dawn with a hard core of worry in my stomach. I had never faced college exams before—had I studied properly? I went out on the dorm's broad porch to breathe the morning air, hoping it would calm my nerves. The porch swing was the closest I could get to a feeling of home.

I sat on the gently squeaking swing in my bathrobe and slippers, looking out as the early morning light sifted through the bare branches of the huge trees filling the quad. I felt utterly alone. But only for a minute. As I sat there, a huge, bumbling wild turkey waddled along the sidewalk, looked up, and then used every ounce of its determination to flap its unwieldy body onto the lowest limb of a nearby oak. It settled, awkward and out of place, proudly surveying its accomplishment, unaware of me. I saw my mountain girl self in that turkey—if that turkey could do it, so could I. For the rest of my college career.

The summer after my junior year presented a unique opportunity for me to make a new place for myself. Up to then, I had come home every summer and lived rent-free with Mom, saving the money I earned by working nearby at World Around Songs, a cottage industry where I made minimum wage running the machinery to bind spiral-bound calendars. But I reached a point where I was ready to step farther away.

The timing was good because Nancy and Randy had bought the Celo Inn, the bed and breakfast where they had married five years before, and this was their first summer season of guests. Nancy was pregnant with a second child; their daughter Lane was two years old. Their family needed help, and they had an extra room in the private wing where I could sleep.

I eagerly agreed to live with them for the summer. In some ways, though I didn't think of it this way at the time, it was a dream come true for me. In the frightening years when Dad was home, I had fantasized about one of my sisters coming to sweep me away, adopting me and letting me live with her. And now I finally got that chance.

Expectations fell short of reality. After all, Nancy was tremendously pregnant. And grumpy. Inn work was nonstop for her all day and into the evening, seven days a week. I made beds, cleaned bathrooms occasionally, and helped out in the kitchen, but the bulk of innkeeping weighed heavily on my already overburdened sister.

My primary job was to keep two-year-old Lane entertained, and there was nothing I would rather do. I had been utterly enthralled with her since the moment, two years before, when I had come home for Thanksgiving break from Guilford and held her in my arms, a fresh new life only hours old. Ever since, she had seemed more real than anything in my college world.

Lane and I read books, sang songs, did puzzles, played games. Our favorite daily activity was walking down the middle of the gravel road along the river singing at the top of our lungs, "Wade in the water, wade in the water, children, now wade," and when we got to the beach, we'd take off our shoes and do just that, hand in hand.

Though I certainly helped by keeping Lane diverted, Nancy must have felt some resentment—after all, I was younger, unencumbered, and worst of all, still light on my feet. She was often angry and impatient with me, especially when I tried to cook a family meal on my assigned days. Nancy was known as a gourmet cook, and my attempts were almost always unqualified failures. I tried, but at some point about two-thirds of the way through the process, the meal fell apart. I would appeal to Nancy for help, and she would huff impatiently, pull herself up out of her chair, and wave me out of the kitchen. She could always resurrect the dish, no matter how ruined it was. Even today I would still rather wash the dishes.

I completed my college years differently than any of my sisters. Linda and Janet both graduated but took multiple leaves of absence, whether to earn money or figure out where they were heading and where they wanted to be. When school didn't feel right to Nancy, she left and never went back. But somehow I didn't feel like I had that option. My job was to be successful—to do well in school, participate in student government and other extracurricular activities, keep my scholarships, and graduate. And that's what I did.

Though I had worried at first about how hard the classes might be (compared to Mountain Heritage High) and whether it would be possible to maintain the B average I needed to keep my honors scholarship, I thrived in the discussion-based courses at Guilford and in general felt more kinship with my professors than I did with my peers. Mom was tickled that I graduated with high honors, with the highest grade point average of anybody in my graduating class. Personally, I was more pleased that my friends were surprised that I was at the top of the class. I had learned the hard lesson in middle school that brainy girls don't have friends, and most of my college friends had no idea I was such a good student. At the time, that meant "success" to me.

After grappling with the decision, I finally sent Dad an invitation to graduation. I knew I would be embarrassed if he actually showed up—what would my friends think of me then? Though our paths rarely crossed, I had lived for four years in fear that he would show up at Guilford, entirely unexpected. And now I was inviting him. But he was my dad.

I got a three-sentence postcard back:

Hi Cindy,
Thanks for the announcement of your graduation.
While I'm not much into academic education anymore, I am proud of
you.
I love you.

He didn't sign the card—didn't need to—and I didn't believe for a minute that he was proud of me. After all I had been through with my dad, it was hard to believe that he loved me. It felt like another slap in the face.

When I left Guilford, it seemed like everybody had a future but me. They were all off to jobs, or law school, or whatever. I was drifting.

Though I had no plans, I knew what lit my fire. I had spent a semester in London my junior year and fallen head over heels in love with Shakespeare's plays. When I came back to campus afterward, I had attached myself to Ellen O'Brien, the Shakespeare scholar at Guilford who taught the plays with an eye towards the stage. I had joined an *Othello* class she was teaching, as a junior "text coach." Ellen taught me how to help the other students understand their lines, and I found that I was not only excited but also good at this task; I noted interesting connections, and complicated passages untangled themselves easily in my hands. The original punctuation of *Othello*, as a key for understanding the character of Emilia, eventually became the subject of my senior honors thesis. The work thrilled me.

During that time Ellen went to California each summer, serving as text and voice coach for Shakespeare Santa Cruz, the repertory theater at the university there. I had initially hoped that I could work with her for a summer after graduation, but when she discouraged the idea I made plans to return to Celo and work as the shopkeeper at Toe River Crafts. It was a quiet job—I mostly sat and read—but I tried to make the best of it. I told a friend, "I'll make five dollars an hour!" It seemed like a lot to me, but he wasn't impressed. I left college feeling deflated.

A couple of weeks after I got home, I got a call from Ellen, who had spoken to the director at Shakespeare Santa Cruz. She invited me to come as an intern for the summer—no money, no academic credit. She would be Associate Director for *Julius Caesar* and *Antony and Cleopatra*, and I could work on those plays with her. Though it wasn't exactly an enthusiastic invitation, I jumped at the chance and bought a plane ticket.

When I think of that trip to California, the phrase "half-cocked" comes to mind. Judi McGahey, the old friend from Celo who had intervened directly with Dad years before, kindly recruited her mom to meet me at the San Jose airport, put me up for that first night, and drive me the hour to Santa Cruz. I had a plane ticket, $300, a suitcase so large I couldn't even carry it, and that was it. I had no idea where I would stay when I got there, but I figured Ellen wouldn't let me sleep on the street.

Judi's mother was straightforward and incredibly warm, filled me up with food, gave me a comfy bed, and drove me capably over the mountain to Santa Cruz. When we got there, we found the performing arts center on campus, I dragged my mammoth blue suitcase out of her trunk, and she drove away. I had arrived. My first real test was only minutes away.

I quickly found Ellen in the darkened theater, rehearsals already underway.

"You made it! Where are you staying?"

"I don't know yet—I was hoping to stay wherever you are for a couple of nights until I can find a place."

"Oh, no. I'm sleeping on someone else's couch already—there's really no room there and I wouldn't want to impose."

"Oh, shit," I thought.

The rehearsal break ended, Ellen turned her attention back to the stage, and I carefully swallowed the large rock in my throat and went out for some air and to ponder my options.

The University of California at Santa Cruz is an amazing place. Up on a mountain overlooking the sea, its buildings are tucked discreetly among the redwoods. I emerged from the dark theater into the brightness, found a small rock to hold in my hand to keep me grounded, and sat down on a larger one to think.

Four words came into my head immediately: "WHAT—HAVE—I—DONE?" Everyone I knew and loved was three thousand miles away.

I was three hours out of sync and could feel it down to my cells. I had never been truly on my own, and now I had jumped off the edge of a cliff, expecting to be caught. It was a long way down, and the waves were crashing on the rocks.

I remembered that I needed to consider my options. I had a tiny slip of paper buried somewhere in my bag that had the name and phone number of another Celo connection: a cousin of Donna Jean Dreyer, my friend Robin's mother. I dug it out and found a pay phone so I could call this woman.

I had her work number and it turned out that she was a physical therapist and was with a patient. The receptionist told me to try back in forty-five minutes, so I went back to my rock to wait, breathing carefully.

At this point, I noticed a herd of animals grazing in the field below me. Like everything else here, they seemed foreign. Light brown coat, slender legs, graceful heads, short tails. After several minutes of pondering, I finally realized that they were a herd of garden-variety deer, like the ones we used to see bounding into the woods behind our house, but utterly tame and unfrightened. They were completely familiar yet entirely unknown. Like me in Santa Cruz.

Many quarters in the phone slot later, I finally reached Donna Jean's cousin and explained my predicament. "Well," she responded, "we're going out of town in the morning, so you can't stay with us, but you can come for dinner, and maybe I can help you figure something out."

My dinner host helped me find temporary lodging, and within a few days I found a room to rent: a former Shakespeare Santa Cruz stage manager, Mary Grabowski, had a room available in her house a few blocks from the bay. The house was modest and the room small, but I didn't need much, and I was thrilled that I could walk just two blocks to the ocean. It was a beautiful walk over the cliffs along the bay to a little brick lighthouse. I culminated my moving-in ritual by carefully smoothing the greens and whites of my high school graduation quilt across the narrow futon on the floor. I had finally landed.

I quickly figured out how to navigate the Santa Cruz bus system so I could get up the hill to rehearsals every day, and eagerly dove into the world of Antony, Brutus, and Cleopatra and her court of women. Love, loyalty, war, sex, betrayal, death—plenty of drama, but none to rival what happened behind the scenes and off the stage. I found I had little patience for actor histrionics. Nor did I really have a role there; I ran lines with some of the actors occasionally, and the kind actress who played Cleopatra graciously allowed me to do a little text coaching with her. But mostly I sat in the theater and figured out that this was not actually my bliss.

I had only been in Santa Cruz a month when I faced the nearby origins of my half-brother, whose name I now knew was Josh.

We had heard over the years that Josh's mother Dana had gone back to her old boyfriend before Josh was born, and they had moved to Washington state. I wondered about Josh sometimes, and Dad had shown me a picture of him. I secretly thought that my little brother, with his red hair and square jaw, looked a little like me. But I preferred not to think about him much. He wasn't a part of our lives and probably never would be.

In Santa Cruz, though, I couldn't help thinking about those days long ago, when Dad had written me the letter and described the view from his and Dana's windows. His descriptions seemed uncomfortably familiar now. I wondered where he lived, where he went, what he did. Finally tired of wondering, I wrote to him and asked.

When Dad wrote back, he managed to floor me once again. The house where he and Dana had lived, which at that time was a hippie cooperative house, was now none other than Epworth-by-the-Sea, the beautiful Victorian "events location" overlooking the bay. I had walked past it several times a week since I arrived—it was on the corner at the end of my street, where I turned right onto Westcliff Drive on my excursions along the cliffs to the lighthouse. I always admired its generous porches and gingerbread trim, but never thought it had any special significance for me.

The lights in the windows now took on a whole new cast. Which window was their room, where Dad found the note from Dana saying that she was gone and never coming back? I didn't figure it out, of course, but I stared intently at that house every time I passed it from then on. Eventually Epworth-by-the-Sea became what it had been for me in the beginning: just a house. Something in me opened up and let it fly away. I walked on.

Another day I was out sunning in the backyard when I noticed a cat that had bounded over our fence to stalk a butterfly. I watched for a while as the cat inched closer, taking its time, not yet ready to pounce, enjoying the hunt. I wondered: what if the cat actually catches it? It's not like the butterfly would taste good—probably dusty and crackly in the cat's mouth. The point was clearly not the catching. For the cat, the point was the joy of going after the butterfly.

It was one of those moments when something that everybody else seemed to know from birth finally came to light in my brain. I decided to try it out.

Leaving the backyard, I went inside and put on my black cotton sundress with the tiny buttons all the way up the front. The dropped V waist hugged my slim frame—I could feel myself filling my body in a new way.

And then I set out.

I walked the block and a half down our street to the bay, turning right at Dad's old house and along the cliffs toward the lighthouse. I walked slowly, enjoying the feel of my young body, the sun on my shoulders, the breeze in my hair. Just a few feet along Westcliff, I came to a set of steps that led down the rocky cliffs to the water, one of the entry points for the many surfers who bobbed in the waves. A cute guy was coming up with his blonde curls dripping, board under his arm. As he topped the stairs and I walked by, our eyes met. They locked. The electricity crackled. I kept going and he crossed behind me. I could feel his eyes burning into my back. The cat and the butterfly. It was a first for me.

At the end of the summer, for lack of any other concrete plans, I decided that I liked Santa Cruz and would stay. I used the second half of my round-trip plane ticket to fly back to North Carolina so I could get my car and belongings, and then drove across the country with my brother-in-law Randy, who wanted to visit a friend north of San Francisco. We had a fun bonding trip, but when I dropped him off at a street corner in San Francisco, I had the same feeling of panic that overtook me when Ellen had no place for me to live. Yes, this time I knew where I'd lay my head when I got to Santa Cruz. My quilt was already there. And my baggage was easily transportable on the four wheels of my car. But for the first time, I had to find a way to support myself. I had no money and no résumé. I had never had a real job. I was flying solo, with no parachute except the one my housemate Mary had draped artistically on the ceiling of my bedroom.

Many hand-typed resumes and dead-end applications later, as my meager savings drifted toward the pennies column, I landed a job at M. Jacobs & Associates, a geotechnical engineering firm where the slogan was "Dirt is our life." I quickly felt bored and overqualified, but I was still desperately grateful for the steady income. Except for the fun technicians, geologist, and junior engineer, all of whom who were out in the field most of every day, the office was deadly boring. The silence between clock ticks was interminable.

Not surprisingly, my eye wandered when the workload was light, and I was eager to act on my new self-discovery. My eye landed on a cute, unattached technician: Tom. He was unattached in that he was recently divorced with three young kids. Clearly not unencumbered. But I was bored and naïve. In the beginning of December at the Jacobs & Associates Christmas party, I ended up spending most of the evening at the bar talking to Tom and was delighted when he offered to drive me home. Since I had ridden to the party with another friend, I was free to accept.

"Look at me!" I thought as we drove through the dark. "The cat and the butterfly!"

We dated some after that, though he had made it clear that he wasn't looking for a serious, long-term relationship. But I was still me, even in the faraway land of California. Though I tried to be relaxed and easygoing, I couldn't wrap my mind around the concept of spending a long evening kissing and caressing, and then letting it all go and not thinking about it the next day. I wasn't wired that way. Tom started calling less, becoming unavailable. I started pining and hated myself for it. The relationship, or whatever it was, finally petered out completely. By the time Tom left for a job with another firm at the end of February, I was glad to see him go. I was tired of pining.

About that time, I started thinking about what might come next. I felt like I had been successful at Guilford—maybe academia was my place. There was one performance-oriented Shakespeare professor in the English department at the University of North Carolina at Chapel Hill, and it would be inexpensive to go there if I could still get in-state tuition. I took the GRE, applied to UNC-CH, got accepted, and had a plan. My California friends thought I was nuts to head back to the South. Deep inside me, my roots understood, even if my friends didn't.

My friend Gretchen rode with me back across the country—she was heading east for graduate school, too. It was a great trip. I was wide-eyed on the first day, when we drove through the middle of Reno's glitz and glamour. A few days later, Gretchen was driving a little too fast along the straight highway in Missouri, and a state trooper taught us about his state motto: "*show me* your license; *show me* your registration."

We ate sloppy barbecue on soggy white bread with men in business suits at Arthur Bryant's in the sketchy part of downtown Kansas City.

We stood quietly by Elvis's grave at Graceland, watching the mascara slide down the face of a weeping woman in an overstuffed polyester pantsuit, as she clung tightly to her Elvis impersonator husband.

It was an American pilgrimage. And when we got to the green of Celo, I knew I was home.

I had a month to catch my breath before I needed to be in Chapel Hill for the beginning of the semester, giving me time to reset my internal clock and take stock of who I was, this post-California Cindy back in the homeland. I also had time for a family week at the lake in Georgia. For the second time, my cousin David invited his friend Robert.

David had first brought Robert to the lake right before I went to London my junior year of college. On our final at the lake, Robert had kissed me, and I had over-interpreted it, as I tended to do. Robert was an au pair in Germany that fall, and when I visited him there from London, our "relationship" had ended badly. It was another pining experience for me, and not something I was eager to repeat. During this visit, I was determined not to let his presence ruin my favorite place on the planet. After all, the sun was still hot, the lake was still cool, and the waterfall still splashed down on the rocks. I was in my happy place. And once again, I must have seemed irresistible. Robert and I had a great time— just flirting, nothing else. Somehow, just this once, I managed to keep it simple. After all, I looked forward to the excitement of moving to a new place, finding a place to live, settling in, starting a new life.

I ended up renting a house in Chapel Hill, sight unseen, that was owned by the parents of a Celo friend. It was within walking distance of campus, and if I found a housemate, I could afford the rent. When I finally drove up to that tiny log cabin on Purefoy Road, I immediately fell in love. It was right out of a fairy tale—a straight gravel walk led to the woodpecker knocker on the front door, two windows peeping out at me on either side. It was a perfect symmetrical house.

Once classes started, though, I found that graduate school was not such an easy fit. After the small, informal seminar classes at Guilford, I was taken aback to come to graduate school and be thrown into large, lecture-style survey courses. The English department parties tended to be an awkward combination of beer drinking and literary one-upmanship, neither of which I particularly enjoyed. Robert kept writing me letters, eventually deciding to come to Celo for the Henry/Moore family Thanksgiving.

I stayed in the cottage at the Celo Inn the night before Thanksgiving, telling Mom that it made the most sense since her siblings and their spouses would stay at her house the next night and I didn't want to have to move. My real motive, of course, was that Robert was coming. I wanted privacy.

By the time he got there, it was late. I was already in my flannel nightgown, the fire crackling in the cottage woodstove. He walked in and gave me a hug, and I laid the cards on the table. I wasn't playing games.

"There's a bed downstairs, and one upstairs. I'll be in the one upstairs. Feel free to sleep in either one." That night, we made love for the first time, and I finally understood what the phrase meant.

By the middle of December, our relationship was serious. Robert talked about coming to Chapel Hill for the summer and living with me. I planned a trip to Jacksonville to see him after Christmas. My phone bill was through the roof. I was deliriously happy—an actual boyfriend at last. So *this* was what it felt like.

Our after-Christmas visit took me to increasing heights. His mother liked me. We went to St. Augustine and stayed in a hotel, walking on the beach, taking silly pictures of ourselves, looking into each other's eyes, making love, and holding each other close.

Finally, I thought, I'm allowed to experience what it seems like everybody else has had a taste of but me. Finally I somehow deserve it. Finally I'm good enough.

But by the end of January, I felt the end coming. When I said "I love you" at the end of a phone call, Robert said, "good-bye." I knew it was over, though it took me a while to admit it to myself. He came to visit for Valentine's Day and made it official. His final reason for the break-up couldn't have been more clearly stated: "You have too much baggage." How could I argue with that?

All I had left to think about was graduate school, and by that time it was clearer than ever: this was not my calling. But for once I didn't try to be something I wasn't, didn't try to fit in and be like everybody else, didn't even try to excel. I recognized my situation in graduate school for what it was: not a good match. It was a new kind of revelation for me.

But I hung in there. I have never been a quitter. I got a mindless clerical job on campus to get me through the summer, and then the school year started again. By this point I knew I wouldn't continue on for a PhD; I considered the master's program a two-year holding pattern with expensive tickets. But I was already a year into it, so I decided not to throw away the investment I'd already made. I would put my head down and get through.

Starting the semester with my head down, it was easy to notice people's shoes. One pair in the English department grad student lounge jumped out at me: size thirteen fluorescent orange Chuck Taylor high-top sneakers. And when my eye went upwards, up and up and up, I found a nice pair of smiling eyes at the top. How could I not notice?

Soon "the guy with the orange tennis shoes" became "John McMahon," though I wasn't sure I was pronouncing his last name right. I enjoyed chatting with him in the lounge—he was funny, and unlike most of the graduate students in the department, he seemed like a real person.

One day I was in the lounge talking to my friend Nancy about our plans for that evening. We had tickets to a "Thistle and Shamrock" concert on campus, and were deciding where to go for dinner beforehand. John strolled up. "Oh!" I said, a little too obviously, "You're a Mac—I bet you'd like this concert, too. You should get a ticket and go with us!" We pulled out our tickets to show him where we were sitting— he had strict instructions to get a seat next to us. He left, and then came back with a ticket for the seat in the row behind us. Couldn't he even follow directions?

My friend Nancy, hardly a wilting lily herself, was somewhat appalled at my unbridled flirting with John during dinner. But I figured I couldn't blow it any worse than I had in the past—what did I have to lose? By the time Dougie McClean's first song came to a close, it was obvious that no one was coming to sit in the empty seat next to me. I gestured to John, and his long legs easily stepped over the seat to join me. By intermission we were holding hands. The next night he came to my house for dinner, and we sat on the floor of my log cabin and kissed, my calico cat purring on the rug between us.

The next morning, a Saturday, I got up early to study on campus. As I walked I thought, entirely unrealistically, "I should see John now." I knew it made no sense—the huge campus was deserted and nothing about his laid-back style said "early riser." But as I rounded the corner of a building to cross the brick pit near the library, there he came from the opposite direction, up the steps from his dorm. There was not another soul in sight. Every cell in my body screamed, "*This is right!*" I shushed them and smiled.

We never looked back after that, with the exception of one brief moment. It was the moment I started realizing that our relationship was truly something special. I had never been interested in a man who made me feel so good about being me. I wasn't self-conscious. I wasn't over-analyzing our connection. Everything about us felt easy and right. And *that* was frightening. Finally, sitting in my living room one afternoon, I leveled with him.

"John, I really like you."

"And I like you."

"But you need to know—I have a lot of baggage. I had a pretty rotten childhood, my dad's crazy, I'm still really mad at him, and sometimes that comes out in weird ways. If you have a problem with baggage, there's the door. You won't have to explain anything, I won't blame you for leaving, and I promise there will be no hard feelings. But if you do have a problem with baggage, please just leave now before this goes any further."

"Who doesn't have baggage?"

I've loved the man ever since. Six months later he moved in with me, six months after that we got engaged, and six months later my dear sweet mama walked me down the aisle so I could promise to be true "as long as we both shall live" in the sunshine at the Celo Inn. We invited Dad, but as with graduation, his response was that he didn't "believe in the institution of marriage," but wished us all the best. This time it was uncomplicated: I was purely relieved that he didn't come.

A highlight of our wedding was the now-traditional wedding quilt. Wedding quilts in our family are "friendship quilts," with different squares made by different people, then stitched lovingly together into a patchwork tapestry to grace the marriage bed. In our case, the friendship squares lined the edges: appliquéd tadpoles from Mom; embroidered pictures of "Chicken Big and Chicken Little," the names Janet and I called each other; a replica of our sweet log cabin on Purefoy Road; images of the books from our master's theses; a pieced log cabin square that Nancy made, echoing the pattern of my high school graduation quilt; and many others. Truly a gift of love.

Our early years of marriage were stereotypically blissful. We found another, slightly larger log cabin to move into, this one about ten miles out of town on ten acres of land, with a big front porch, dive-bombing hummingbirds, and a pond with ducks on the surface of the water and huge catfish underneath. John planted a garden, and when he came into the house with his first full-sized watermelon cradled in his arms, I did the obvious thing: put a red-haired wig on the melon and took his picture as he held it in the sun. We had close friends through the woods on both sides of us, community woodcutting parties, and hardly anything to complain about. For the first time since I had passed puberty, my love life had nothing to offer as a target for my angst. After a decade of irony, being totally preoccupied with the fervent wish for something that I was one hundred percent convinced that I was neither worthy of nor capable of, I had actually found true love. Two out of three girls from violent homes grow up to partner themselves with abusers, but I had beaten the odds by falling in love with the gentlest man on the planet. I had found my home at last, and it was inside my own skin.

But somehow it wasn't enough to be happy. I found love but didn't feel the credits rolling. The end-of-story music wasn't swelling for me. Did I dare wish for more? I focused my attention on my career.

After finishing my master's degree, I had continued to work at the UNC Center for Gastrointestinal Biology and Disease, where I had started as a secretary the summer before I met John. My supervisor left as I was graduating, so I stepped comfortably into his position, which, as it turned out, offered little more in the way of a challenge than the clerical work I had already been doing. Terry, my departed boss, had made it *look* complicated and important—that was his special gift. When I was sitting behind the desk, the job no longer looked interesting. But I loved my new boss, and the job paid the bills.

To keep my brain cells stimulated, I volunteered as a tutor for the Orange County Literacy Council and started thinking more seriously about a career in nonprofits. Before long, the Executive Director of the Literacy Council resigned. Knowing it was a long shot with my complete lack of nonprofit and leadership experience, I applied for her job. I envisioned many fun possibilities for the Literacy Council. I was hired.

In many ways, though I was seemingly unqualified, my job at the Literacy Council was the perfect position for me. It brought together my love of reading, my early Montessori experiences, my up-to-then undiscovered public speaking skills, and most important, my basic belief in the potential for all people and all organizations, no matter how they might be struggling. I was finally in a position to use my natural leadership skills; I could stretch my arms as far as they would reach. During those years, the Literacy Council and I both began to grow toward the sun.

But somehow being successful in my job wasn't enough, either. Before I met John, I had always imagined myself as a career-obsessed spinster and figured that having a rewarding career would have to be my life. But now that I had love *and* a career that made me feel like I was making a difference in the world, it seemed like I could even imagine having more. Me? A mother? Well, why not? The idea sounded good to John, so we decided to start a family.

This time, though, what I wanted didn't fall into my lap quite as easily as I had come to expect. Getting pregnant wasn't hard—John could practically turn to me with that amorous look in his eye, and the next thing I knew the drugstore stick would come up positive. But holding on to my babies was another thing. We faced the heartbreak of two miscarriages in quick succession, by far the most wrenching experience we had yet shared. I decided that the log cabin was to blame for the miscarriages—we needed to buy a house and move. John didn't object.

We finally found a beautiful salt-box style house with breathtaking views across a lake in Cedar Grove, about twenty-five miles north of Chapel Hill. We knew no one in the neighborhood, but it was gorgeous there, and we felt sure that our friends would flock to visit us. I met someone who told me she'd had a successful pregnancy after six miscarriages thanks to acupuncture, and I decided to see what the needles could do for me. By the time John gave me a canoe for my thirtieth birthday, I was six months pregnant, but I hopped into the boat anyway and paddled off across the lake.

I worked right up to my due date, took a three-month maternity leave, and then was back in the Literacy Council, breast pump in hand. Caleb Henry McMahon, the redheaded wonder who was born on my sister Janet's birthday, stayed with a babysitter while I worked. We got into a routine. John was working at the university by then, and we rode together to our jobs. I sat in the back with Caleb and nursed him in his car seat on the way to town, we went in our separate directions for the day, and then we'd do the reverse as the sun set at the end of the day. It was exhausting, but we made it work.

But then life intervened in the form of sobering news. I wrote about it in my journal on Caleb's first birthday, as John was driving his dad, David, to the airport after a visit at our house: "We've known for about 2½ weeks that David has prostate cancer. We've known for almost one week that it has spread to his bones. We've known for about 4 days that it has spread to lots of his bones. He doesn't really know yet what his outlook is, but it doesn't look good."

The routines of our daily lives took on a different sort of significance. I had less patience for my work. The gravity of our priorities shifted: since moving, we had rarely seen our friends, and it felt important to be close to family. John loved Celo, but I knew I couldn't live there—too many ghosts. I decided to start looking for a job in Asheville, which was close to Celo but not too close, and a real city with plenty of fun things going on. My sister Janet, who lived in Asheville already, was thrilled. Though the job market was tight, I quickly landed a job offer at United Way of Asheville and Buncombe County, the heart of the nonprofit world.

But the transition to Asheville wasn't easy. John still had his job at UNC Chapel Hill, and there was no way we could sell our house by the time I had to start my new job at United Way. Janet graciously offered the extra bedroom at her house: we figured Caleb and I could stay with her while John finished up in Chapel Hill, he could visit us on the weekends, and hopefully our house would sell soon so we could afford to buy something in Asheville. It wasn't ideal, but it was a way to make the transition.

After three months, John moved to Asheville, maintaining his Chapel Hill job by telecommuting. Our house still hadn't sold, but we put all our furniture in a storage unit in Asheville, and he set up a desk so he could work from Janet's living room. All the while, the medical reports from Massachusetts sounded increasingly dire—it didn't look like David would be with us much longer. Grief stricken though he was, John was loving and steady.

Finally, the long winter subsided. The real estate market picked up in the Triangle, and our lakeside house shone in all its glory. The house sold, and we found the perfect place to buy in Asheville. UNC arranged an office for John at the local community college, and life began to feel almost normal. Three months later, on Caleb's second birthday, I found out I was pregnant again.

Still happily married, living in our own house in Asheville, gainfully employed, and managing my now expanding job of motherhood was still not enough for me. My job at United Way was steady, but I wanted to be closer to the front lines of human services work.

In recent months, I had gotten to know Holly Jones, the energetic, upbeat Executive Director of the YWCA. I felt like the mission of the YWCA—*to empower women and eliminate racism*—dovetailed with my DNA, speaking to my family history in interesting and ironic ways. At the same time I'd been watching the Chief Operations Officer of United Way and thinking that such a second-in-command position might be the right place for me, since my heart was more in management than fundraising and marketing, the primary responsibilities of the top dog.

Holly, nearly overwhelmed with her job at the helm of the foundering YWCA, was about to take on a major capital campaign; I'd been telling her for a while that she needed someone to be her first mate.

She finally convinced her Board of Directors, and they agreed to let her hire more help. She called to let me know the opening was listed in the newspaper.

Though invited to apply, I was hardly a shoo-in for the job. Fifty-five people applied, including one YWCA board member and several who had more local experience than I did. It was a rigorous application process. I had to create sample meeting agendas, a facilities assessment plan, and a comprehensive outcomes measurement plan for the after-school program, a key YWCA feature. I could plan agendas, and I had learned a lot about outcomes in my job at United Way. But I had no experience with facilities management or any of the wide spectrum of programs the YWCA offered. Still, I wanted the job. Why should I let a little inexperience stop me? And it didn't. Holly called me as I was getting ready for bed one night, and I gladly accepted her offer. In January 1999, I started my new job.

As is often the case with such things, the YW (as it was called, to distinguish it from the YMCA, which always seemed to trump us) was in far worse shape than I imagined. I knew money was tight, the facility was old and overstressed, and programs were struggling to stay afloat. What surprised me was the dismal employee morale. Holly, in spite of the upbeat face she showed the world, was utterly threadbare after three years of working desperately to keep the YWCA's doors open to its members. The staff turnover rate was astronomical. My role was to turn that around, supervise all program staff, and keep the roof over our heads from leaking and the walls from caving in while Holly mobilized volunteers to raise enough money to completely refurbish the building.

Amid staggering daily drama, Holly operated in crisis mode, critical program staff members quit constantly, and I was expected to replace and train employees. Until I found new workers, I had to do the jobs. Certain directors didn't get along with each other and maintained an undercurrent of tension. State licensing inspectors threatened to close our day care center. One day a swim lesson instructor came to work obviously drunk. Impoverished parents screamed at us when we confronted them about long-overdue tuition fees, and then slapped their children as they walked out the front doors. And when the situation looked most dire, Holly's "hair would catch on fire," as she described it. We all tiptoed around her, hoping to prevent the explosion. Echoes of my past.

It was my job to maintain peace, get out the bandages, soothe the injured spirits, and keep the programs going. I was pregnant, with a toddler at home and a husband grieving his faraway dying father. Holly, who was nearing forty and painfully lacking a significant other herself, had no patience for my family needs. In May of that year, Katie was born. I felt terribly guilty about staying home for two months of maternity leave, and came back to put her in the YW's beleaguered day care down the hall from my office. Now, on top of everything else, I nursed off and on all day and could hear Katie when she cried.

Four months later, on All Saints' Day 1999, after an incredibly difficult two years of fighting cancer throughout his body, David McMahon finally succumbed. John's mom had died before I met him; now all he had left were his two younger brothers. After all I'd been through in my life, nothing had approached the pain of seeing my gentle John go through so much grief. It was devastating for both of us.

At work, the only successful aspect of the YWCA was the capital campaign. Holly and the campaign committee met their fundraising goal, and by 2001, we were ready to break ground for the new addition and start the phased renovation. I took on the additional responsibilities of managing the three-million-dollar construction process, which literally happened under our noses. Finally hope was in the air, but the short run would be tough. Describing a typical day, I wrote in my journal,

> Here's the current situation at the YWCA: construction all around us. Things not working that are supposed to be working because a wire's been cut, a hair dryer was removed prematurely, etc. Extra high level of [state day care licensing] vigilance because of construction. No footprints allowed in the lobby—we have constant footprints in the lobby. Everybody crammed into offices together, and some working off-site because there's no room for them at the YW. Boxes of paper in what little hallway is left, waiting for me to sort through them and catalog

their contents. Stressed-out receptionists because it's swim sign-up week, the phone is ringing off the hook, and parents are ticked off because the pool viewing area is closed. On and on and on.

Then, when I'm home, Caleb and Katie are needling each other and squabbling constantly. John goes to Romania in 2½ weeks, and I haven't made any back-up plans to help me get through. Caleb's birthday party is this weekend. Gerry [John's brother] and Melissa arrive Friday night.

And I ask myself why I'm not able to relax and enjoy myself?

In June of that year, with no warning whatsoever, Janet forwarded an email to Nancy, Linda, and me. She had received a message from our half-brother, Josh.

Dear Janet,

It is a bit hard to figure an appropriate way to start this letter, but I suppose I'll just jump right in and hope that all that I say falls in the right places. Al Henry is my biological father, which makes you my biological half sister. The term biological feels a bit impersonal, but since we've never met and share no history, I think that the term is appropriate until we find some common stories between us.

I'm looking forward to having a relationship with you and yours, and having sisters to call my own. I have three brothers, all with red hair, so you can imagine the fascination for me of what a difference it will make to have older sisters in my life.

As for Al, I am still unsure of what place he will hold in my life. I enjoy knowing him and am open to wherever our relationship may lead, but his role as a father in my life is hard for me to justify. I have been angry, sad, and confused with him and the situation involving my conception and birth for many years, and am only now coming to terms and working through these complex emotions and thought patterns. I have a whole life, including a wonderful man that I call Dad here at home, and the notion of where to put Al in that picture is hard for me. But I see him when I am around, and try to keep in touch when I can— and that is enough for me right now—a big step from not even being sure I even wanted to ever know him.

I have many more feelings about Al, and feel that I will have a much better picture of him after meeting you and your sisters and hearing about the parts of his life that he hasn't mentioned yet.

216

The whole situation has been difficult for me from the day it was revealed to me 12 years ago, a reality that any 8 year old boy would find confusing. But I feel that the saving grace of all of this will be the healing of all involved and the relationships that will develop. I have heard many wonderful things about you and I have a feeling that we will have a strong connection....

I have lots of questions about your life, and much to tell you about my own, but I imagine that there will be more time for that soon enough. I will be in your neck of the woods this summer and I am hoping that we can arrange to meet and spend some time together....

Your brother,

Joshua Paul Henry Cutler (but you can call me Josh)

We were all shocked. Our brother Josh, whom we had imagined for years but had never thought we'd actually meet, had decided he was ready to join our family and invited us to come meet him at ARE Camp. Whatever that might mean. Strange though it was, I felt ready to welcome him.

Janet and I drove to the camp, a familiar trip from our distant past, on Saturday, August 18, 2001. We had no idea what to expect. As we pulled into Rural Retreat, Virginia, we agreed we should stop. Get gas. Buy a snack. Catch our breath. But then we could put it off no longer. We drove the familiar miles into the crossroads of Cedar Springs, and then turned down the gravel road into Mountain Valley farm. Neither of us had been there for twenty years. It looked very much the same. I forced myself to breathe, carefully in and out, as we drove down the narrow road between the trees. I tried to figure out where we had camped by the little creek, where the cows had trampled our cooking pots and we had held each other close in the rhododendron thicket, as Mom and Dad screamed at each other by the campfire. I couldn't find it.

Finally we stopped in the gravel parking lot next to the director's cabin. As we got out of the car, a man came toward us and we recognized Philip Morgan, an old friend from our camp days, who happened to also be Josh's uncle, his mother's stepbrother. Putting an arm around each of us, he led us toward the camp kitchen. It was a long few steps.

I was the first through the screen door, and my eyes had to adjust as I stepped out of the sunshine. But there he was, a tall, beautiful young man standing next to the big stove, smiling at me. Our eyes met, and I saw a face astonishingly similar to my own—the red hair, the square jaw, the twinkly eyes. Younger, yes, and decidedly male. But of all Dad's offspring, clearly Josh and I looked the most like him. It was a moment in time I'll never forget. I loved him instantly.

We took Josh back to Asheville with us the next day, and I spent as much time with him as I could manage. One evening he came over for dinner, and I dug out old pictures of Dad from when he was Josh's age. Josh had never imagined Dad as anything other than an old bearded man who didn't bathe often enough, and he was astounded by the handsome man in the photos. My sisters and I all noted the carbon-copy resemblance between Josh and our father at age twenty. Josh took the picture into the bathroom and stood staring at the two of them, side by side, in the mirror. If he had ever wanted to doubt the truth about his origins, there was no question now.

~ ~ ~ ~ ~ ~

On this journey of writing my memoir, I have reached out to many of my parents' old friends who have, almost without exception, welcomed me with open arms. Nearly all of them have warmly embraced my life-changing project.

The only exception was another Janet, a friend of Mom's from our Atlanta days. Since she lives across the country, I sent her an email. Janet's reply to my initial email was the usual warm response I had come to expect, full of light and love for Mom. She was sympathetic about Mom's dementia, having been through a similar experience with her own mother. She recounted fond memories, including one about a musical recorder group my mother attended. She'd brought me along, and Janet said the group marveled at my good behavior and Mom's gentle care of me. To Janet, our interactions "showed that Carol was so good at inspiring little children to be their best. She and you had such a good rapport. You trusted her, and cooperated with her softly spoken suggestions, which were thought-out and appropriate for you." My response to Janet's kind email, only the second time she had heard from me, was probably insensitive. Eager to find out more about how others viewed my parents' relationship, I went too far too quickly.

> Through the years, you seemed to have a sense that things were difficult for Mom and Dad. Did she ever mention the extent of it, or talk about his violence? Were you ever aware of bruises or scars? Did she ever talk about the fear? It's interesting to me that she had several very close women friends during that time, people that she apparently confided in, but nobody who I've spoken to so far had much sense of just how controlling and violent Dad became. Did you know?

Janet's response was unequivocal. Not only was she completely unaware of the violence, but she wondered if I had imagined it. And she cautioned me to tread lightly if my parents' relationship was a violent one, reminding me that "Carol wanted to preserve her dignity, and also Al's." I was dumbfounded. Without exception, my parents' friends had been shocked and saddened to learn of the hidden violence in our family. But this was the first time I had faced blatant disbelief along with the implication that, by writing my story, I was somehow destroying Mom's dignity!

Janet's words forced me to face the question head-on: is this journey ultimately a betrayal of the person I have held most dear my entire life?

I knew I could never write this book if Mom were herself—she wouldn't like our secrets to be told, and I wouldn't want to upset her to that degree. But she's beyond that now. She no longer remembers who Dad was, what happened, or what her motives might have been for hiding the truth. I love her and have always loved her, and I think our story needs to be told.

After our difficult email conversation, Janet sent a package that brought healing. Long ago, she wrote, when she was first friends with Mom and our family lived at Cabbagetown, she bought a quilt from the trunk of Mom's old car. Mom was making quilts with the women from Cabbagetown and selling them to support the community. Janet kept the quilt through the years, wrapping her sons in it, infusing it with their family's love. Her boys grown and gone, she felt ready to pass it on. So she boxed up the quilt and mailed it across the country to me. I opened the box and saw my mother inside. I buried my face in the folds of yellow and blue, and wept. The pattern was pinwheel, my mama's favorite.

All quilts, however artfully constructed, start with a pile of scraps. Some of them are rags, some are cherished remnants. They contain bits of memories: an old blouse, a dancing skirt, the backing from another quilt. From time immemorial, women have taken what we have to work with, meager though it may be, and created works of warmth, comfort, and beauty. It's what we do. We take what we have on hand, what we're given, what we've managed to scrape together, and do the best we can with it. We pray for strength and forgiveness, feel gratitude for insight when it comes, and snuggle down with those we love. I've done it, and so did my mama.

We all do the best we can.

And ultimately, the result is beautiful.

10

Flight

We all know where we were when it happened. I was at the YWCA, where I spent most of my waking hours. It was just a few weeks after we met Josh for the first time, and the YWCA was full steam ahead with the renovation.

We were working in a construction zone—staff squeezed into smaller and smaller areas, sharing tiny offices, breathing fumes, climbing over each other to get to our daily work, which we somehow did through the din of power tools. It was my job to manage it all: make sure the members knew where to go as traffic patterns continually shifted in the building; keep the after-school kids safe (our day care had closed for the construction); apprise the remaining staff of what was happening and try to respond to their complaints; and put the fifty-gallon trash can under the roof leak when the water came pouring in.

On that day, though, the main thing on my mind was the looming progress report deadline for a multi-year grant that was helping us stay afloat. First, as always, I checked in with Mark, the balding, barrel-shaped construction supervisor out in the job trailer, my new favorite place to be. In the trailer I could let it all hang out, let the cuss words fly, and for a few golden moments not worry about whose feelings might get hurt.

But I had to get back inside. As I walked through the front doors, Hazel, the grandmotherly receptionist on the morning shift, stopped me, wide-eyed.

"Cindy, a plane just flew into one of the Twin Towers in New York!"

Barely breaking my stride, I remarked, "What a terrible accident!"

I had a report to write.

Fifteen minutes later, Hazel buzzed me on my telephone intercom. "Cindy, it wasn't an accident. The other tower has been hit."

I reacted as I'm sure many others did. I didn't want to believe it. It was too scary, too out of control. I tried to stay focused on my paperwork, but then came word of other crashes: the Pentagon with a flaming gash in its side, and in Pennsylvania, a downed plane that officials believed was headed for the White House. The day was a blur of smoke, death, and disbelief.

As always, I soon turned to my journal to sort out my thoughts:

> This has been an unsettling time, to say the least. Planes flying into buildings, fire, death, grief, fear. What will they do next—what will we do next? Why did this happen? How can anyone have that much hatred?
>
> War seems inevitable and it feels so wrong. It feels like vengeance and proving we're not wimps—schoolyard level responses to bullying. But with no teacher or principal to step in and tell everybody why we don't allow fighting in school. I wouldn't mind a little justice for the people who did these horrific things—but I don't want vengeance.
>
> Today after work we go to Mom's for the weekend. I am looking forward to spending a few days in the bosom of that valley.

Sometimes nothing but the green of Celo could soothe my soul. And full-fledged grownup though I might be, there were still times when I needed my mama's arms to hold me close.

A year later, we came to the end of the YWCA construction chaos. With renovations of old buildings, you never know what you'll find, and we had our share of snafus and challenges. But we negotiated our way through the maze of sanitation inspectors, fire marshals, and child-care licensing specialists, and finally got our permanent Certificate of Occupancy. It was time to celebrate. My journal had a different ring the morning of our big Grand Opening:

> I am proud of my part in this undertaking. I have asked questions, I have understood. I have projected the impact of construction on the programs, and participated in decisions to allow them to keep running or to close them (in the case of the day care) for the safety of the children. I

have learned tremendous amounts of child care licensing, fire regulations, building codes, HVAC systems, plumbing, on and on. I have asked questions. I have understood. I have put pressure on when it was required, and let it off when things didn't matter. I have built good relationships with the architect, engineers, contractors, and subs. I have asked questions. I have understood.

In the midst of all of it, I have strived for balance. I have nurtured my marriage and spent quality time with my children. I have found ways to keep myself healthy—working out, going to acupuncture, writing in my journal, confiding in friends and sisters, taking time off when I could.

And now here I am. The building is built. It shines. And so can I. It's time to celebrate....

I came home at the end of 11 hours of prepping the YW totally fried. I had just yelled at the supervisor of the night cleaning crew and I was furious. John handed me a glass of wine, a plate of dinner, and a sympathetic ear (not on the plate). After dinner, the kids and I went out on the porch, and John soon joined us. Candles and crickets. We sang— all of us together, two of us, one of us at a time. Caleb fell asleep on my lap. A golden shining moment.

The Grand Opening was all that we hoped it would be: sunshine, music, speeches, food, and a long chain of loving YWCA supporters, connected by the multi-colored, multi-knotted threads of our ribbon-tying ceremony. Other organizations mark new buildings and new beginnings with big scissors; ours was a day of unity.

Six days later, the United States Congress gave President Bush the authority to attack Iraq if Saddam Hussein refused to give up weapons of mass destruction. In the wider world, the era of vengeance continued.

And though it seemed in October that the dark days of the YWCA were behind us and we faced a brighter future, by December I was having bad dreams about work and waking up with stomachaches on a regular basis. Christmas morning I woke up in pain after dreaming that I had given my resignation notice, the scariest dream of all. I could sense that staff morale was bottoming out again, and I felt helpless. Despite the YW's facelift, the financial situation was still dire.

At a board/staff strategic planning retreat in January 2002, I burst into tears in front of the whole group, convinced that there was no way I could be successful in my job. It was too much, too hard. On the way home from an out-of-town meeting of another board that I served on, a close friend listened to my woes and asked me point blank: "Cindy, where are you heading?" The question echoed through my body. I had no answer.

Towards the end of January, Holly left the YWCA in my hands for six weeks so that she could start her own family: she was going to Guatemala to adopt a daughter. Though Holly's absence put me in the seat of responsibility with even more worries on my tired shoulders, we soon got good news. We learned that both our day care and afterschool programs had received three-star child-care licenses. It had been a long, uphill battle to prod the program directors to apply for the licenses, but we met our goal of reaching the three-star level. Our program income would increase as a result. It was a taste of success I desperately needed.

Meanwhile, the bottom was falling out in my personal life.

Dad was still living in Virginia Beach. We knew he wasn't doing well, but I never thought about what would happen when he could no longer take care of himself. He had lived on the outskirts of society all these years—some part of me figured that when he neared the end, he'd simply follow the paths of the wild animals he so admired and wander off into the woods to die alone.

No.

His tent was in a friend's backyard, a man named Bruce whom we'd known since I was a child. Janet had visited Dad occasionally over the years, so Bruce called her to say he was worried about Dad: his memory was fading, and Bruce couldn't be responsible for him. Janet met Linda in Virginia Beach, and they decided that the only solution was for Janet to bring Dad back to Asheville. This time he would stay.

My first thought was, "This can't be happening." Asheville was my home. Dad lived in Virginia Beach. The two places were far apart. By design.

My second thought was born of panic: "John's still employed by UNC-Chapel Hill, so we could live there. I'll quit my job. We'll move back."

Thought number three brought me back to earth. "This extreme flight reaction could be a red flag. Maybe it's time to find a therapist."

Janet had to deal with the issue in a more concrete way. Until we made other arrangements, Dad would stay at her house. Her first line of attack was simply the smell: she made him take off his many layers of clothes so she would wash them, probably for the first time in years. As she pulled the clothes apart and emptied the pockets, she laid aside little stashes of money and notes. When she finally got it all organized, she was astounded. Dad had been carrying, on his person, more than ten thousand dollars. His response made strange sense when she talked to him about the danger of carrying that much cash: "I look like a homeless person. Who would think I had any money?"

About that time, Mom suffered her first mini-stroke. She woke up one morning disoriented and frustrated by the fact that she had no associations with the names of people written on her calendar for the upcoming week. She called Nancy, who agreed that it sounded odd, but the disorientation passed, and Mom quickly remembered her friends. The incident seemed relatively unimportant at the time.

At the beginning of March, Holly returned from Guatemala, and I gladly handed back the YW reins with a sigh of relief.

Internationally, the US invaded Iraq just two weeks later, hell-bent on toppling Saddam Hussein and his regime, operating on the basis of what turned out to be "false intelligence" and gross misrepresentations. Vengeance, misguided though it may have been, mattered most.

For me, that spring and summer were just about getting by.

At work, the recovering alcoholic housekeeper (whom I had nurtured and believed in throughout her recovery) was within days of passing her final GED test when she ran off with her landlady's car and got arrested for drugs. I had to let her go, and I scrambled to find ways to keep the building clean without her, my heart breaking with disappointment.

The director of our state-funded program for displaced homemakers quit with no notice when I finally put her on probation for not doing her job. It was left to me to piece the program back together, on top of my other responsibilities, as I desperately searched for someone to fill the position. I found myself facilitating support groups and struggling to compile long-overdue statistical reports based on incomplete records.

A teacher in the day care infant room alleged that another teacher had hit a child on the back of the head for biting—not just once, but three times. When confronted directly, the accused's only response was that she "couldn't remember" if she had done it or not.

Roughhousing among kids in summer camp turned into an all-out fight, and angry parents called the Department of Social Services to report it. The allegation of neglect was substantiated, a crucial blow to our school-age program's shiny new three-star license.

Money continued to be incredibly tight—every month was a nail-biter. Would we make payroll?

And on and on and on.

Personally, life was no less complicated or intense.

After three weeks at Janet's house, Dad had moved downtown to a low-income apartment building for the elderly. His building, the former elegant Battery Park Hotel, presided over the city—I could see it from almost anywhere I went, including the second-story windows of the YWCA. I began to avoid going downtown for lunch or shopping, fearing I might run into him when I least expected it.

It was excruciating for me to visit him, and yet I wrestled with my sense of obligation.

Monday 3/31/03

I've been grappling with what is my "duty" toward my dad—how much do I "owe" him—how much should I be doing to help? Cleaning, stocking his refrigerator, visiting, etc. I've been feeling increasingly resentful—he didn't live up to any of his fatherly responsibilities, so why should I do my daughterly ones? I've also been feeling like I'm being selfish and petty—a tit for a tat—I should be turning the other cheek. But there's something else inside me that says NO. Mom turned the other cheek for twenty years. It wasn't right. Forgiving and forgetting feels like condoning. Yes, he was mentally ill—but does that absolve him? He could have gotten help, medication, whatever. But instead he put his own ego, fears, whatever, first. He came first, and we suffered.

I don't want to condone what he did. But how can I heal my own wounds?

I tried to think of him as "Granddaddy Al," the name my children called him, as a way to bring our relationship into the present and distance myself from the old, haunting feelings. After all, he was completely different now. Stuck in the repeating loops of his foggy mind, he somehow seemed saner than ever before. He even said to me, "I used to be so into studying all that complicated stuff all the time—now I can't even remember why it mattered that much." With the help of my therapist, I imagined myself as an adult, stepping in to break up those long-ago fights, setting limits, telling him, "STOP. This is not okay. You need to get yourself together and leave here. You cannot come back until you are calm. And I will still be here." Now that he was frail, I figured I could take him in a fight if I had to.

Beyond the anger, hurt, and rigidity, I finally reached overwhelming, huge tidal waves of sadness. "This is a journey," I wrote. "I wish I knew where it was going. I don't feel like I packed the right stuff. I feel helpless and adrift. I want to drive it, make it better, get it over with. I want to understand. And I don't."

That April, John and I took a ten-day trip to Ireland, just the two of us. We had never done anything like that before, and it was exactly what I needed. A flight to the other side of the world. Cozy bed and breakfasts. Dark, foamy stout. Beautiful vistas.

And yet even the preparations for that romantic getaway felt stressful, adding to my already teetering cairn of worries. Finally I reminded myself that "traveling is about going with the flow, enjoying it, soaking it up. It absolutely is not going to go the way I think it is down to every little detail. And if I wig out about it every time, I will not enjoy myself—it'll be a wasted trip." I got the message as it related to our trip to Ireland, and we had a fabulous time. But somehow the life message didn't sink in.

By May, my angry feelings towards Dad were beginning to overwhelm me. After taking the kids to visit him one day after work, I came home and told John, "I hate him. It feels like a festering, cankerous, dark place inside me, and I don't like it, but I don't know what to do. I don't want to be the kind of person who has feelings like that for anybody. I want to be a loving person." I knew my feelings were rooted in the past, not the present—Dad was now a gentle, harmless old man. But I couldn't seem to change the way I felt.

John responded with the story of Buddha, who said that anger is a hot coal we hold tightly; it burns nobody but ourselves. I didn't know how to put down the ember, or even open my clenched hand. It seared my skin.

At the end of May, my sister Linda traveled south again to face the Herculean task of emptying Dad's disintegrating tent in Virginia Beach and transporting the contents to Asheville. She arrived in time for my birthday weekend, logically expecting me to help sort through it all with Dad, so that he could decide what was worth keeping. At that stage, though, he wasn't mentally capable of making such decisions, and I wasn't emotionally capable of helping. I blew up at Linda, and finally realized why birthdays had always felt so sacred to me: I wasn't allowed to have birthday celebrations growing up, and if we managed to celebrate one, it was full of secrecy and guilt. Never being allowed to celebrate my life was a heavy restriction for a girl whose conception was a mistake in the first place.

I had also decided that this was a good time for surgery. John and I had long since decided that two kids were enough. I had hoped that John would have a vasectomy so we could avoid birth control, but I finally realized that he wouldn't do it. If I needed for one of us to have the surgery, it would have to be me.

Both physically and emotionally, ending my child-bearing years was a much bigger deal than I expected. I cried and felt the physical pain deeply. But eventually I recognized that we were only changing one small letter—going from the child-*bearing* years to the child-*rearing* years. I was still young. There was much fun to be had. Maybe even more, I realized, now that our lovemaking could be more carefree. The incision gradually healed, and I got through it.

Getting through it—it was all I could do with everything in my life. But by the end of the summer, "getting by" had settled into a serious case of the blahs. The kids went back to school, and the relentless intensity of summer began to ease into fall. Suddenly, my friend's question from the beginning of the year came ricocheting back. "Cindy, where are you headed?" I wanted to feel inspired, to wake up feeling excited about each day, but instead I simply felt empty.

Remembering my most reliable personal resource, I turned my infallible logic towards the problem. What was the real issue? How could I break it down? How could I fix it? I quickly landed on three possible solutions:

1. plod along at work, and focus my energy on the margins of my days;
2. make a big change, leave the YW, do something totally different; or
3. get re-inspired about the YW, make it more fulfilling, work towards excellence.

I quickly and easily dismissed number two, feeling like I was far too attached to the YWCA. Caleb was in the after-school program. John exercised there daily. Most of all, I couldn't fathom the thought of not belonging there, not having my own place, not having a say about what happened. I couldn't face the idea of giving up my master key to the building. So I decided on a combination of numbers one and three: I'd start new projects at home and begin thinking about the future, while doing what I could to make the YW more fun and interesting.

A few weeks later, I got the opportunity to attend a national YWCA conference with a board member and my coworker friend Mary Beth. The conference was held, of all places, in a hotel at Virginia Beach. Since Dad no longer lived there, I had no hesitations about going. Mary Beth found us a cheap flight, and we took off.

When we got there, though, I found that the ghosts of my old feelings still congregated in Virginia Beach. We passed several of Dad's former haunts on the way, including the ARE Library (Edgar Cayce's Association for Research and Enlightenment, where Dad spent most of his waking hours). Each place made me catch my breath. The full moon on the beach that first night, with Dad's astrological constellations all around it, was more than I could face. I hurried back inside the sterile hotel, where all the ghosts had been scrubbed away.

The conference workshops left me cold—I had come with budding enthusiasm for the possibilities we could achieve if we set our minds on excellence, and was met with others' bitterness and doubt. So I went to the beach.

I set out with my journal on September 11, two years after the planes had crashed into the Twin Towers, planning to have my own workshop, set my own course for YWCA excellence, find professional inspiration. Instead, the professional and personal collided in the air above me, and I found I couldn't write. So I walked the beach for hours instead.

As I walked along my father's beach, a decision began to take shape. It was born in the soles of my feet, where they touched the sand and water. Then it gradually made its way up my body, along the muscles of my calves, across the hollows behind my knees, up towards the core of my being. It wound its way gradually through my intestines as I walked, inching its way toward my chest and heart, where it stopped. As I finally walked back toward the hotel, I breathed more deeply, the breaths reaching down past my chest, filling me up. But I didn't yet know why. Instead, I felt the breeze on my skin, drank in the salty ocean smells, and listened to the calls of the sea birds winging back and forth over my head. Part of me was in the air with them, looking down on the stretch of sand below. From that perspective, all my worries and grief blended with the grains of sand.

It wasn't until I was back home nearly a week later that I realized the decision had been made. I woke up in the silvery early morning light, my stomach unusually relaxed and unclenched before a day of work.

After I rehashed my most recent disappointments—the failure of our DSS appeal and the subsequent threat of losing our three-star license for the after-school program—the decision I had already made stepped forward and revealed itself. This time, I was able to write.

> What if I say to myself that I won't be there for another summer camp? I will use this year to do the customer service thing, get after-school back on its feet, make everybody not so dependent on me, and scope out other potential jobs. I'll take next summer off. And then get another job.
>
> Whoa. How does that feel? Could we do it financially? How would it be to sever those ties? I would miss the camaraderie, the feeling that I "belong" there, and at least the feeling (if not the reality) of having some control over what happens. But it does feel like it's time for me to move on. And I do want the place to be in good shape for a smooth transition.
>
> But oh, the idea of a summer off! I could really connect with the kids, spend time with Mom, get projects done, feel light. It's what I need.

By the time I dropped Caleb at school and was on the road to work, the excitement was overwhelming. I knew I would do it. The only question was *how*.

It wasn't a smooth process—I had some underlying grief about the idea of saying good-bye. One morning soon after my realization, I woke up with a dream still fresh in my head. I had dreamed that John and I had decided to date other people and stay married. In the dream, I had mixed feelings. On the one hand, dating was fun and exciting—new, challenging, self-affirming. But on the other hand, I could feel my heart breaking that our strong bond had dissolved. Fortunately, in my waking life I knew that my marriage was rock solid, and I curled myself around John in bed that morning to reassure myself. But my other primary relationship, one that had consumed most of my waking hours for the last five years, was coming to an end. The day began with deep sadness.

I told only a couple of my closest friends about my decision, focusing my attention on developing a new customer service program for the YW, an initiative born out of our strategic planning process at the beginning of the year. It was a great opportunity for me to funnel vitality into the organization before I left, and I channeled my best energy into developing the project. It was my going-away present. The planning was well underway by the end of December when I finally told Holly that I would leave at the end of the school year. Our meeting ended with a hug, and I announced my decision to the rest of the staff that afternoon.

The fall had been difficult for my family. I continued to struggle with old feelings of anger and fear towards Dad. My sisters didn't understand, and I felt them pushing me towards him, trying to get me to spend more time with him. They couldn't comprehend the trauma I was somehow re-experiencing, and their gentle nudging felt to me as if they were holding my hand in the old fire. My reaction to them, too, seemed lodged in the past—not only had they never rescued me, as I had often fantasized they would as a child, but now they were pushing me back towards what felt like danger.

Janet hosted a birthday party for Dad, with the strong expectation that I would come. It was all I could do to get myself there, and every minute was agony. I was burning from the inside out. I couldn't get away fast enough and was breathing hard when I left.

Church provided a balm during that time, a new community that welcomed us with open arms and drew us close. I finally realized that, like chocolate, grandparents, and sugar, church was another of life's delights that Dad had angrily denied us throughout my childhood. Finally, I allowed myself to savor its sweetness. I often felt tears slide down my cheeks during Sunday worship.

And then Dad got sick.

It seemed like a stomach bug at first. He complained of nausea, and Janet noticed that he wasn't eating the food she left in his fridge. There were signs of diarrhea when she took his laundry home to wash. We tried to get him to eat, to drink. He wouldn't.

After a week or so, Janet suggested that she take him to see a doctor. Not surprisingly, he refused. He had long since sworn off the medical system and hadn't seen a doctor in decades. He wasn't about to start now.

We made sure that one of us visited every day, and Janet, Nancy, and I communicated after each visit. We left out a plate of saltines where he could easily get to them, and kept close track of the number of crackers that disappeared. "How many were there for your visit? Were there any signs of him drinking juice, or even water?"

He was taking nothing in. He got progressively thinner and weaker. He stopped getting out of bed.

As this went on, with Dad still refusing to see a doctor, we wondered what we were supposed to do. None of us wanted to force him to get medical treatment against his will, but it was obvious that he wasn't getting better. Was it neglectful of us to let him waste away? All my angst about the past now seemed utterly irrelevant—the crisis was in the present. And none of us knew what to do.

Finally Matt, Janet's levelheaded boyfriend, talked to his neighbor, a social worker with Adult Protective Services at the county Department of Social Services. She recommended that we call DSS—perhaps they could help assess the situation.

A social worker came out with a nurse. True to his lifelong pattern, when outsiders walked in, Dad rose to the occasion, this time literally. He was dressed and out of bed during their visit, raising his cognitive and social performance several notches. Though the nurse found that he was severely dehydrated, he convinced her that he was still able to make self-care decisions. He was not incompetent, the social worker declared, and she advised that we let him continue to decide his treatment or the lack thereof. We were frustrated.

Not long after, it was my turn to visit Dad, and I couldn't face seeing him. Work was consuming, I had back-to-back meetings all day, and I simply couldn't bring myself to ride the elevator up to his apartment, not knowing what I'd find when I got there. John, my knight in shining armor, agreed to go for me.

When John arrived at Dad's apartment that day, he knocked on the locked door. "Al? It's John, coming to visit. Could you let me in?" He could faintly hear Dad's genteel southern voice responding through the door. "Nope, I'm sorry I can't do that. Now's not a good time—you'd better come back later." His voice sounded strangely close to the door, and yet far away. Something didn't feel right. John knocked again, but Dad wouldn't come. John went downstairs to find the building manager.

When the manager came back and unlocked the door, John knew he had done the right thing. Dad was lying on his stomach on the floor in the doorway to the small living room, mostly naked. The smell of diarrhea hung in the air. John thanked the building manager, who gratefully turned to go, and John got a sheet to cover Dad.

"Al," he said, "can you get up?"

"No, I'm just fine right here, thanks."

"Well, it seems like maybe you need to see a doctor."

"Oh, no, I don't think so. Don't you worry about me. I don't need to see a doctor."

At a loss, John went in the other room to call members of the family. Matt was the only one he could reach, and he suggested that maybe it was time to call DSS again. John remembers that as he walked back into the room where Dad still lay on the floor, Dad's southern manners were strangely intact as he said, "Why, you have such a light tread! I didn't even hear you come back into the room."

Matt and the social worker arrived quickly after John's calls. The social worker leaned down to Dad and said, "Mr. Henry? Can you get up?" Again he replied, "Oh, no, I'm fine here, thanks." Echoing John, she said, "Well, it looks to me like you need to see a doctor."

After steadfastly refusing any kind of help for weeks, Dad finally made an abrupt about-face. "Well, ma'am, if you think so, I reckon you're probably right."

John recalls his own uncharacteristic urge to give Dad a swift kick in his naked rump.

They called an ambulance, and Dad willingly went to the hospital. Matt had been able to reach Janet by this time, too, and she rode along.

Dad was in the hospital for a week. The initial diagnosis was severe dehydration and malnutrition, and they immediately put him on intravenous fluids and a feeding tube. Nothing changed. Tubes, wires, bright lights, machines everywhere—the scene was chaotic and alien, with my bearded, frail father in the middle of the confusion. Though he couldn't speak, this was clearly not the place he wanted to be.

Linda flew down from Massachusetts when she got the news. Nancy and Mom drove in from Celo. For a short time, we all crowded together, the six of us in the small hospital room. Mom was beginning to show more signs of her own fogginess, and she looked old and small as she held Dad's hand one last time in the high-tech hospital room. I couldn't hold back my tears.

Finally the doctor met with us, explaining that Dad's lack of response to the feeding tube indicated that something much more serious was going on, probably an aggressive cancer. It was too late to treat it. The doctor recommended that we stop all interventions and shift to palliative care—he was dying. We were all relieved that he could finally be disconnected from the torturous tubes and wires. And we were even more grateful when we learned of an available bed at the local hospice facility. Dad could leave the hospital and go to a place of peace and comfort. And we could go with him.

At first, with Dad in the hospital, I felt the pull of my work responsibilities. I had meetings, appointments, deadlines. I went back and forth—sitting with Dad but feeling like I should be at work, and then back at work, wondering what I was doing there. Finally, when he got to hospice, I let it go. Dad was dying. The YWCA could survive without me for a little while.

After a year of not wanting to visit Dad, I was surprised to find that I wanted to be with him at hospice. I had no specific needs—I didn't need to take care of him, didn't want him to hurry up and die, and didn't particularly feel like I wanted to be there when he passed. But somehow I knew I needed to be there for the process, so I stayed.

We lucked into a suite of sorts at hospice; Dad had one of the only rooms with a sitting room attached, furnished with a couch and chair where the family could be while Dad breathed laboriously with his oxygen machine just through the open door. It was March and springtime was on its way—birds chattered cheerfully outside the partially open window, and I brought a vase of sunny yellow daffodils to grace the sill of the sitting room. I found a jigsaw puzzle in one of the lounges and spread it out on the low coffee table. The intuitive, tactile, mindless activity of the puzzle—slow piece by slow piece, colors and textures gradually coalescing—soothed my soul. My sisters came and went. We sang songs now and then. The hospice staff quietly and lovingly took care of all of us. Peace prevailed. Dad rebounded a little, responding to the comfort of his new surroundings.

On our second day at hospice, I realized that something had shifted. Dad was comfortable but no longer able to speak, still breathing slowly and regularly. He was able to respond to us, but only with his eyebrows. When he liked something—a song, a touch, or the sound of our voices—his eyebrows went up. When he was uncomfortable or didn't like something, they would drop severely.

I felt a light bulb go off above me, cartoon-style. "This is my day! I can say whatever I want to him, knowing that he will hear it, but there's nothing he can do. He can't yell at me, or disagree, or make me feel bad, or even walk away. He is a completely captive audience. This is my chance!"

So I took it. For the first time in my life, I had the courage to say what had never been acknowledged between us before. I sat in the chair beside his bed, looked in his face, and said, "Dad, because of you, I had a really scary childhood." The eyebrows went down—I knew he heard me. "It wasn't a good way to grow up, never being sure when you were going to yell, or throw things, or hit Mom, or try to choke her. But you know what, Dad? I'm working on letting it go."

I took a break then, returning to my puzzle in the sunny sitting room, until another thought came, and I went back to his bedside. "Oh, and Dad, there's something else." Eyebrows back down. "I felt abandoned when you left. You'd be gone for months, and I missed you so much. Sometimes we didn't even know where you were. I loved you, and didn't even know if you loved me or not."

But then a thought occurred to me, an idea I had never considered. "You know, Dad, maybe you were leaving to protect me from yourself—maybe you knew that was the only way to keep us safe. Maybe you left because you did love me so much. It was a sacrifice. Thank you for that, Dad." His eyebrows finally relaxed into place. I held his hand in silence.

After that, I felt different. I left hospice for a day to hike in Celo and then came back to find him still there, slowly breathing in and out. I spent more time at home by myself, just being, knowing Dad's time was close but not knowing when it would come.

And then it did. On Tuesday afternoon, March 16, Janet was alone with Dad. The window was open and fresh spring air filled the room. She held his hand and sang a few songs to him. His breathing was ragged now, and she was the right one to be there, saying the words he needed to hear.

"We'll be okay, Dad. We don't need you to stay. You've done what you needed to do here, and it's your time to go. Don't you worry about us—we'll be fine. We all love you, and we'll be fine."

After a few more ragged breaths, Dad's chest stopped moving. Out the open window and into the treetops, he took his final flight.

A big life lived, now over.

There were certainly moments of fear for Dad in the dying process—he spoke to the devil of his childhood religion more than once before he lost the ability to form words. But if it's possible to die and heal at the same time, that's what Dad did. He finally found the peace he had sought all his life. Peace at last.

Soon it would be time for me to take flight as well.

The months after Dad's death were a period of numbness for me, as I kept asking the question, "How do you grieve something you're not going to miss?" I felt unfocused, and the phrase "at a loss" began recurring in my journal. Can you lose something you never really wanted in the first place?

It wasn't just my conscious mind that was preoccupied with the loss. When I tried to escape the feelings by plunging back into my last months of work at the YWCA, I was stopped short by melodies that floated through my mind and heart. Strains of what Grandmama Moore called her "little songs" reminded me to slow down and let the grieving process take its course.

Be still and listen, the master speaks to thee…
Be still and listen, He speaks so tenderly…

And another:

Have you heard the wind in the pines?
Have you seen the dew on a rose?
Do you know the colors in a butterfly's wings?
All these are gifts of God,
All gifts from the hand of God.

One morning I woke up remembering a vivid dream. In it, Janet and I had gone to Virginia Beach for a memorial service for Dad. When we got there, the room was filled with prim, well-dressed church ladies, not Dad's kind of people. It was a quiet affair, with different ones of them saying sweet, loving things about what a good man he'd been. After sitting with my mouth clamped shut for some time, I finally burst out in a rage. "What are you talking about? He was crazy! He was a terrible father, violent and absent! He wasn't a wonderful person at all!" I felt humiliated by my outburst, and ran from the room in tears.

In the dream, Janet and I left the memorial service to go to the airport and fly home. When it was time to collect our suitcases at the conveyor belt, other people's luggage came out, piece by piece in an orderly fashion, but mine didn't. I waited and waited, walking around to see if I was in the wrong place, but nothing came. Why did everyone else have their bags? Finally my suitcases began to arrive, shooting out in all directions—I couldn't begin to catch them as they flew into the air, landing heavily on the shiny airport floor. I ducked and dodged, feeling bombarded. The situation was out of control.

I woke up at that point and puzzled over such an odd dream. Then it hit me, and I lay there giggling on my pillow, first thing in the early morning. "I get it! *BAGGAGE!*" Emotions still seemed to be all or nothing with me.

Springtime took on special significance for me that year, as I moved toward the end of my time at the YWCA. The greening of the trees marked time passing, and I watched them closely. Finally the world was transformed, decked out in full leafy glory. It was time for me to say good-bye.

When you leave well, it feels a bit like a wake. Everybody reminisced and sang my praises; I felt incredibly well loved. And ready to go. As it turned out, I hadn't arranged a job to step into at the end of the summer—I was truly taking a huge leap of faith, something I had never considered possible. As the reality began to sink in the next day, I celebrated my birthday. John's card, in his own handwriting, said it all:

Happy Birthday
my love
Let's float away
to new heights,
new vistas, dreams
realized (and dreamed)
and always you
and me
John

His birthday gift to me was something I'd wanted for a long time: a ride for the two of us in a hot-air balloon. I wasn't leaping. I was just lifting off.

I thought the balloon ride would be exciting, but it was one of the most peaceful experiences I've ever had. Since you travel the same speed as the wind and the blast of hot air is only occasional, the silence in a balloon can be profound. That day, the tourists who had also plopped down the big bucks for their time in the sky couldn't make it, so there were only five in the basket: the pilot, the two of us, and two men who had grown up in the same valley—a father and his adult son.

There wasn't much wind that day, so we didn't go far. Instead, we traveled in time as we gently brushed the treetops, with the old father telling stories of who used to own that land over there, and how that barn there was the most modern construction when it was built in 1955. Now that developers have gotten interested in that whole beautiful valley, his family's deep connection to the land will soon be stripped away.

When we landed on the roadside it was church time, but I didn't see how being in church could make me feel any closer to God than caressing the treetops and listening to stories about the soil.

I was still grieving my dad's death. I hadn't even finished being angry with him. But I had opened my fist and willingly returned the master key to the YWCA. I surrendered the sense of control—whatever modicum of control it ever was—and trusted the universe to guide me. Dad would have been proud. And for once, that was fine with me.

~ ~ ~ ~ ~ ~

I end at the beginning. Genesis.

> And Isaac digged again the wells of water, which they had digged in the days of Abraham his father; for the Philistines had stopped them after the death of Abraham: and he called their names after the names by which his father had called them.
>
> And Isaac's servants digged in the valley, and found there a well of springing water.
>
> And the herdmen of Gerar did strive with Isaac's herdmen, saying, The water is ours: and he called the name of the well Esek [Contention]; because they strove with him.
>
> And they digged another well, and strove for that also: and he called the name of it Sitnah [Enmity].
>
> And he removed from thence, and digged another well; and for that they strove not: and he called the name of it Rehoboth [Expanse]; and he said, For now the Lord hath made room for us, and we shall be fruitful in the land. (Genesis 26:18-22, KJV)

Granddaddy Moore had foretold my story on the morning of my birth, hours before the pains of labor began. Contention. Enmity. Expanse.

It is only by rising gently above the familiar, curving, blue and green expanse of my own story that I finally see it clearly. Contention is first—discord, fighting, violence, terror. The next well is enmity—bitterness, resentment, long-held anger. These first two wells are deep, and it's easy to fall in and get lost.

But beyond the two of them, if we can ever get there, is the warm expanse of forgiveness. It's not the same as justifying, condoning, or even forgetting. Even justice becomes somehow irrelevant. It is instead a loving remembrance and release.

Old wells. Fresh water.

Fly like a bird to the mountain.

Epilogue

Much has changed since I started writing this story.

The landmark blue steel roof and the solid building of Pilgrim Congregational Church, on the well-to-do side of Birmingham, Alabama, have been pulled down, the peaceful glade of evergreens toppled, to make way for a well-heeled housing development. The congregation has renamed itself "Pilgrim Church" and now worships in a renovated former office building. They have a flat roof.

With just three simple and emphatic words—*yes, we can*—our country finally burst through an eternity of racial strife, only to hand our brilliant new president one of the worst economic crises in our nation's history, along with two wars underway. The peace of Rehobeth seems unlikely in our wider world, no matter how we may pray for it.

Mom finally let go. It wasn't quick or easy.

After the excruciatingly slow process of curling in her chrysalis and losing contact with the outside world (including all of us), she finally forgot how to swallow and one day aspirated her lunch. The facility called me and I rushed to her bedside; all I could do was hold her hand as she gasped for breath. Her panic-stricken eyes locked with mine. Of all the scary times we had been through together, that moment was one of the worst.

When I went to the hallway with my cell phone to let the family know, it felt like the end must be imminent at last. But the kind nurses got her breathing easily again, and she held on for another ten days, giving everyone time to gather from points north and south to sing hymns and tell stories by her bedside. She didn't let go until we all left her alone for a bit. Early on a Sunday morning, she finally drifted away. She always was a morning person, and Sunday mornings were her special time.

We gathered for warm stew at the Celo Inn that day, and as I sat in the midst of our loving family I found that Mom's obituary was already in my head, complete and ready to go. All I had to do was write it down.

Carol Henry's strong, loving heart stopped beating at dawn on Sunday, March 4, 2012. Her spirit is with us still.

Her spirit blooms in the Hudsonia montana, a rare wildflower on a craggy outcropping now protected thanks to her keen eye.

Her spirit offers a firm foundation for hundreds of people in Mitchell and Yancey Counties—she was a founder of Mitchell-Yancey Habitat for Humanity, and the Stitch and Chat group that gathered around her table has raised more than $25,000 by selling colorful patchwork potholders.

Her spirit lingers in the mind's eyes of hundreds of now-grown Spruce Pine Montessori kids. With Ms. Carol's gentle guidance they learned to sound out words, recognize trees, sing songs, and make new friends.

Her spirit sings with the Celo Sacred Harpers. Her title is clear and she's homeward bound.

Her spirit fills the hearts of her family and a multitude of friends. Celebrating her loving spirit are her four daughters (Linda Henry, Nancy Raskin, Janet Henry, and Cindy McMahon) and their families (Bob and Emma Snope; Randy, Lane, and Evan Raskin; Matt Revis; and John, Caleb, and Katie McMahon) as well as her brother Walter Moore, Jr., his wife Marian and their children and grandchildren.

Just a few days later, smoke crept over the Celo valley, and word got around that the Forest Service was doing a controlled burn on nearby Singecat Ridge. We worried; that was the ridge where Mom discovered the rare and delicate Hudsonia montana. Would it survive the flames? But then this small announcement appeared in the morning paper:

> The prescribed burn in the Singecat area of the Pisgah National Forest in McDowell County went well this week, burning about 1,800 of the projected 2,100 acres, according to U.S. Forest Services. The burn accomplished the primary objective of protecting habitat for the endangered Hudsonia montana, a type of mountain heather.

Mom had only been gone for four days. We figured she was smiling.

And then there's me. Anyone who has read the chapters of this book has watched my transformation. I'm grateful that I found what I was hoping for when I started this journey—the cool water of forgiveness running lightly across my fingers. The hot coal has finally lifted away. And most days I'm lighter, in the present, as a result.

Yes, I still have my days. I'm still human, thank goodness. And still learning, laughing, loving.

Amen.

Acknowledgments

I owe a huge debt of gratitude to the institutions and individuals whose openness made this book possible. Thank you to the Jack Tarver Library at Mercer University for access to my grandfather's papers, and to the Robert W. Woodruff Library at Emory University for access to those of Frances Pauley. Thank you to Vineville Baptist Church, Pilgrim Church, Koinonia, and Celo Community for opening the doors of your archives to me. And many, many thanks to the friends and family who so generously shared their memories and stories: my sisters and brother (Linda Henry, Nancy Raskin, Janet Henry, and Josh Cutler); Marian and Walter "Buddy" Moore, Jr.; Randy Raskin; Nisbet Kendrick, Jr.; Irvin Cheney; Sam Oni; Ray and Ruth Brewster; Loyd Landrum; Jack and Mary Lib Causey; Pat Chetelat, Ethel Owen, and Fran Feazel; Ed Brown; Lenny Jordan; Millard and Linda Fuller; Broadus and Lib Willoughby; Schley Gatewood, Jr.; Gene Singletery; Tim and Mary Yoder; Don and Judy Bender; Dave Shields; Betty O'Berry; Waldie Unger; Bill Breyer; Janet Rinard; Alan Hoskins; Bob and Marian Sigmon; Hector, Susie, Rose, Aggie, and Annie Black; Dale Moody; Ben Geouge; Robin Dreyer and Tammy Hitchcock; Bob and Geeta McGahey; Marnie Walters; and Bob and Dot Barrus. Finally, thank you to John. You are steadfast, amazing, and a great editor and proofreader.

Works Consulted

Bayor, Ronald H. *Race and the Shaping of Twentieth-Century Atlanta*. Chapel Hill: University of North Carolina, 1996.

Campbell, Will D. *The Stem of Jesse: The Cost of Community at a 1960s Southern School*. Macon, GA: Mercer University, 1995.

Davis, Murphy. *Frances Pauley: Stories of Struggle and Triumph*. Atlanta, GA: The Open Door Community, 1996.

Elliott, Ralph H. *The "Genesis Controversy" and Continuity in Southern Baptist Chaos: A Eulogy for a Great Tradition*. Macon, GA: Mercer University, 1992.

Eskew, Glenn T. *But for Birmingham: The Local and National Movements in the Civil Rights Struggle*. Chapel Hill: University of North Carolina, 1997.

Garrow, David. *Bearing the Cross: Martin Luther King, Jr. and the Southern Christian Leadership Conference*. New York: William Morrow, 2004.

Hall, Jacquelyn. Interview with Frances Pauley, July 18, 1944. [G-0046] Chapel Hill, NC: Documenting the American South, 1974. http://docsouth.unc.edu/sohp/

Hicks, George L. *Experimental Americans: Celo and Utopian Community in the Twentieth Century*. Urbana: University of Illinois, 2001.

Jordan, Clarence. *The Cotton Patch Version of Luke and Acts: Jesus' Doings and the Happenings*. New York: Association Press, 1969.

———. *Sermon on the Mount*. Valley Forge, PA: Judson Press, 1952.

Lee, Dallas. *The Cotton Patch Evidence: The Story of Clarence Jordan and the Koinonia Farm Experiment (1942-1970)*. Americus, GA: Koinonia Partners, 1971.

Manis, Andrew M. *Macon Black and White: An Unutterable Separation in the American Century*. Macon, GA: Mercer University, 2004.

McWhorter, Diane. *Carry Me Home: Birmingham, Alabama: The Climactic Battle of the Civil Rights Revolution*. New York: Simon and Schuster, 2001.